More Lives Than One

More Lives Than One

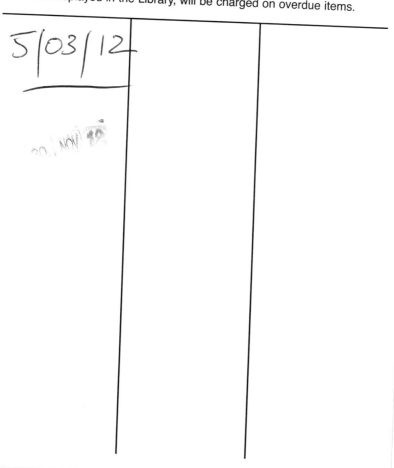

First published in 2011 by
The Collins Press
West Link Park
Doughcloyne
Wilton
Cork

British Library Cataloguing in Publication Data

Hanberry, Gerard.
   More lives than one : the remarkable Wilde family
   through the generations
   1. Wilde, Oscar, 1854-1900—Family. 2. Wilde, W. R.
   (William Robert), 1815-1876. 3. Wilde, Lady, 1826-1896.
   4. Wilde, Constance, 1858-1898. 5. Authors, Irish—19th
   century—Family relationships.
   I. Title
   828.8'09-dc22
   ISBN-13: 9781848891203

Typesetting by Patricia Hope, Dublin
Typeset in Bembo
Printed in Sweden by ScandBook A/B

CONTENTS

Acknowledgements

I would like to thank my family – my wife, Kerry, sons Jamie, Daniel and Gregory and daughter Jane – for their support and tolerance over the years while I worked on this book. I particularly want to thank Gregory for his invaluable assistance on the IT front. He always responded patiently to my many cries for help when my computer refused to act as it should.

I am indebted to Siobhan Campbell of Kingston University for her support and encouragement over many drafts of the manuscript and for her constant belief that it would eventually become a worthwhile book. I also wish to thank Professor Adrian Frazier of the National University of Ireland, Galway, for his encouragement and for giving me the confidence to continue. Also Dr Éibhear Walshe of University College Cork and Denise Bukowski of Toronto for their valuable suggestions, which helped improve the manuscript. I wish to include The Collins Press for accepting the manuscript and editor Laurence Fenton for his excellent work. I would like to extend a special word of gratitude to Stephen Wall of Cong for giving so generously of his time and for sharing his knowledge of the locality that played such a large part in the life of Sir William Wilde. Likewise I am most grateful to my good friends Liam Madden and his wife Carol for their encouragement and more specifically for their practical assistance in sharing both their vast knowledge of the lake and their lovely cruiser *Witchhazel* in the days when I was attempting to retrace the route taken by Sir William in his book *Lough Corrib, its Shores and Islands*. I wish to thank Scott Jacobs of the William Andrews Clarke Memorial Library, UCLA, and Orla Sweeney and Honora Faul of the National Library of Ireland for their kind and helpful assistance in locating photographs for publication.

I would like to include my friends and colleagues at St Enda's College, Salthill, for their encouragement and also the members of The Talking Stick Writers' Group, Geraldine Mills, Hugo Kelly, Hedi Gibbons Lynott, James Martyn Joyce, Siobhan Shine and Alan McMonagle who have always been there with positive words of advice over the years.

THE WILDE FAMILY TREE

(partly based on Brian de Breffny 'The Paternal Ancestry of Oscar Wilde', *The Irish Ancestor* Vol 5:2, 1973)

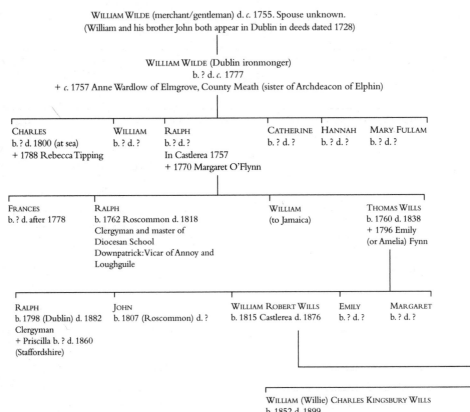

WILLIAM WILDE (merchant/gentleman) d. *c.* 1755. Spouse unknown.
(William and his brother John both appear in Dublin in deeds dated 1728)

WILLIAM WILDE (Dublin ironmonger)
b. ? d. *c.* 1777
+ *c.* 1757 Anne Wardlow of Elmgrove, County Meath (sister of Archdeacon of Elphin)

CHARLES
b. ? d. 1800 (at sea)
+ 1788 Rebecca Tipping

WILLIAM
b. ? d. ?

RALPH
b. ? d. ?
In Castlerea 1757
+ 1770 Margaret O'Flynn

CATHERINE
b. ? d. ?

HANNAH
b. ? d. ?

MARY FULLAM
b. ? d. ?

FRANCES
b. ? d. after 1778

RALPH
b. 1762 Roscommon d. 1818
Clergyman and master of
Diocesan School
Downpatrick: Vicar of Annoy and
Loughguile

WILLIAM
(to Jamaica)

THOMAS WILLS
b. 1760 d. 1838
+ 1796 Emily
(or Amelia) Fynn

RALPH
b. 1798 (Dublin) d. 1882
Clergyman
+ Priscilla b. ? d. 1860
(Staffordshire)

JOHN
b. 1807 (Roscommon) d. ?

WILLIAM ROBERT WILLS
b. 1815 Castlerea d. 1876

EMILY
b. ? d. ?

MARGARET
b. ? d. ?

WILLIAM (Willie) CHARLES KINGSBURY WILLS
b. 1852 d. 1899
+ 1891 Miriam Florence (née Folline)
Frank Leslie (b. 1836 New Orleans d. 1914
New York) divorced 1893

+1893 Sophie (Lily) Lees

DOROTHY (Dolly)
b. 1895 d. 1941

THE ELGEE FAMILY TREE

(partly based on Brian de Breffny 'The Maternal Lineage of Oscar Wilde', *The Irish Ancestor* Vol 4:2, 1972)

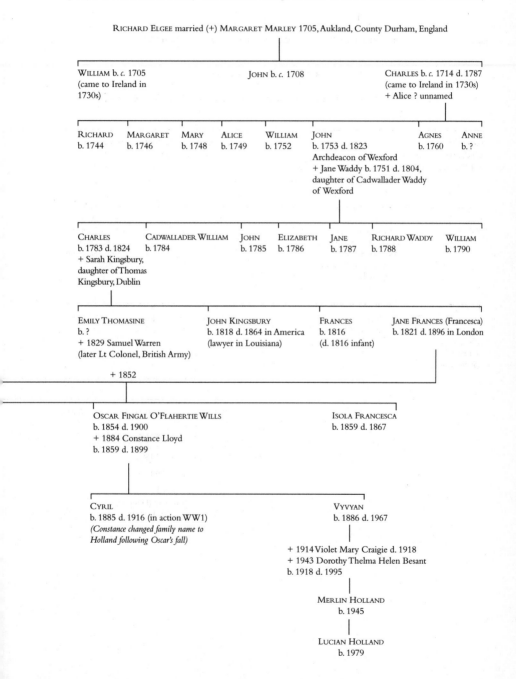

RICHARD ELGEE married (+) MARGARET MARLEY 1705, Aukland, County Durham, England

WILLIAM b. *c.* 1705
(came to Ireland in
1730s)

JOHN b. *c.* 1708

CHARLES b. *c.* 1714 d. 1787
(came to Ireland in 1730s)
+ Alice ? unnamed

RICHARD
b. 1744

MARGARET
b. 1746

MARY
b. 1748

ALICE
b. 1749

WILLIAM
b. 1752

JOHN
b. 1753 d. 1823
Archdeacon of Wexford
+ Jane Waddy b. 1751 d. 1804,
daughter of Cadwallader Waddy
of Wexford

AGNES
b. 1760

ANNE
b. ?

CHARLES
b. 1783 d. 1824
+ Sarah Kingsbury,
daughter of Thomas
Kingsbury, Dublin

CADWALLADER WILLIAM
b. 1784

JOHN
b. 1785

ELIZABETH
b. 1786

JANE
b. 1787

RICHARD WADDY
b. 1788

WILLIAM
b. 1790

EMILY THOMASINE
b. ?
+ 1829 Samuel Warren
(later Lt Colonel, British Army)

JOHN KINGSBURY
b. 1818 d. 1864 in America
(lawyer in Louisiana)

FRANCES
b. 1816
(d. 1816 infant)

JANE FRANCES (Francesca)
b. 1821 d. 1896 in London

+ 1852

OSCAR FINGAL O'FLAHERTIE WILLS
b. 1854 d. 1900
+ 1884 Constance Lloyd
b. 1859 d. 1899

ISOLA FRANCESCA
b. 1859 d. 1867

CYRIL
b. 1885 d. 1916 (in action WW1)
*(Constance changed family name to
Holland following Oscar's fall)*

VYVYAN
b. 1886 d. 1967

+ 1914 Violet Mary Craigie d. 1918
+ 1943 Dorothy Thelma Helen Besant
b. 1918 d. 1995

MERLIN HOLLAND
b. 1945

LUCIAN HOLLAND
b. 1979

Prologue

When Oscar Wilde was fifteen years of age and a boarder at Portora Royal School, Enniskillen, in what is today Northern Ireland, he became fascinated by a high-profile prosecution then under way in England. He told his fellow students that it would be wonderful if some day he too were 'to go down to posterity as the defendant in such a case as "Regina versus Wilde"'.[1] This wish to be at the centre of a legal sensation would be eventually granted with catastrophic results.

It was at half past three on the afternoon of Saturday 25 May 1895 that the jury in the second criminal trial of Oscar Wilde retired to consider its verdict. They returned two hours later but only to query some minor detail of evidence before withdrawing again. The Prosecutor turned to Sir Edward Clarke, Council for the Defence, and whispered 'You'll dine your man in Paris tomorrow.' Sir Edward, in his mid-fifties and one of England's most respected barristers, was less optimistic. Long, pointed side-whiskers brushed his high shirt-collar as he replied 'No, no, no'. Clarke had done his best but his arguments were 'fatally weakened with each new witness that the prosecution produced'.[2]

Sir Edward's task had been made all the more difficult by Oscar's co-defendant, Alfred Taylor, being found guilty of the same charge just days before. Nevertheless, the experienced barrister had delivered an excellent closing statement and nothing was certain. He told the jury:

If on an examination of the evidence you, therefore, feel it your duty to say that the charges against the prisoner have not been proved, then I am sure you will be glad that the brilliant promise which has been clouded by these accusations, and the bright reputation which was so nearly quenched in the torrent of prejudice which a few weeks ago was sweeping through the press, have been saved by your verdict from absolute ruin; and that it leaves him, a distinguished man of letters and a brilliant Irishman, to live among us a life of honour and repute, and to give in the maturity of his genius, gifts to our literature, of which he has given only the promise of his early youth.

But the prosecution was left with the final words, and they were damning. Both the Solicitor General Sir Frank Lockwood's speech and the judge's summing-up were couched in most unpleasant terms.

When the jury returned for the second time they had a verdict. Oscar Wilde, they agreed, was guilty of committing indecent acts. Mr Justice Sir Alfred Wills peered from the bench at the two prisoners now standing together in the dock. A pair of wire reading-spectacles sat on the end of a long nose and his lean face looked even more severe than usual. Victorian society, so often wittily satirised by Wilde, would now have its say. The courtroom fell silent for the last time in this sensational case:

Oscar Wilde and Alfred Taylor, the crime of which you have been convicted is so bad that one has to put stern restraint upon one's self to prevent one's self from describing, in language which I would rather not use, the sentiments which must rise to the breast of every man of honour who had heard the details of these two terrible trials. That the jury have arrived at a correct verdict in this case I cannot persuade myself to entertain the shadow of a doubt; and I hope, at all events that those who sometimes imagine that a judge is half-hearted in the cause of decency and morality because he takes care no

prejudice shall enter into the case, may see this is consistent
at least with the common sense of indignation at the horrible
charges brought home to both of you. It is no use for me to
address you. People who can do these things must be dead
to all sense of shame, and one cannot hope to produce any
effect upon them. It is the worst case I have ever tried. That
you, Taylor, kept a kind of male brothel it is impossible to
doubt. And that you, Wilde, have been the centre of a circle
of extensive corruption of the most hideous kind among
young men, it is equally impossible to doubt.

I shall, under such circumstances, be expected to pass
the severest sentence that the law allows. In my judgement
it is totally inadequate for such a case as this. The sentence
of the Court is that each of you be imprisoned and kept
to hard labour for two years.

Wilde, pale-faced, uttered 'My God, my God!' and tried to say more
but his words were lost in the uproar and the judge waved him away.
The warders caught his swaying bulk and took him down, with the
slight-framed Taylor following like a bit player in the tragedy. The
Marquis of Queensberry, the bellicose father of Oscar's lover Lord
Alfred Douglas, and his circle of cronies were delighted, but the cry
of 'Shame' was also heard ringing through the courtroom.

Sentencing over, Wilde and his co-defendant Taylor were
immediately taken from court and held at Newgate Prison while the
warrants for their detention were being prepared. From there they
were conducted by prison van to Holloway Prison where their
possessions were taken from them. Wilde was told to strip and had his
appearance and physical condition closely noted, after which he was
ordered to take a bath. He was then given a full suit and cap of grey
prison clothes complete with black arrows and shown to his cell.
Soon after, he tasted his first prison meal as a convict, a plate of thin
porridge and a small brown loaf. Oscar would later recall the moment
in *De Profundis*, the long reflection he wrote towards the end of his
sentence. 'I sat amidst the ruins of my wonderful life, crushed by
anguish, bewildered with terror, dazed through pain.'[3]

In early June Oscar was moved from Holloway to Pentonville Prison. Here the fallen 'Lord of Words' was introduced to the treadmill, a bare plank bed and meagre prison rations. Oscar's destruction was total, and he would serve his full two years without any remission. All pleas on his behalf for even a slight mitigation of his sentence were ignored.

In *The Ballad of Reading Gaol*, composed shortly after his release, he wrote:

> And for all the woe that moved him so
> That he gave that bitter cry,
> And the wild regrets, and the bloody sweats,
> None knew so well as I:
> For he who lives more lives than one
> More deaths than one must die.

If Oscar died for the first time that terrible evening in Holloway Prison, he was to experience many more 'deaths' before his final days in the Hotel d'Alsace, Paris, where he passed away on the afternoon of 30 November 1900, the most famous man of English letters of his day, reduced to an impoverished exile, abandoned by all but a few loyal friends.

Towards the end of his prison sentence, Oscar had been allowed improved access to pen and ink by Major J. O. Nelson, the newly appointed warden of Reading Gaol, to which he had been transferred in late 1895. From January to March 1897 he managed to write an autobiographical account of the time spent with his lover, Lord Alfred Douglas, in which he reflects on the events leading to the ruinous trials and the resulting anguish of his incarceration. In order to circumvent prison rules, the text – eventually published as *De Profundis* – was written in the form of an emotionally charged letter to Douglas. It was, according to Oscar, 'the psychological explanation of a course of conduct that from the outside seems a combination of absolute idiocy with vulgar bravado'.[4] In a letter to his loyal friend Robert Ross, Oscar reveals another reason for trying to elucidate what he calls his 'extraordinary behaviour': 'I am not prepared to sit in the grotesque gallery they put me into for all time; for the simple reason that I inherited from my father and mother a name of high distinction in literature and art, and I cannot for eternity allow that name to be degraded. I do not defend my conduct, I explain it.'[5]

Oscar was especially close to his mother, Lady Jane Wilde. In *De Profundis* he tells of her lonely death while he languished behind bars and of his torment at having disgraced the proud family name:

> I am transferred here [to Reading Gaol]. Three more months go over and my mother dies. No one knows better than you how deeply I loved and honoured her. Her death was terrible to me; but I, once a lord of language, have no words in which to express my anguish and my shame. Never even in the most perfect days of my development as an artist could I have found words fit to bear so august a burden; or to move with sufficient stateliness of music through the purple pageant of my incommunicable woe. She and my father had bequeathed me a name they had made noble and honoured, not merely in literature, art, archaeology, and science, but in the public history of my own country, in its evolution as a nation. I had disgraced that name eternally. I had made it a low byword among low people. I had dragged it through the very mire. I had given it to brutes that they might make it brutal, and to fools that they might turn it into a synonym for folly. What I suffered then, and still suffer, is not for pen to write or paper to record.[6]

In her time, Jane Wilde had been adored by the masses in her native land – Ireland. As the young revolutionary poet 'Speranza' she had stirred a nation with fiery verses for the rebellious Young Ireland movement of the 1840s.[7] Later, as Lady Jane Wilde, wife of Sir William Wilde, she would meet with royalty and be the mistress of one of Dublin city's finest mansions. Sir William and Lady Wilde loved to entertain, and Oscar and his older brother Willie learned the art of conversation at first hand when, as children, they were allowed to sit in silence at the end of their parents' dining table, where they were introduced to many leading figures of the day. But Jane also experienced great personal tragedy and despair. In the end, Oscar's success was her only source of comfort, and even that was taken from her.

Lady Wilde bequeathed many of her qualities to her two sons, Willie and Oscar. They received her large frame, her extravagance, her sense of self-importance and her humour. Her friend, the scholar and famous mathematician Sir William Rowan Hamilton, once told a colleague that 'she is quite a genius, and thoroughly aware of it'.[8] From his father, Oscar inherited a quick intelligence and also a certain disregard for the conventional.

Sir William Wilde was only sixty-one years old when he passed away on 19 April 1876, while Oscar was still attending Oxford University. He had been an eminent eye and ear surgeon in Dublin, and was the founder of St Mark's Ophthalmic Hospital in Park Street. He was the Surgeon Oculist in Ordinary to the Queen in Ireland and ran a busy private practice. He also lectured in his field, with students coming from as far away as America to attend St Mark's and learn about his treatments. Sir William's book *Practical Observations on Aural Surgery and the Nature and Treatment of Diseases of the Ear* remained the standard textbook for many years on both sides of the Atlantic.

Sir William's reputation went far beyond Ireland and did not rest solely in the field of medicine. He was a noted antiquarian and archaeologist with several books on these subjects to his name. He also published two popular and successful travel books, together with many articles on history and folklore as well as on medicine. Because of his superb powers of observation and description, and his extraordinary ability to handle data, Sir William was appointed Medical Commissioner for the Irish Census. It was primarily for his work in this area that he received a knighthood from Queen Victoria in 1864. On top of all that, he took upon himself the enormous task of cataloguing the many artefacts in the museum of the Royal Irish Academy.

Sir William was well respected by Dublin's poor as a caring doctor, but he was often the subject of rhymes, jokes and vulgar street ballads, mostly related to his reputation as a womaniser. According to popular rumour he had 'a child in every farmhouse'. Exaggerated reports of his philandering were not without some basis, and it is known that he fathered at least three children – a son and two daughters – outside of wedlock. Sir William also became implicated in a sensational court case involving alleged sexual misconduct with a younger woman; the account of proceedings reads like a strange foreshadowing of the terrible lawsuit that would destroy his son a generation later. Many of the ingredients are there – a hastily written note, an action for libel, sex, scandal and private lives laid bare before an eager press and a packed public gallery.

This book tells the story of a remarkable family from their veiled origins in the early 1700s to the present day. It examines the lives of Sir William and his wife Lady Wilde, extraordinary people who experienced both the lofty heights of triumph and tragedy's deep troughs. By linking the generations, and placing the life of Oscar in the context of his family background, a more complete picture emerges of this brilliant Irishman whose wit and works still dazzle and whose tragic fall still breaks the reader's heart.

Part 1

Origins

'The man who could call a spade a spade should be compelled to use one. It is the only thing he is fit for.'

The Picture of Dorian Gray

1

Veiled Roots

Jane 'Francesca' Wilde believed that a creative mind must be free to live like 'a pine upon the mountain', high above the mundane considerations of the day-to-day, but her lofty world often included much that was fanciful. When it came to explaining her ancestral origins she claimed her family name of Elgee could be traced to sixteenth-century Italy and that it was actually a corruption of the name Algiatia. In her more flamboyant moments she went so far as to mention a familial connection with the poet Dante Alighieri himself. For this reason she chose 'Speranza', Italian for 'Hope', as a *nom de plume* when, in her early twenties, she began writing for the Young Ireland newspaper, the *Nation*. With her dark eyes and long black hair, this romantic Italian fantasy was almost conceivable, and besides, who would dare to question her? Even if such a foolhardy inquisitor existed, Jane's claims could not be challenged because her birth was never registered: the law did not require it at the time.

The reality of Jane's family background is much more commonplace. Her great-grandfather was neither Italian nor a poet. His name was Charles Elgee and he was a bricklayer from Raby in County Durham in England where he was born in 1714 to a Richard Elgee who on 15 May 1705 had married Margaret Marley in St Helen's Church, Auckland, Durham. Richard and Margaret had two other children, William born sometime around 1705 and John born about 1708. John stayed in England while his two brothers, William a carpenter and builder and Charles the bricklayer, came to Dundalk, County Louth, during Ireland's building boom of the 1730s where they both prospered. Their children and grandchildren married well and the Elgees climbed the social ladder, up and away from 'trade'. 'From a label there is no escape!' Lord Henry Wotton exclaims in *The Picture of Dorian Gray*, but Jane Elgee, ever conscious of class and status, a trait she passed on to her sons, could not be associated with carpenters from Durham, hence her fanciful attempt to escape into a fictitious Italian background.

As for her husband's surname, she liked to believe the Wilde name arrived in Ireland with an officer in the Cromwellian army who remained on after the wars. Oliver Cromwell is still widely hated in Ireland where his name is synonymous with cruelty and anti-Catholic bigotry following his Irish Campaign of 1649–50. It is interesting that Jane would prefer to be associated with the detested Cromwell rather than with a 'trade'. Vyvyan Holland, Oscar Wilde's son, maintained the name came from a Dutch army officer called de Wilde who served with the armies of William of Orange, who as Protestant King William III of England fought Catholic King James II at the Battle of the Boyne in 1690. Hostilities over, de Wilde is supposed to have settled in Castlerea, County Roscommon. There is, however, no evidence to support either of these claims.

So what is known about the origins of the Wilde family? Lord Alfred Douglas, Oscar's lover, snobbishly remarked in his 1914 biography *Oscar Wilde and Myself* that 'Wilde's father was certainly a knight; but heaven alone knows who his grandfather was.'[1] Douglas, of course, was being characteristically snide.

Sir William Wilde's father was Dr Thomas Wills Wilde, a general practitioner based near Castlerea, County Roscommon, in the west of Ireland. Dr Wilde was a familiar figure in a caped riding coat, doing the rounds of his wide-ranging country practice on horseback until he died on 1 January 1838 at seventy-eight years of age. He is buried in the Holy Trinity Church of Ireland graveyard, Castlerea, and his tombstone states that 'he practised as a Physician in this town for upwards of 30 years'. Dr Wilde's father was Ralph Wilde, a 'dealer' and agent for an aristocratic family – the Lord Mount Sandfords of

Castlerea House and estate – who then prospered and acquired property in the locality. Ralph married Margaret O'Flynn, the daughter of a distinguished Gaelic family whose ancestors gave their name to a district in Roscommon. He eventually became known as a farmer and then a gentleman in his own right.

But where did this Ralph Wilde come from? He appears as Lord Mount Sandford's Roscommon agent in the middle of the eighteenth century but from there the trail to his origins becomes uncertain. One study points to the possibility of Ralph being 'a son of a Dublin merchant named John Wilde who belonged to a family of merchants, ironmongers and property developers'.[2] It points to the fact that when Sir William received his knighthood in 1864 an article appeared in *Duffy's Hibernian Sixpenny Magazine* linking him with a certain Richard Wilde who lived in Dublin towards the end of the 1700s. Richard Wilde was 'a man of high commercial standing in Dublin'. He was also involved with the Society of United Irishmen, a secret organisation behind the Irish uprising of 1798. Richard had to flee to America following the failure of that rebellion. There, his son, Richard Henry Wilde, went on to become a poet, writer, lawyer and member of the US Congress for the state of Georgia. Richard Henry Wilde's claim to even greater fame rests on the fact that he discovered a lost portrait of Dante in the Bargello Palace in Florence, which was attributed to Giotto or to the school of Giotto, while researching a book on the life of the Italian poet Tasso, which he published in 1842.

Sir William Wilde, who liked to be associated with influential people, did claim a connection between his family and this famous American politician and author. However, there was no evidence to support the link and nothing was ever said about Richard Henry Wilde's father, the Irish rebel and ironmonger who lived at 12 High Street and later at 73 Thomas Street in Dublin before making his getaway to America. Perhaps the anonymous writer of the 1864 article was trying, for political reasons, to forge a link between the new knight, the Protestant Sir William Wilde, and Irish nationalism. After all, Sir William's wife had once been the great nationalist poet Speranza. But this connection with the American Wildes does not ring true. William Wilde's politics had never been nationalist. He was a Protestant supporter of the link with the British Empire, the son of a doctor and the grandson of an agent for an aristocratic family. It is difficult to see a close family connection with the rebellious United Irishmen and with a rebel who had to take flight.

On the other hand, Terence de Vere White in his book *The Parents of Oscar Wilde* is quite definite about William Wilde's family history. The parish register in Wolsingham in the county of Durham, England, where the Wilde name is common, shows that a William Wilde was baptised there on 28 March 1656 and that a 'Ralph Wilde is given as one of the twenty-four in the parish of Wolsingham in 1713 . . . Either this Ralph or one of his sons settled in Connaught.'[3] He also offers as proof the fact that 'In a door window of a house opposite the National Bank, Castlerea, County Roscommon, there could be seen written on the glass "R. Wilde July 16, 1758, old English."'

Brian de Breffny's work 'The Paternal Ancestry of Oscar Wilde' (*The Irish Ancestor* Vol 5:2 1973) sheds some light on the father and possible grandfather of Ralph Wilde, Dr Thomas Wills Wilde's father. His discoveries lead one to believe that Ralph Wilde who married Margaret O'Flynn of Roscommon was the son of William Wilde, a Dublin ironmonger who about 1757 married Anne Wardlow, the daughter of Charles Wardlow of Elmgrove, County Meath, *c.* 1757. She was also the sister of the Reverend John Wardlow, Archdeacon of Elphin. This would supply the Roscommon connection. This William Wilde, who died in 1777, had three sons – Charles, William and Ralph – and also three daughters – Catherine, Hannah and Mary. He was the son of a Dublin gentleman and merchant also called William Wilde whose spouse is unknown, as are his origins, but he had a brother called John, maybe the John Wilde mentioned earlier as being the possible father of Ralph. He died in 1755. Perhaps it was this man or his father who arrived from England.

So there never was a Cromwellian officer or a Dutch soldier called de Wilde. The truth appears to be that a Ralph or William Wilde, possibly a builder from Durham in the north of England, was attracted by the construction boom of the early eighteenth century and arrived in Ireland. He prospered and his sons and grandsons married well. They climbed the social ladder and managed to obscure their humble origins along the way. The reality, distasteful as it may be for a professional family from Merrion Square, is of a background where an honest living was earned by the sweat of one's brow, be it as a Dublin ironmonger or a Durham builder.

What would Lord Alfred Douglas have made of this revelation? As for Oscar, if he ever discovered there was a drop of carpenter's blood in his veins, the great conversationalist would probably have attempted to include it in the story of a brilliant star and three wise kings bearing gifts. If the Durham connection is the correct one, then, by an amazing coincidence, when William Wilde came to marry Jane Frances (she preferred Francesca, it being more Italian) Elgee in November 1851, he was taking as his wife not only a poet of national standing but a woman whose veiled roots were the very same as his own.

2

Marry Well

When Oscar crowned his successes at Trinity College, Dublin, in 1874 by winning the Berkeley Gold Medal for Greek, he was following in the footsteps of the eldest son of Ralph Wilde, the Castlerea land agent, also called Ralph, who had been awarded that very same prize two generations before. Thus begins the almost eerie foreshadowing of events that is a feature of the story of the Wilde family through the generations.

Ralph Wilde, the land agent, had three sons. The eldest was Ralph, the Berkeley gold medal-winner, born in 1758. He entered Holy Orders becoming curate of Inch and later took a position running a school at Downpatrick. The third son, William, went off to Jamaica and the middle son, Thomas Wills, born in 1760, became a doctor and settled down to practise first in the rural town of Loughrea in County Galway and later in the small town of Castlerea, County Roscommon.

Lord Alfred Douglas had a point, although he did not know it, when he raised questions about Oscar's paternal grandfather, Thomas Wills Wilde. Biographers have always been happy to swiftly brush past the figure of Dr Wilde doing his rounds on horseback, pleased to have established him as a general practitioner (GP) of medicine with a rural practice in Roscommon. But this is not the full story. Previously unpublished facts have recently come to light concerning Thomas Wills Wilde's medical qualifications.[1] It appears that he was almost fifty years of age before he qualified as a GP and little is known about his life up to that point. He received his Doctor of Medicine (MD) degree from the University of St Andrews in Scotland on 27 January 1809 on the recommendation of two other MDs and the payment of a fee that was normally £25. This was not an unusual practice for the time. His two sponsors were James Cleghorn, MD, sometime president of the King's and Queen's College of Physicians of Ireland, and John Pentland, MD of Dublin. They were in a position to state that Thomas 'attended and completed a course of Lectures on the General Branches of Medicine in Trinity College Dublin, has received a Liberal Education, is a Respectable Character, and from personal knowledge we judge him worthy of the honour of a degree in Medicine'.

It is known that in 1796, at the age of thirty-six, Thomas Wills Wilde married Miss Emily or Amelia Fynn, whose family held a large estate at Ballymagibbon, near Cong in County Mayo. It would be another thirteen years before Thomas managed to qualify as a doctor and his whereabouts or occupation up to that point remain unknown. Emily Fynn Wilde would eventually keep house for her youngest son, William, in Westland Row, Dublin, when he in turn set out on his own medical career years later. There were three sons from this marriage: Ralph, born in 1798, John, born in 1807, and William, Oscar's father, born in March 1815 in Kilkeevin, near Castlerea. There were also at least two daughters from this marriage, Margaret and Emily, whose birth dates were not recorded, in keeping with the times.

The two eldest brothers both entered the church. Ralph held various appointments both in England and Ireland over a long lifetime. His final position was as Rector of Hollymount, County Down, and he died at Downpatrick on 10 January 1882. He was the clergyman who christened Oscar at St Mark's on 26 April 1855. John was appointed Vicar of West Ashby in Lincolnshire, England. Oscar, as a student in Oxford, occasionally visited with his clergyman uncle where they had lively discussions on matters of religion, Oscar having leanings towards Rome. In a letter to his Oxford friend Reginald Harding dated 5 July 1876, Oscar recounts a visit with his uncle John Wilde when he 'examined schools in geography and history, sang glees, ate strawberries and argued fiercely with my poor uncle, who revenged himself on Sunday by preaching on Rome in the morning, and on humility in the evening. Both very "nasty ones" for me'.[2]

Both the Elgees and the Wildes 'married well', as the saying goes. When Thomas Wilde took Emily Fynn as his wife he was looked upon as her social inferior. The Fynns, being landed gentry, were connected to some of the most distinguished families in Connaught, such as the Surridges, noted for their scholarship, and the Ouseleys, one of whom became the British Ambassador to Persia.[3] Such is the intricacies of Irish genealogy, that the Fynn family was also connected to the great native Gaelic clan of the 'ferocious' O' Flahertys, whose ruined castles today dot the Connemara landscape. The O'Flahertys had been the dominant family or clan in Connaught for centuries before the Normans arrived into Ireland in 1169, sweeping the old order before them. The O'Flahertys then settled in Connemara, the remote mountainous region west of Lough Corrib, where they once again established their control. Jane marked this association with the old Gaelic chieftains of Connemara when the time came to give baby Oscar his names by including O'Flaherty on the list, thereby suggesting that her son had some tentative link to an ancient Celtic past.

Writing in the less politically correct world of the 1940s, Sir William's biographer T. G. Wilson is interesting on the topic of the Wilde/Fynn gene pool. 'The division between genius and madness is very narrow,' he wrote. 'The Fynnes were undoubtedly very unstable mentally, and there can be no doubt that much of the later peculiarities of the Wilde family, and perhaps much of their genius, can be traced to the Fynne strain in their blood. John Fynne was an enthusiastic member of the sect of "Dippers". It is said that he used to bribe impecunious peasants to allow him to baptise them in a spring near his house.'[4] Wilson goes on to quote from a popular ballad referring to the Fynns:

> If you were in Ballymagibbon
> Convenient to Cross,
> It's there you would see them
> Like water-rats creepin',
> When they were baptised
> By the Tyrant, John Fynne

The Fynn estate at Ballymagibbon covered about 2,000 acres along the northern shores of Lough Corrib near Cong, County Mayo. A young William Wilde travelled regularly from Roscommon to his grandparent's estate although his grandfather was no longer alive. John Fynn of Mayo had married Elizabeth Donaldson of Lucan, County Dublin, in 1779 and had died in Lucan in 1796. Young William was greatly influenced by all he encountered at Ballymagibbon. Today the old Fynn mansion is an ivy-clad ruin, hidden from sight and forgotten in the middle of green fields outside the village of Cross.

Sir William would continue to be drawn back to the west of Ireland frequently. In the early 1850s he managed to fulfil an ambition when he acquired Illaunroe, a fishing lodge in a remote district of Connemara, off to the west near the Atlantic coast. Ten years later he was in a position to do even better and succeeded in purchasing 170 acres of Ballymagibbon lands when his aunt, a Miss Fynn, was certified insane and had to be committed into care. There, on a green hilltop overlooking Lough Corrib, Sir William built his beloved Moytura House, a comfortable gabled lodge that still stands today at the end of a half-mile driveway.[5] It became his haven in the west, the place where the busy eye and ear surgeon was happiest. Here his family came for holidays to escape the unhealthy environment of the city with young Willie and Oscar fishing and boating on the nearby lakes and little Isola, their beloved golden-haired younger sister, toddling around the walled garden. Here a young Oscar experienced the ancient Gaelic culture and traditions at first hand. He would have heard the Gaelic language spoken by the tenantry and would have listened to the enchanting stories as told by local folk, such as Frank Houlihan who worked for Sir William at Moytura. Such exposure at an early age to this rich oral tradition must have had a big influence on the boy who would grow up to be one of the world's greatest storytellers. Oscar had a deep fund of Irish folk tales according to the writer Vincent O'Sullivan, who befriended the fallen author in his final years.

On Jane's side, her great-grandfather, the builder Charles Elgee who had come over from Durham with his brother in the 1730s, obviously prospered. He is known to have built a large residence in Dundalk called Cumberland Castle while his brother William built the Dundalk Court House. Charles and his wife Alice had eight children but John Elgee was the only son to survive. He entered the church and was appointed curate in Wexford, a strong Protestant town at the time. In 1782 he married Jane Waddy, a daughter of Cadwallader Waddy of Wexford. They had seven children, the eldest being Charles Elgee, Lady Jane Wilde's father. In 1795 John was promoted to Rector and was still there three years later when rebellion broke out in Ireland and Wexford became the scene of the worst atrocities in that most brutal uprising. Ireland had never been content to settle down under rule from England. It had remained loyal to the Church of Rome while England embraced the reformation. As English and Scottish Protestant planters gradually replaced the native Irish Catholic landowning population, a disgruntled, alienated class continued to be a thorn in the establishment's side. This disaffected populace occasionally found expression in violent rebellion.

Years later, Jane told how her grandfather escaped being murdered by the 1798 rebels when they captured the town of Wexford. His reprieve was put down to a kindness he had earlier shown to some Catholics in the area, possibly to a prisoner or prisoners he had befriended while visiting Wexford jail. According to the story she had been told, the Reverend Elgee returned home from administering the sacraments to his terrified congregation only to find that insurgents had taken possession of his house. He was seized, put on his knees and surrounded by armed pike-men ready to strike but the leader stepped forward, laid his hands on the kneeling Rector and ordered that his life be spared. The rebels even placed a guard on the Rector's home to protect both his family and his property. The family went unmolested during the three bloody weeks the rebels held the town.

John Elgee and his family came through the horrors of the 1798 rebellion unscathed, whatever the full truth of Jane's account. They remained indoors in the rectory during that month of terror when other Protestant clergymen and their flocks were tortured and put to death on the bridge over the River Slaney. It was there on the same bridge that the ringleaders of the rebellion were later hanged from the iron lamp bracket when General Lake retook the town. In 1804 John was appointed Archdeacon of Wexford, the same year his wife Jane passed away. Today the old graveyard of Rathaspeck just outside the town contains the tombstones of the many Elgees who have lived and died in that corner of Ireland, including Jane Waddy Elgee, John's 'beloved and lamented' wife and great-grandmother of Oscar Wilde.

Archdeacon Elgee's eldest son, Charles, did not follow his father into the Church; instead he studied law and became a solicitor. He began working in Dublin where, in keeping with the family pattern of marrying well, he met and wedded Sara Kingsbury, one of the most beautiful girls in the city and a member of a very prosperous and well connected Protestant family. Charles Elgee and Sarah had four children: Emily Thomasine, John, Francis, who died as an infant, and Jane. Sara Kingsbury had two sisters, Elizabeth who married a baronet, Sir Charles Montagu Ormsby, and Henrietta who married the eccentric clergyman and writer Charles Maturin. Although Jane was very young when Charles Maturin died in 1824 at the age of forty-four, she was always conscious of her aunt and uncle's unusual lifestyle and knew about Maturin's literary achievements. Jane would later keep a bust of Maturin in her own family home on Merrion Square.

As well as being aware of Aunt Henrietta and her husband Charles Maturin's antics, Jane would have heard stories of other larger-than-life characters from that era including the blind ballad singer 'Zozimus' and the writer Lady Morgan who hosted a famous salon on Kildare Street. Lady Morgan was perhaps best known for her novels *The Wild Irish Girl*, a romance with political overtones, and *O'Donnell*, which contains some wonderfully vivid descriptions of the country's poorer classes. Jane and later Oscar would have read these novels and been influenced by them and by their flamboyant author. Lady Morgan wrote under her maiden name, Sydney Owenson, and her entertaining gatherings included radical politicians, writers, performers and any celebrity who might be in town. Charles Maturin attended regularly at those lively salons and was remembered for his unconventional behaviour, sometimes wandering in absent-mindedly in his dressing gown and slippers. Jane would host her own salons years later along the same lines. Jane's system of inviting guests would not, however, be as idiosyncratic as the one used by Lady Morgan who had the habit of calling the names and the hour from her Kildare Street balcony, which happened to be just across the street from one of the city's most fashionable clubs.

This family connection with Charles Maturin, the clergyman and writer of gothic plays and novels, albeit as an uncle through marriage, was another definite influence on Jane and later on Oscar. An avid reader, Jane would have been familiar with Maturin's literary output, with his unorthodox beliefs and fantasies, as well as the many anecdotes surrounding the colourful behaviour of both himself and his wife. Maturin liked to claim he had escaped from the Bastille where he was incarcerated, having been found on a Paris street dressed in rich clothes. Jane, of course, had her own Italian fantasy. Maturin and his wife, though never wealthy, could be very extravagant and were given to entertaining their friends lavishly, sometimes on borrowed money. On one occasion the pair threw an elaborate party with Henrietta, Jane's aunt, welcoming their guests while seated on a throne even though the party was financed with £50 given by Lady Morgan's husband, Sir Thomas Morgan, to help tide them over a difficult time. Jane would have approved, as would Oscar.

Maturin liked to entertain his guests by candlelight, with the window shutters and drapes closed even on bright sunny days. This was another practice Jane would later adopt for her own Saturday afternoon 'At Homes' in Dublin and later, less successfully, in London. Jane also shared Maturin's liking for dressing up in fantastic costumes and they both had a habit of reciting aloud from works of literature as they went about.

The Elgee and Kingsbury families, like most of the other Anglo-Irish families in their circle, were Protestants who believed in the political union of Ireland with England. Anglo-Irish is a term used to describe a privileged social class, usually Anglican Church of Ireland, with ties of kinship or residency to both England and Ireland.

Maturin, although a Protestant clergyman, was a nationalist and did not support the 1801 Act of Union, which created the United Kingdom of Great Britain and Ireland, believing that Ireland received few if any benefits from its political connection with its larger neighbour. Jane would also come to reject her own family's strong Protestant-unionist politics, pouring her nationalist thoughts and feelings into the stirring poetry she published in the *Nation*. Nationalist opinion encompassed a range of opinion from people who believed that Ireland should have a say over their own domestic affairs while keeping the link with England and the monarchy to those who held the more radical opinion that the island of Ireland should sever all links with the United Kingdom and become 'a nation once again'. The Elgee family members were, of course, horrified when they found out who the rebellious nationalist poet Speranza actually was.

Charles Maturin and his work also had a definite influence on Oscar Wilde. This is particularly evident in Wilde's novel *The Picture of Dorian Gray*. Sebastian Melmoth, the hero of Maturin's only great success, *Melmoth the Wanderer*, published in 1820, exchanged his soul for 150 years of life. After many years of wandering Melmoth eventually returned to his native Wicklow where his youthful features disappeared as his bargained time came to a close. Meanwhile, his brother's descendant came across a strange portrait, felt its sinister power and resolved to destroy it. The ingredients for *Dorian Gray* are all there. When Oscar Wilde was released from prison in 1897 he immediately crossed to France and spent his few remaining years exiled in Paris with occasional wanderings south to the coast or to Italy and Switzerland. During this distressing final period he regularly used the name Sebastian Melmoth, the hero of Maturin's novel, in order, as he put it himself, 'to avoid the prying eye and the foolish tongue'.[6]

3

A Rural Boyhood

Oscar's father, William Wilde, was a complex man: a Protestant and a unionist but with an attachment to native Irish culture and a strong desire to see Ireland and the Irish prosper. Unlike many others of his class, William understood the customs of the Irish peasantry and appreciated their fondness for story and legendary romance. Born in March 1815, William's childhood years were spent romping through the fields around Elphin and Castlerea where his father had his practice. This brought him into close contact with the local tenantry and he became well versed in the old Gaelic folk tales and superstitions. But William was the Protestant grandson of a land agent and the son of the local doctor and was well aware that he was of different stock.

Having a dissimilar background did not blind him to the harsh conditions being experienced by the native Irish in that difficult period after the Napoleonic Wars when prices for agricultural produce fell dramatically and public executions ran at about 800 every year. William Wilde lived through some of the country's most traumatic events and witnessed rebellion, epidemics and famine at first hand. Though always sympathetic to the plight of the rural Irish, he could not support lawlessness and was horrified when the legitimate frustrations and discontent of the peasant manifested itself in acts of violence. One manifestation of the frustrations of the rural poor was Ribbonism, the umbrella name given to the banding together of young peasants into secret organisations with passwords, oaths and strange names such as Peep-O'Day Boys, White-Boys or Hearts-of-Steel. Many such secret societies sprang up in rural Ireland when William was a boy. Their nocturnal activities involved mutilating stock, attacking tithe-proctors and police barracks and other forms of lawlessness and intimidation.

In 1852, at the age of thirty-seven, William Wilde published a book called *Irish Popular Superstitions*. It is an important work because it contains an account of William's early childhood spent in and about the countryside around Elphin, County Roscommon, and includes the story of a tragic event involving Ribbonmen in the locality. It tells of William's friendship with a local peasant farmer and 'roving blade' called Paddy Welsh, the first of three men who played influential roles in the life of the sometimes precocious young son of the local doctor. In parts this is a charming little book with its somewhat idyllic descriptions of the lives of the country folk in the 1820s and 1830s, but it also includes scenes of cruelty and hardship and goes on to give a startling account of the horrors of the Famine of the 1840s.

Paddy Welsh lived with his wife and son in a thatched cabin beside the River Suck in a place called Castlecoote, close to where Dr Thomas Wilde had his practice. Here young William spent many happy days learning to make fishing flies as he listened to Welsh planning his adventures or playing his fiddle and telling fantastic tales that filled William's impressionable mind with excitement. William obviously idealised Welsh who appears to have had an exceptional understanding of distilling, hunting, fishing and fiddle-playing as well as the more mundane pursuits of tilling, churning and shoeing horses. Paddy Welsh was a larger-than-life character and was blamed for keeping his young friend from his formal education at the local Diocesan School. According to William himself:

> he was one of the quaintest companions, and the most astute fisherman that frequented the banks of the Suck for many a long year . . . During our own boyhood, when watching his practised hand throwing a red-tackle, or a black-and-orange, over the very nose of a trout . . . with his light whip-rod springing from the very wheel, and at least

five and thirty yards of line out – or listening with gaping
avidity to the doctrines he enunciated . . . complacently
viewing our efforts to imitate his casting . . . we regarded
him with reverence approaching to awe.[1]

Paddy Welsh died of a fever when William was only eight years old
but the seeds of a love for the ways of the country had been sown.

Soon after Paddy Welsh's death a series of terrifying events took
place in County Roscommon. They stayed forever in William's mind.
It was known that Paddy, being a hunter and sporting type, kept a gun
in his cottage. One night a large band of Ribbonmen called at
Widow Welsh's door. They wanted her son Michael to join in their
night's business and they wanted the gun they knew was in the house.
The leader and his men had come all the way from Galway and many
others of the gang also came from outside the district and would not
have known Paddy Welsh personally. William tells his readers that
Michael had been expecting some calamity because he had recently
received a strange warning of impending doom while paying a
nocturnal visit to the ruined castle at Ballintober. There a ghostly
spectre known as the Thivish (from the Gaelic word *taibhse*, meaning
ghost) appeared to the terrified youth who afterwards came to believe
that a curse was upon him. Oscar, incidentally, would have been
influenced by such tales heard in his own youth and believed in such
forewarnings and was always very superstitious. Even though he
understood that such ideas were 'the opponents of common sense',
he also held that 'common sense is the enemy of romance'.

The promised doom soon arrived for Michael in the form of
the Ribbonmen who press-ganged him into joining them in their
planned attack upon the barracks near Ballintober. The youths did
not know that the police had been alerted and were ready and
waiting in the ruins of Ballintober Castle, listening for the band of
Ribbonmen to arrive in the moonlight. Their white shirts and
ribboned hats made them easy targets. The police allowed about a
third of the gang of several hundred to pass and then opened fire.
Seized with panic, the party scattered and fled in all directions leaving
young Michael Welsh dead on the roadway. Two more youths later

died of their wounds and others were captured but the terrible story does not end there.

On the following Monday morning, two poles forming a gallows were erected in the market square of Roscommon town. From these the body of Paddy Welsh's son was suspended by the hands and a placard with the word 'RIBBONMAN' scrawled across it attached to a decorated hat fixed by the hangman on the dead youth's head. At that time the hangman for the Connaught Circuit was a woman known as 'Lady Betty'. She had actually been sentenced to death for killing her own son and stealing his savings but then escaped the hangman's noose by volunteering to fill the vacancy that existed for a hangman. She proved her ability to carry out the required duties and was quickly appointed to hang and flog those convicted at the Connaught courts.

About noon Michael's body was taken down from the gallows and tied in a sitting position in a cart that then set off at the head of a grisly procession through the town. Three horses and carts followed. Bound at the tailboard of each cart was a man sentenced to flogging. The military lined the streets and the procession moved through at flogging pace. 'Lady Betty' was involved in hanging young Michael Welsh from the gallows but was not called upon to officiate at the floggings on this occasion. In her place a young Sicilian carried out the punishments together with some drummers from army regiments in the province. William describes the scene vividly – the floggers, the military, the police, the cavalcade of magistrates, many on horseback, and the Major who ordered and directed the proceedings sitting in an open chariot. By the Major's side 'lolled a large, unwieldy person, with bloated face and slavering lip – the ruler of Connaught . . . the great gauger-maker of the west, The Right Honourable'. Here William falls silent and refrains from naming the grotesque figure, 'the ruler of Connaught,' a Member of Parliament (MP) called Denis Browne. Instead William shows his disgust by stating simply 'Let us drop the curtain. If this was not Connaught, it was hell.' But then the outraged William Wilde pulls himself together, his unionist background reasserting itself: 'Well – it was a frightful spectacle, horrifying and demoralising; but perhaps applicable to the time and circumstances.'

He concludes by saying that 'it completely put an end to ribbonism in that district for many a year'.[2]

The love of fishing and country life picked up from Paddy Welsh in Roscommon was further nurtured during William's regular visits to his grandparents' estates at Ballymagibbon. Even today the countryside around Cong with its lakes and rivers and mysterious prehistoric sites is a magical place and was the ideal playground for a boy like William with his vivid imagination and intellectual curiosity. Here, among the ancient cairns and stone circles with their associated legends and supernatural connotations, the enthusiasm that would later drive William Wilde to climb to the top of an Egyptian pyramid or to tunnel into the suffocating depths of a mummy's tomb was fired.

Still later, a tiring Sir William, by then a respected author and antiquarian as well as a renowned medical man, would spend much of his time in a close study of those same ruins he fondly remembered from his youth. When his sons Oscar and Willie were free from school, Sir William liked to have them accompany him as he poked around the ruins and sites, measuring, examining and sketching. Later, Oscar attempted to make use of this familiarity with archaeological practices when in 1879 he wrote to the Professor of Comparative Philology at Oxford, A. H. Sayce, enquiring about the possibility of an archaeological studentship. He told the professor that he had experience 'and from my boyhood have been accustomed, through my Father, to visiting and reporting on ancient sites, taking rubbings and measurements and all the techniques of open air archaeological – it is of course a subject of intense interest to me'.[3] Nothing came of Oscar's idea, however.

Young William was not only stimulated by the mysterious cairns and the standing stones, he also encountered some inspiring characters around Ballymagibbon. One of those was a Catholic priest, Fr Peter Prendergast, the very last Abbot of Cong Abbey, who befriended the visiting youngster from Roscommon. It was said that the Fynn family had given shelter to the Canons Regular and members of the Order of St Augustine when they were driven from their monastery at Cong and so it came to pass that the very last Abbot was at that time living in a farmhouse known as Abbotstown on Ballymagibbon lands. He was 'a very fine, courteous, white–haired old man . . . he did not nominate a successor, nor was such appointed by any Irish chapter, or by the General Abbot at Rome'.[4] Fr Prendergast lived a long life and died on 28 January 1829 at the age of eighty-eight when William was thirteen years old.

The Abbot possessed several valuable relics, among them the Shrine of St Patrick's Tooth, known as *Fiachal Phádraig*, and a piece of linen called *Foil-a-Rí* (King's Blood) said to have been dipped in the blood of King Charles I at the time of his decapitation at Whitehall in 1649 and believed to have the royal or Stewart faculty of curing the King's Evil.[5] People came in large numbers to be touched by Fr Prendergast and his relics and he took particular pride in showing them to William and elucidating on their various powers. The young grandson of the estate owners found the old priest and his stories fascinating and perhaps this explains William's lifelong interest in artefacts.

Incredibly, Fr Prendergast was the keeper of one of Ireland's great national treasures, the priceless Cross of Cong. William remembers seeing the beautiful cross 'in the possession of Abbot Prendergast, who kept it with the other relics already mentioned, in a three-cornered cupboard in his little sittingroom'.[6] Every Christmas Day and Easter Day he set up the Cross on the altar at Cong, where thousands of people from the surrounding villages would come to see the precious and holy object. The Cross of Cong is now on permanent display in the National Museum of Ireland and is one of its most prized possessions. It is an oaken cross, 30 inches high by 19 inches across the arms, covered with bronze and silver plates, washed with gold and most beautifully enriched with intricate engraving using blue and white enamel with exquisite gold filigree work, and the edges are studded with precious stones. Turlough Mór O'Conor, King of Ireland, whose name is punched into the silver plate around the sides, commissioned the cross in 1123 as a fitting place to enshrine a portion of the true cross sent to him from Rome.[7] When Fr Prendergast died his successor as parish priest of Cong, Fr Waldron, found the precious object left casually in the press in the old Abbot's home.[8]

Abbot Prendergast came to own one of his other relics, the *Fiachal Phádraig*, in a somewhat irregular manner. The story goes that the Abbot, a formidable character by all accounts, happened upon the custodian of the shrine, a man named Reilly, who was making a living for himself by going about the countryside performing cures with the relic both on animals and on humans. The Abbot asked him if he might know who the rightful holders were and was told the Canons of Cong once owned the relic. To the amazement of Reilly, the Abbot snatched it and rode off with the cry that he was the last of the Augustinian Canons of the monastery and therefore would be keeping it. William Wilde would be equally cavalier and had no qualms about taking skulls from tombs in Jerusalem or removing urns and bones from the depths of ancient cairns. And the death mask of Jonathan Swift, the satirist and author of *Gulliver's Travels* who was also Dean of St Patrick's Cathedral in Dublin, disappeared while in William's possession, only to surface many years after his death when it was offered for sale by his son Willie.

Visitors to the ruined abbey at Cong in a village of the same name on the northern shores of Lough Corrib can today see the face of Fr Peter Prendergast carved in limestone above the arched gateway leading down to the Monks' Fishing House. The carving is probably not an exact likeness, however, as it dates from the early 1860s when Sir Benjamin L. Guinness of the famous brewing family had restoration works carried out on the ancient abbey. He had recently purchased the nearby Ashford Castle estate, today a world-famous luxury hotel.

The restoration or conservation of national monuments and historical buildings was far from a priority in nineteenth-century Ireland but Sir William Wilde was among a small number of antiquarians who passionately believed in the importance of recording and preserving the country's ancient ruins and prehistoric sites, many of which were in an appalling condition.[8]

If the young William Wilde was impressed by Fr Prendergast's stories and his precious relics he was also influenced by a local youth called Dick Blake who helped him refine his hunting and fishing skills and the other talents William had picked up from Paddy Welsh back in Roscommon. Years later, when Sir William was engaged in travelling about the locality gathering information and inspecting sites for a book he was planning to write, which would detail the ancient monuments found around Lough Corrib, he would be unexpectedly reminded of his boyhood friend Dick Blake. It happened while he was conducting a survey of the old church of St Fraughaun's, which today can be found on the grounds of the Dowagh estate just north of the village of Cross.[9] He was surprised to discover a relatively recent grave behind the crumbling western gable of the ancient ruin. It was the final resting place of Dick Blake, William's companion from the long-ago days when he used to come as a boy to visit with his grandparents at Ballymagibbon.

Sir William included the following as a footnote to his account of St. Fraughaun's: 'Within the precincts of this little church stands the tomb of a very memorable man in his day and generation, and by his life affording a type of many of the gentry of the West during the past century and a half. Well, with all your faults, Dick Blake, I cannot but remember how well you taught me to ride, keeping my "hands down low on the saddle" – what skilful directions for shooting, and training setters and pointers, you gave me; and with what pride you used to see me shoot the rising trout from off the bridge of Cross . . . years ago.' Because Dick Blake was mentor to young William Wilde when he came to stay at his grandparents estate in Mayo, it is only natural to think of him as being older than his pupil, perhaps with something of the character of Paddy Welsh. It is therefore surprising to read on what is today a cracked and overgrown gravestone that William Richard Blake died in 1847 at the age of thirty-one. They were boyhood friends of almost exactly the same age. The headstone is also inscribed with the old Blake family crest, which means that Dick came from a branch of one of the leading families in the area.

Oscar and his brother, Willie, would have heard their father discuss his findings and possibly knew about the discovery of the grave of his childhood friend. Sir William did not reveal Dick Blake's precise faults but they were probably those usually associated with the boisterous country gentry he represented whose talents often did not extend far beyond excessive gambling, drinking and carousing. One is reminded of George Eliot's Squire Cass and his two pathetic sons. Years later, in *A Woman of No Importance*, Oscar would describe gentlemen who enjoyed foxhunting as 'the unspeakable in full pursuit of the uneatable'. Perhaps Dick Blake was still galloping somewhere through the great playwright's subconscious.

4

City Girl

If young William Wilde enjoyed the countryside and its pursuits, Jane Elgee was a city girl through and through. Born and brought up in Dublin, she matured to be a striking young lady, tall with dark luminous eyes and jet-black hair tumbling to her shoulders. Jane's father, Charles Elgee, the eldest son of the Archdeacon of Wexford, had just commenced practising as a solicitor in Dublin in 1807 when his eyes fell upon the beautiful and wealthy Sara Kingsbury. Her family lived in the splendid Lisle House on Molesworth Street, close to the Duke of Leinster's mansion that today houses the Irish Parliament. Sara's prosperous father, Thomas Kingsbury, was the Commissioner of Bankruptcy and also the Vicar of Kildare. The Kingsburys were Protestant gentry, staunch supporters of the union with Britain. Sara's grandfather had been President of the Royal College of Physicians and a friend of Dean Swift.

Charles Elgee and Sara Kingsbury were married in the church of St Iberius on Wexford's High Street two days before Christmas in 1809. Yuletide and wedding festivities merged in that southern town before the couple returned to Dublin to begin their married life in the house on Essex Bridge where Charles had been lodging. The following year their first child, Emily Thomasine, was born and in 1811 they moved to an address on fashionable Leeson Street. Stability was not to be a feature of this marriage, however, and within a year they had moved once again, this time to 4 St James's Street East where their second child, John, was born in 1812.

Charles got himself into some kind of financial difficulties and in 1814 a deed had to be drawn up giving him £130 from his wife's resources to pay off debts. However, in order for him to obtain what was then a sizeable sum, Charles had to sign over any future interest he might have in his wealthy wife's inheritance. Apparently, he would be helped once and once only. It looks as if the marriage was under strain at this point as the deed also clarifies Sara's financial position should she decide to separate from her husband. The couple got through this turbulent period and in 1815 returned to Leeson Street, this time to number 3. Sara gave birth to their third child, Frances. Sadly, this baby died in Wexford three months later. Two years later and the nomadic pair are on the move once more, but only a few doors down to 6 Leeson Street. The name of Elgee remains on the Leeson Street directory for the next seven years but disappears abruptly in 1822 only to reappear twenty-one years later when Sara Elgee is listed as the tenant of 34 Leeson Street.

What became of Jane's father, Charles Elgee, and what is the explanation for his sudden disappearance in 1822? An obituary, which appeared in the *Freeman's Journal* of 4 February 1825, goes some way towards an explanation. It reads: 'On the 13th August last, at Bangalore, in the East Indies, Charles Elgee, esquire, the eldest son of the late venerable Archdeacon Elgee of Wexford.' Charles had taken himself off to India, then the land of opportunity and part of the British Empire, for reasons unknown. If this note had not appeared in the paper his fate would have been as mysterious as his motives because Jane, throughout her life, remained curiously silent on the subject of her father. Perhaps there was someone else in his life or maybe he had run up further debts and this time could not draw upon the Kingsbury fortune. Whatever the reasons, Charles Elgee left his young wife and family behind in Dublin while he took off for distant shores. But his plans, such as they were, did not work out and he died in India in the summer of 1824. Given the constant changes of address, the borrowing of monies, the deed and his sudden departure, it is not unreasonable to suggest there may have been a feckless strain in the maternal grandfather of Oscar Wilde.

The obituary also sheds some light on one other issue. Jane liked people to believe that she was born in 1826, a date widely accepted by her contemporaries. Her father, however, was already dead by this time. Confusion over Jane's age should not be a surprise. She would have fully agreed with Lady Bracknell's declaration on the issue: 'No woman should ever be quite accurate about her age. It looks so calculating.' Unfortunately, Jane would eventually be forced by harsh circumstances to become more 'calculating'. When the wolf of poverty eventually arrived at her door in the difficult years following her husband's death, Lady Wilde found it necessary to apply to the Royal Literary Fund for a grant. Because age would help her case she gave her date of birth as 27 December 1821, a time more in keeping with events.

It has been suggested that Jane might have been illegitimate, but this is highly improbable, and besides, she had the large physique associated with the Elgee family, a feature she bequeathed to her two sons. It is much more likely that Jane, for reasons of vanity, simply wanted to lop a good five years from her age. This idiosyncrasy was among the many she would pass on to Oscar who also liked people to believe he was younger than he actually was. What seems a harmless foible of vanity actually played against Oscar when, at the opening session of his lawsuit against the Marquess of Queensberry for libel which precipitated his ruin, he was caught out in the lie and was made to appear untrustworthy by a clever lawyer who knew his true age.

Unlike William Wilde, Jane wrote little about her childhood so it is impossible to say where exactly the widowed Sara raised her family, but given her Kingsbury background and inheritance it is doubtful that they experienced any hardship, even with an absent father. Perhaps Sara eventually joined forces with her sister Henrietta, whose husband Charles Maturin also died in 1824. The two sisters had always got along and Sara was a regular visitor when Maturin was alive. Jane may also have spent time visiting with her uncle the Reverend Richard Waddy Elgee, curate and later Rector in Wexford, which could help explain Speranza's ability to empathise so well with rural Ireland. However, given the fact that Jane was never really enthusiastic about rural living, it is fair to assume that she was raised mainly in Dublin where the granddaughter of the wealthy Kingsburys would have enjoyed the privileges of her class.

Jane was very bright and received an excellent education from private tutors. Years later, Jane's own young children would also be educated at home. Oscar received a private education until he was almost ten years old. He was then sent off to boarding school with his brother, Willie. Jane was fond of the Classics and literature, another attribute she would bestow upon her son, but she really excelled in the study of languages and would eventually become highly respected as a translator of both fiction and poetry. As an adult she added Swedish to her list of languages when she became acquainted with Rosalie Olivecrona who edited a magazine for women in Stockholm. Jane also made friends with Rosalie's wider Swedish circle, which included Baron Robert von Kraemer, governor of Uppsala, and his daughter Lotton. She visited Sweden with her husband on a number of occasions giving rise to one more Dublin rumour about Sir William's sexual prowess. A story went around to the effect that William had operated on the future King Oscar of Sweden's eye. To add sauce to the tale, while the future King was temporarily incapacitated, William was supposed to have seduced his wife. This well-known bit of gossip was, of course, totally groundless, but is indicative of the kind of rumour-mongering to which the Wildes were often subjected.

Jane kept up a correspondence with her Swedish friends over many years and a large number of her letters are today in the Royal Library of Sweden. If her ability with languages was exceptional it is, however, clear from her letters that her handwriting never improved and remained a lifelong weak point. Jane ensured that both her sons and her daughter, Isola, would likewise be proficient in languages and to that end employed a succession of European governesses. One came from Germany, another was Swiss and she once asked her Swedish friend if she could locate a governess there. Oscar had fluent French and little Isola by the age of nine knew German and Swedish. Jane boasted to Lotten von Kraemer that Isola 'took great delight in reading the Swedish testament to me'. Jane's children were her pride and joy.

Life in Dublin during the 1820s and 1830s would have been pleasant for a single girl of Jane Elgee's class. Grafton Street had its selection of fashionable shops and St Stephen's Green with its tree-lined walks was a pleasant place to take a stroll. Across the River Liffey, the open spaces of the Phoenix Park were perfect for picnic outings or horse-riding and the scene of occasional military displays with soldiers in fancy uniforms marching in formation or dashing about on horseback while cannons blazed away. Dublin had two theatres and Jane would have enjoyed attending concerts as well as going to lunch and tea parties or to the popular musical soirées. Then there were the private balls where young officers from the Royal Barracks came to dance with the beautiful daughters of the city's notables. It was wittily remarked at the time that the function of Dublin's large army barracks was not to garrison the country but to provide dancing partners for the young ladies of the city.

The highlight of Dublin's social calendar at that time was 'the Castle Season', when most of Ireland's society came to town to spend the six festive weeks in early spring attending the many balls, functions and drawing rooms as well as the more formal court presentations hosted by the Lord Lieutenant, the Crown's representative in Ireland. Girls came from all parts of the country in the hope of attracting the eye of someone of suitable rank who just might propose. Jane Elgee loved the drama and dressing-up associated with attending Castle functions and continued to enjoy those glittering occasions even as Speranza of the *Nation* and later as the flamboyant Lady Wilde.

Dublin was a bustling city in the early decades of the nineteenth century with students attending Trinity College mingling with dragoons from the Royal Barracks and seamen up from the busy port. It was, however, a city in slow decline, both economically and politically. Many of the Protestant ascendancy class, the 'real aristocracy', left Ireland altogether when the country voted itself out of existence with the 1801 Act of Union. The aim of this Act was to unite the Kingdom of Great Britain and the Kingdom of Ireland to create the Kingdom of Great Britain and Ireland. The Irish Parliament, which up to this point had its sittings in Dublin, also merged with the British Parliament sitting in Westminster. Dublin as a city had been demoted by the Act of Union. The aristocracy rented or more often sold their great townhouses, making room on the elegant eighteenth-century Georgian squares and boulevards for a rising middle class of professionals, which would eventually include Sir William Wilde and his family.

If Dublin had its elegant side it also had more than its fair share of poverty. Once the second city in the United Kingdom, it would in due course drop to tenth place and be overtaken even by Belfast. Side-street slums expanded and some of the city's once-beautiful townhouses were converted into tenements. Eventually, inner-city Dublin came to have the worst slums in Europe with entire families subsisting in single rooms. When Queen Victoria visited Ireland in August 1849, she wrote from the Viceregal Lodge in the Phoenix Park to her uncle King Leopold of Belgium stating that 'you see more ragged and wretched people here than ever I saw anywhere else'. The Queen failed to mention the terrible Famine that was ravishing the Irish countryside at that very time, driving people into the city and swelling the numbers of destitute already roaming the streets.

Another feature on the streets of Dublin when Jane was young were the many ballad singers, the most famous of all being blind Michael Moran, better known as 'Zozimus', whose special talent was turning the news of the day into verse that he then bawled out to the passing public. His favourite pitch was Essex Bridge where Charles Elgee first brought his new wife to live.

The young Jane Elgee, like the rest of her class, would have been shielded by her position from any real appreciation of the city's slum life. As the youngest by far in her family she probably spent a good deal of her time alone and this would have furthered her interest in literature and learning. She was eight years old when her nineteen-year-old sister, Emily Thomasine, married Captain Samuel Warren of the 65th Regiment, a member of a prominent Dublin family whose grandfather had been Lord Mayor. Two years later in 1831 she watched her brother, John, marry Matilda Duff and leave soon after for Louisiana with his wife and baby daughter where he became a successful lawyer, eventually rising to a judgeship in New Orleans and growing very wealthy. Interestingly, when he died there in 1864 at the age of fifty-two, he mentioned his sister Emily Thomasine and even his nurse in his will but for some reason left nothing to Jane. Her independent spirit and nationalist views always meant there would be tensions between Jane and her unionist family.

Dublin had one other claim to fame in the early nineteenth century. The city was a renowned centre for medicine and its doctors and scientists were highly respected internationally. When the time came to choose a career for the young William Wilde, the country doctor's son, it was decided to pack him off to Dublin to study surgery under the celebrated Abraham Colles at Dr Steevens' Hospital. Jane Elgee was still only a child of about ten when, in 1832 at the age of seventeen, William arrived in the city to begin training for a career in medicine.

Part 2

Youth's Kingdom

'There is nothing like youth. The middle-aged are mortgaged to Life. The old are in Life's lumber-room. But youth is the Lord of Life. Youth has a kingdom waiting for it.'

A Woman of No Importance

5

The Young Doctor

When William Wilde arrived in Dublin he found a loose educational system and a group of bohemian students much given to revelry and toughened by the horrors the young trainee surgeons were encountering. He was immediately plunged into the turmoil of hospital practice and introduced to the ghastly filth of the operating theatres and the hideous dissecting rooms. This was the era when alcohol or a little opium were the only forms of anaesthetic available to the unfortunate patient who, more often than not, had to be tied down with ropes while the surgeons went about their task accompanied by screams of agony and terror from the very person they were trying to cure. This work required a special type of nerve and William Wilde had it. He was more than equal to the grisly tasks. He took to his studies and got along well with both his peers and his lecturers.

There were two parts to the medical students' studies, a practical element and the medical theory. The actual surgery was taught at Dr Steevens' Hospital under Dr Coles and, for the more academic medical modules, the students had to attend the Park Street School in Lincoln Place where they received instruction from two equally distinguished physicians, Dr William Stokes and the more senior Dr Robert James Graves. Dr Stokes was still only in his late twenties but he had already achieved an illustrious reputation. His interests extended to art and nature and the antiquities of Ireland as well as to medicine. A strong, lifelong friendship developed between the young doctor and his enthusiastic student up from County Roscommon. Dr Graves also befriended William, a friendship that would last until the senior man's death in 1853.

Surgical procedures in those days were basic and operations were usually limited to amputations or the removal of stones from the bladder and the tying of arteries for aneurysm. Above all else, speed was essential, and the better operator was the quicker. The top surgeons had developed their skills to such a degree that if an observer glanced away at the crucial moment he might miss the entire procedure. Surgeons may have understood the importance of speed but they had little or no appreciation for cleanliness or infection and liked to parade around wearing aprons encrusted in blood and gore as proof of their professional experience and ability.

If the operating theatre was not sufficiently gruesome for the youthful students there was always the putrid dissecting room where the cadaver on the table was often partly decomposed. The school was glad to have any corpse for its students regardless of condition and asked few questions from their suppliers as to their sources. As a result of this policy a grim trade had built up to meet the demand from medical schools for bodies. Resurrectionists, as they were known, were busy stealing from graves, mostly from the burial grounds at the nearby Royal Hospital, Kilmainham, where the common folk of the city brought their dead but were too poor to employ night watchmen to make sure their relatives were allowed to rest in peace. The thefts, which were carried out under the cover of darkness and at great speed, involved exposing only the head of the coffin then breaking open the lid and dragging the body out by means of a rope around the neck. The corpse was stripped and the clothes returned to the grave because stealing clothes was a greater offence in law than stealing the body.

William made friends with a number of his fellow students in Dr Steevens' Hospital, including Charles Laver who later deserted medicine for literature. He went on to become a successful novelist and, for a time, edited the *Dublin University Magazine* where William published many articles on a wide array of topics. William was only settling into his studies and to his new life in Dublin when he was recalled back to his home west of the River Shannon following an outbreak of Asiatic cholera in the capital city. The epidemic had been spreading along the trade routes, reaching Dublin in 1832. William's relatives were naturally alarmed and it was decided he would return to stay with his grandparents at Ballymagibbon. As events turned out, County Mayo was not the safest option for William, but, when faced with unexpected danger, the seventeen-year-old proved to be both decisive and brave.

A peddler had taken ill in the village of Kilmaine north of Cong and William, the 'young doctor', was sent for. He hurried to the scene but upon arrival found that the peddler was already dead and the cause of death was, without doubt, cholera. The owner of the lodging house where the peddler had been staying was by now also unwell, having caught the disease himself. Nobody from the locality would enter the house or help in any way. William did what he could. He bravely stayed with his patient and nursed him through the cholera fever but, unfortunately, the lodging house keeper then died from exhaustion. The villagers supplied a coffin but continued to keep their distance. With no assistance forthcoming, William worked on alone. He placed the body in the coffin and, with the help of one drunken pensioner, bore the corpse to the graveyard on a donkey cart. William dug the grave, buried the coffin in quicklime then returned to the house. He burned the beds and clothing, fumigated the building with sulphur and tobacco smoke, best practice at the time, and by so doing would appear to have stamped out the disease in Kilmaine as no further cases were reported.

News of the young man's heroic behaviour reached his teachers in Dublin and Graves gave a full account of the deed in one of his lectures. When the epidemic eventually passed William returned to Dublin and resumed his studies. On a later visit to Ballymagibbon William once again proved his mettle by saving the life of a child with his swift, decisive action. The child was choking on a piece of potato and William, without hesitation, cut open the child's windpipe with the first sharp instrument to hand, which in this case was a pair of scissors. The procedure was a success and the entire village witnessed it because it was Sunday morning and the local folk were on their way to Mass.

If young William had impressed the folk around Ballymagibbon he was also making a name for himself among his teachers in Dublin. He had a naturally inquisitive mind, limitless energy and was in no way squeamish. He could be opinionated and was well able to defend his position without being intimidated by seniority. He also enjoyed the more boisterous side of student life and could drink and carouse with the best of them. In 1836 William Wilde, still an undergraduate, wrote his first medical paper, a treatise on Spina Bifida. The paper so impressed his instructors that he was invited to read the work to the Medical Philosophical Society. It was becoming more and more evident that this young man had a special talent or, to use a phrase that William himself would later employ, he 'possessed the talisman' of his chosen profession, but like many exceptional people he could, at times, push himself too hard with damaging consequences.

Just before taking his final examinations William contracted fever, probably typhus. Against all advice he sat the examinations and answered brilliantly but immediately after the last paper he collapsed. Within a few days his condition was considered hopeless and Dr Graves, William's teacher and friend, was sent for. He prescribed a glass of strong ale to be taken every hour and this medication had the required effect upon the student. The dying youth revived and eventually made a full recovery.

William successfully completed his four-year course in Dr Steevens' Hospital and then decided to spend one additional year studying midwifery at the nearby Rotunda Hospital. Then, on 13 March 1837, at the age of twenty-two, William Wilde became a Licentiate of the Royal College of Surgeons. The Masters at Dr Steevens' Hospital and Park Street School in Lincoln Place were reluctant to let someone of William Wilde's exceptional talent go, so, when he completed his midwifery course, they appointed him as resident clinical clerk and curator of the museum of Dr Steevens' Hospital, a post he retained for some months while he recovered from his illness.

Then, unexpectedly, a great opportunity to travel presented itself. Sir Henry Marsh and Dr Graves required a doctor to attend a wealthy patient of theirs who was about to undertake a voyage to the Mediterranean for medicinal reasons. The patient, a Glaswegian by the name of Robert Meiklam, was a member of the Royal Yacht Squadron and possessed a 130-ton steam yacht called the RYS *Crusader*. It was also believed that William's own health might benefit from a spell in a warmer climate and that this young graduate who bravely faced cholera in Mayo could be relied upon to perform similar deeds if the need arose while abroad.

There may also have been another pressing consideration. The newly qualified doctor was about to become a father and perhaps someone thought it prudent to have him away from the city at such a sensitive time.

6

Voyage of Discovery

On the 24 September 1837 Robert Meiklam's *Crusader* sailed from the Isle of Wight making for sunnier climes. On board, the ship's young doctor patrolled the deck and watched the land fade out of sight. He had armed himself with notebooks and writing materials intending to record the various climates they would encounter along the way with an eye to finding suitable places where invalids might convalesce. If his mind was on the pregnant girl he was leaving behind in Ireland such thoughts did not find their way into his journal at any stage throughout the voyage. The *Crusader* was a sturdy vessel rigged as a topsail schooner and soon both the ship and its young doctor would be put to the test.

They sailed south through open waters and had just entered the Bay of Biscay when the first of several mighty gales struck. William quickly discovered that he was not a very good sailor and had to take to his berth where he lay listening to the groaning and straining of timber all around him as the ship bucked and the wind howled and huge waves splashed across the deck. The mainmast sprung at its base but the vessel managed to limp into port at Corunna (La Coruna) in northern Spain where repairs were carried out.

It was an alarming start but William Wilde was never easily discouraged. He was a young man full of scientific curiosity and he possessed a stout heart. William knew this trip would present him with enormous scope for observation, analysis and research and he rose to the occasion. He soon found his sea legs and began to write. The initial, modest idea of noting the various climates expanded and soon everything was being recorded: the people he came across, the condition of the ports, the history and commerce of the places, the regional dress. Nor did he fail to show an appreciation for the local ladies and the quality of the wine. William adopted the role of explorer, a man of science, investigating the flora and fauna, enquiring into the nature of public institutions and the indigenous customs. He was a born census-maker but gifted with an imagination that ensured he would never be content as a mere statistician. His mind's eye could put flesh back on to bare bones and rebuild ancient cities from the rubble of their scattered ruins.

Repairs completed, the *Crusader* continued on its way, heading south, eventually arriving into the great seaport of Balem (Belem), which today is part of Lisbon. Balem, the name William used, with its fine natural harbour was the starting point for many historical voyages of discovery including those of Vasco de Gama. William records his visit to the 'convent church in Balem' where he found an old tomb hidden away behind the altar. After somehow managing to persuade the sexton to open the lock, William descended into the vault and proceeded to lift the lid of the large trunk-shaped coffin where he found the body of what he claimed to be an old Portuguese royal, Alonzo VI, and noted that it looked well preserved but black and shrivelled.

In Lisbon the little group visited the aqueduct that spans the Valley of Alcantara and made their way across the narrow path 226 feet above ground level. This was a well-known spot for suicides and, sure enough, as they passed by one of the arches they came upon the corpse of a man who had flung himself to his death just hours before, a sight William thought he would never forget. He also mentions the packs of wild dogs that roamed the streets of Lisbon after dark feasting on the day's offal and attacking any stranger foolish enough to be out of doors when their fearful howling began. They were tolerated as scavengers in what he called 'this most filthy of cities'.

From Lisbon they crossed to Madeira where William took detailed notes of the botanical wealth and found the white wine from the south side of the island to be one of the finest he had ever tasted. Next stop was south to Tenerife where William and Meiklam set out with a guide to climb to the top of the island's 13,000-foot volcano. It was a long and arduous ascent by moonlight and it grew so cold that the eggs they brought with them for breakfast became balls of ice. It took twenty hours to complete the ascent, at first on horseback and then on foot, but the climbers were rewarded with a magnificent 200-mile view out to sea. William failed to record the state of his patient's health after this feat of mountaineering, but he did note that the air of Tenerife was possibly better than Madeira for invalids although the island did not have Madeira's lush growth and lacked hospitality and society. The women of Tenerife were, however, 'decidedly the handsomest, generally tall and beautifully formed'.

They sailed from Tenerife and entered the Mediterranean, stopping at Gibraltar and Algiers with William continuing to record all he saw. Gibraltar proved dull but 'the society of some of the fair daughters of England enlivened the monotony of the eternal red coats'. Algiers was under French control at that time and William believed it would have been a much better place if England was in charge of affairs. His attention was drawn to the dress of the Moors and he wondered if the broad cloak or toga, 'without seams, woven from the top throughout', could be the same type of garment worn by Jesus and mentioned in the Bible. As he drew closer to the Holy Land the Bible was much on William's mind and he was also becoming more and more aware of the proud status of 'Mother England' compared with the pitiable conditions of the 'foreigner'.

Even between ports of call William could not be still. As the ship sailed past the coast of Sicily making for Malta they came upon a school of dolphins and William, with some help from the crew, immediately set about catching one. It took 'six or eight stout fellows' and a mighty struggle to haul an eight-foot porpoise aboard. The energetic doctor immediately fell to dissecting the fish and conducting experiments out on the open deck. He spent two days cutting and hacking the specimen, making notes and recording observations he would use much later when he came to write an essay on the subject of suckling in whales and other marine animals. What Mr Meiklam and his wife thought about their indefatigable personal physician's extra-curricular activities went unrecorded.

Then it was on to Egypt where William was to perform deeds that were truly heroic if not downright foolhardy. The Meiklam party set out on a visit to the pyramids and William decided he would like to climb to the top of one of the ancient wonders of the world. The Great Pyramid of Giza has stepped ledges all the way to the peak so William chose the second pyramid, a much more hazardous undertaking, because the coating or outer layer of stones was still smooth and perfectly in place for 140 feet from the top. Two local guides assisted him in this exploit. They had contrived a method of climbing on each other's shoulders, often having to creep some distance to the side in order to find the next foothold, and William was made to follow suit. It was an extremely risky undertaking and if one fell, all three would be dashed on the rocks below. Mr Meiklam and his group could only stand and watch in trepidation as their irrepressible medic risked life and limb 400 feet above the Egyptian sands. At last the climbers reached the top and there, amid much cheering, whooping and backslapping William took in the magnificent views of the River Nile winding through the desert. Far below, Meiklam's party stood waving their hats in celebration, greatly relieved, no doubt, that their audacious companion had survived the ascent. William was normally contemptuous of people who scribbled their names on ancient monuments but when he saw two or three names scratched on the central rock at the pyramid's peak he made an exception and added his own. Perhaps his WRW (the R is for Robert) can still be seen up there to this day under the blazing sun but it will remain unread. Climbing this pyramid is now forbidden because of the large number of people who lost their lives in the attempt over the years.

Not content with conquering the pyramids, the spirited youth decided to spend a little time exploring the desert. He took off alone into the wilderness and when darkness came found a cave where he passed the night in fitful sleep surrounded by local Bedouins. The following day William came upon the mummy pits and, of course, wanted to descend into the narrow, sand-filled tunnels. He had forgotten to bring any lights with him but decided to go into the foul pits anyway, on the basis that if he could not see he could at least feel. The danger of suffocation in the narrow tunnels and vaults was real but he managed to grope and wriggle his way to a chamber with the help of a local guide and found many urns lying about undisturbed. They were able to convey six urns to the surface where William then lay insensible for some minutes. This was no small achievement and, like his other exploits, demanded great courage and determination. He took the urns with him and was eventually able to transport them home to Ireland on board the *Crusader*.

Moving on, William arrived at Alexandria where he came across the famous obelisk known as Cleopatra's Needle lying on the ground among the other shattered fragments scattered around Pompey's Pillar. He took careful notes and made sketches and later wrote an article for *Dublin University Magazine* suggesting that the obelisk would make a fitting tribute to Admiral Nelson if brought to London. This eventually came to pass when Cleopatra's Needle was taken from Egypt in 1878 and erected on the Thames embankment where it still stands today.

Back in Cairo, William visited the asylum for the insane where he found the ragged inmates chained in tiny cells with their hair matted and their nails grown to talons. Recovery, he was told, was rare. He also visited the slave market and took note of the shops at the entrance selling 'koorbags' or Arab whips and learned that Abyssinian girls aged from ten to eighteen were regarded as the better class of slave and fetched $100 whereas $30 or $40 could buy a young Negro girl from Nubia or Dongola. The Abyssinian girls would become concubines while the others would probably be put to work as household servants. William was not outraged by what he saw in the slave market. Instead he calmly reflected on the fact that scripture actually allowed for slavery, noting: 'It was slavery of the primitive Hebrew nations, allowed by Scripture and practised by the patriarchs, but which refinement and Christianity, the well-being of society, and the respect which man owes his fellow, alike forbid.'

More productively, William also spent several days studying the causes and treatment of the eye disease trachoma at a large military hospital and medical school in Cairo. Trachoma was widespread at the time and William was very interested in what he saw of the disease and its treatment. In *Narrative of a Voyage to Madeira . . . and along the shores of the Mediterranean*, the book he later published in which he recounts his travels on the *Crusader*, he wrote that 'the eye of the Arab girl, and more particularly the Egyptian, is so peculiar, and so often caused me to stop and admire its beauties'. His experience of eye disease while in Cairo no doubt influenced the direction his future career would take.

Mr Meiklam, his doctor and his crew sailed from the port of Alexandria on the morning of 7 February 1838 and crossed to Rhodes. On the way they once again encountered fierce storms and, this time, their jib-boom snapped, forcing them to take shelter on the small island of Vurnos in the Gulf of Mymi. When the winds died down the battered schooner made its way back to Rhodes where they were officially met by the dragoman of the British Consul. Indeed, it is interesting to note the amount of times the travellers were received by the Crown's representatives abroad and invited to official receptions and functions – Empire's outposts looking after their own. In Rhodes, William's imagination was sparked by the perfectly paved Street of the Knights. In his mind's eye he could see 'Knights and Christian princes, clad in all the panoply of War'. Down at the harbour William spent time trying to discover where the Colossus might have stood and concluded that the huge figure, another wonder of the ancient world, must have reached a height of at least 150 feet if ships were to sail under it.

Repairs carried out, the *Crusader* made for Cyprus where it had to lie in quarantine for three days before being allowed ashore because fever was so prevalent at the time. Then it was on towards the coast of Lebanon where another terrifying hurricane struck. William was thrown from his bunk and climbed on deck to see a sky darker than any he had ever before witnessed. He described the fearful sight, 'when one spot, if anything, darker than the rest, opened in the centre, and thence shone out a blaze of livid light that appeared to give us momentarily a glimpse into another world; from whose refulgent portals were hurled the sheets of fire that skimmed along the deep, brightening in their transit every nook and cranny of the vessel, and throwing a lurid glare upon the anxious faces of us all'.

They made it through and reached Tyre where William once more allowed his imagination run riot as he recalled the story of Alexander's ferocious attack on the city, even though nothing now remained of 'the strong city of Tyre; the mother of Carthage; the correspondent of Egean; which pushed her colonies beyond the pillars of Hercules, even to the isles of the west'. Standing there amid the ruins, William at last remembered his own Irish background: 'As an Irishman I felt no small degree of interest on first touching the motherland, whose colony we claim to be.' Origins and identity were never far from the surface of William's thoughts. Tyre, however, with its 'prostrate columns, its crumbling walls, its deserted cothon' was disappointing. William would soon be equally shocked at the condition of once-glorious Athens. Lessons about the value of one's own national heritage were being learned, and William would in future years become one of his own country's leading antiquarians and a stout campaigner for the preservation of its ancient sites.

Eventually, the sailors reached their intended destination, the Holy Land. They were met in Jaffa by the British Consul and provided with mules and horses for the journey inland to Jerusalem. 'Our party, which consists of ten persons, all armed and accoutred, made a very formidable cavalcade as we left the town at about twelve o'clock at noon.' They rode across the Plain of Sharon and William's head was filled with visions of proud knights and Crusaders galloping towards the Holy City. It was the Christian Sabbath and many of the inhabitants were sitting out in the sunshine as the riders passed. William noted that 'the women both here and in Joppa, cover their faces entirely with a dark coloured handkerchief – although, if young and pretty, they take particular care to give you, by accident, a look at their features in passing'. They crossed the hill country of the Philistines and reached Jerusalem where they found poor accommodation in a Latin convent. The rooms were cold and dark and the convent wine was not the best but, on learning that William was an Irishman and therefore more than likely a Roman Catholic, the curate Fr Benjamin appeared most days with a bottle of good wine hidden in his cloak.

William and his companions visited all the Christian sites such as the Holy Sepulchre, the Via Dolorosa, the Mount of Olives and Gethsemane and encountered the usual combination of devotion and extortion associated with places of pilgrimage. He questioned the authenticity of some sites such as 'the stable of Bethlehem' where his poking about angered the assisting friar, but overall he preferred to accept their legitimacy in the absence of solid proof to the contrary. William spent much of his time in a state of high excitement: 'in the holy city I slept little, except from sheer bodily fatigue. So exciting were the scenes witnessed in the day, and so perfectly absorbed was my mind in the object of my visit, that it seemed as if I were insulated from the rest of the world.'

While visiting the Field of Blood, the graveyard said to have been purchased with the thirty pieces of silver given to Judas, William heard of a tomb only recently discovered and opened by the Arabs. He made his way to the spot and found that it contained many skulls, but none of them appeared to William to be Jewish. Ignoring the dangers if caught, he snatched four skulls from the tomb and made off with them on horseback. Old Fr Prendergast from Cong would have been proud. He later managed to store them with the urns on board the *Crusader* and brought them home to Ireland for expert examination. Ethnology would also become an area of great interest to William.

The girls of Bethlehem were 'the most beautiful of their sex that we met in the east'. Once more it is their eyes that hold William's attention: 'Such eyes! Long, shadowy, with their languid fall of the fring'd lids.' The wine was once again declared to be the best he had yet tasted. William later said that the scene of greatest interest he had encountered on the entire journey was 'a Jew mourning over the stones of Jerusalem'. Origins, identity, homeland are all bound up in this image and, on reflection, it is not surprising that William Wilde selected this incident out of the many dramatic moments of the voyage.

Near Jerusalem, William and his companions met an old man who begged them to take his youngest son back with them to England. His other sons were either dead or conscripted or had fled as outlaws and the father believed his last surviving son could have a better life if he could make it to the safety of England. William wrote that he felt 'the pride of being an Englishman so strong at that moment. Thrice happy land; even at that distance, and at the very gate of Jerusalem has the poor Arab heard of your freedom and looks to you as shield to the desolate and the oppressed – the Judah of the gentile world!'[1] William, at this time, had travelled far from the green fields of Roscommon and obviously saw himself as an English gentleman abroad among the pitiable foreigners. He would later come to realise the relationship between Ireland and England meant he had inherited a more complicated identity. Oscar would also come to learn a lesson about identity when travelling in America, where he quickly found out how useful it was to be identified as the son of Speranza, the great Irish rebel poet, rather than the Oxford aesthete he was supposed to be.

As the party of English sailors and travellers rode back through the gates of Jaffa an Egyptian soldier threw a pebble that hit William in the face. The young doctor turned and struck the soldier with his whip forcing him to retreat behind the gate. A sentry appeared and he too received a blow from William's 'koorbag'. William's companions then drew up 'in strong muster' forcing the entire guard to retreat. Once more the Crown was successful against the rebellious natives. William never thought to question the motive behind the casting of that first pebble.

Stopping off at Athens on their return voyage, William was disappointed to find that visitors to the Acropolis had to 'wade through the mud and dirt of narrow streets and lanes' and that some of the city's ancient ruins now 'form the side and gables of modern buildings'. It would appear that the party at this stage was growing weary and beginning to wish for 'the home and table of a Briton happy, no matter under what clime he may be placed'. They stayed eight days in Athens visiting all the usual sites. The Meiklams then decided to leave their shipmates and travel east on a visit to Constantinople, allowing the schooner with its crew and doctor to make its weary way back home.

The *Crusader* entered Kingstown Harbour (present-day Dún Laoghaire) just south of Dublin on the morning of 3 June 1838 and William was overjoyed to be back. To William's eye, Ireland looked:

> More dear in its storms, its clouds and its showers,
> Than the rest of this world in its sunniest hours.[2]

7

In Business

On returning to Dublin, William rented rooms at 199 Great
Brunswick Street, now Pearse Street, and began sorting through
the many notes and observations he had diligently recorded while away
on the trip. The Royal Irish Academy asked him to give a series of talks
on his adventures abroad and William once more rose to the occasion.
He proved to be a fine lecturer with a wonderful speaking voice and
was invited by the British Association and the Royal Dublin Society to
give further talks on his travels. William, never slow to recognise an
opportunity, realised that he could probably turn out an interesting and
successful book, given the popularity of these lectures and the amount
of material gathered on the trip. With this in mind he set to work with
his usual diligence in the rented rooms in Great Brunswick Street and
soon had a complete manuscript of what would be his first published
book, *Narrative of a Voyage to Madeira, Teneriffe, and along the shores of the
Mediterranean, including a visit to Algiers, Egypt, Palestyne, Tyre, Rhodes and the
Holy Land.* Long titles were in vogue at the time.

William's style of writing is elaborate, full of 'purple prose' and
moments of high emotion. But the voice is that of a courageous young
man with much determination and self-belief. Nothing is allowed to
get in the way of the brash youth's relentless pursuit of knowledge.
William's opinions, usually the result of much observation and
experimentation, once formed are firmly held, even if they happen to
contradict authority or the accepted norms of the day. He often gets it

right, but he sometimes gets it very wrong. This independence of mind, running occasionally to arrogance, was to be a lifelong trait and could at times lead him into conflict with colleagues.

The young author was paid £250 outright for the manuscript, which was published by William Curry in Dublin and Longman, Orme, Browne and Co. in London. It ran to two volumes with maps and engravings after William's own drawings. It turned out to be a commercial success with the first edition of 1,250 copies quickly selling out. William, displaying good sense and perhaps being also well advised, decided to devote the proceeds of his book to postgraduate study abroad, but there was also another pressing matter. While William was away on the high seas his child was born, a baby boy who was given the name Henry Wilson. The identity of the child's mother has never been revealed but William always kept in contact with his son and paid for his education. This was the norm among the ever-practical Victorians. Fathers were not expected to marry outside their class but they were certainly expected to provide financially for the upbringing and education of a child born out of wedlock. Henry Wilson was well looked after. He eventually studied medicine and became an eye surgeon and a partner in his father's practice. Oscar and Willie discreetly referred to him as their cousin and it was whispered that the name of Wilson was derived from 'Wilde's son'.

William Wilde, through his lectures and his writing, was making a name for himself as a person with a deep interest in archaeology and antiquity, one who had a rare sensitivity and an ability to observe keenly and vividly describe in detail the sites he explored. He soon came to the attention of the famous artist, historian, musicologist and antiquarian George Petrie, like Wilde another polymath, who was about to undertake a very important archaeological study of a site at Lagore, near Dunshaughlin, County Meath. Petrie invited the young and enthusiastic medic to take part in the survey. The archaeological study of Lagore proved highly significant, turning out to be the site of the first lake dwelling ever discovered in Ireland. Even before the survey began vast quantities of bones, up to 150 cartloads, had already been removed from the site and sold as fertiliser to Scotland. As well as bones, the dig uncovered many valuable artefacts and other materials. George Petrie, who was in his mid-forties at this time, passed the artefacts on to the museum of the Royal Irish Academy. William, meanwhile, published a short paper on the many bones recovered. The enthusiastic newcomer impressed his colleagues on the survey and a lifelong friendship was established between the middle-aged antiquarian and the young doctor, although one colleague at least noted 'the mutual jealousies of Petrie and Wilde' as the two multi-talented men sized each other up at the time of Lagore.[1]

With the survey concluded, William could now set off on his postgraduate studies abroad. He first went to England to study eye surgery at the Royal Ophthalmic Hospital in London. Better known as Moorfields, it remains to this day the oldest and one of the most respected centres for ophthalmic treatment, teaching and research in the world. The new student from Ireland worked hard as usual and formed a friendship with Sir James Clark, the court physician, who introduced him to fashionable London society where he made his mark. While in London, William found time between studying and socialising to write a biographical essay on the eighteenth-century doctor Sir Thomas Molyneaux, which was published serially in the *Dublin University Magazine*. This was to be William Wilde's modus operandi for the rest of his busy life; preparing lectures and writing papers and articles that would later be gathered together and published in book form, while at the same time running a busy medical practice.

From London, William travelled on to Vienna to improve his knowledge of ophthalmic and aural surgery at that city's world famous hospital and school. He spent six months there refining his practical eye-surgery skills and, as usual, the Irish student did not neglect the social side of life in what must have been a strange and exciting environment on the banks of the Danube. He attended balls and salons and visited the famous Eliseum, a type of nightclub in a vast number of cellars excavated beneath several city streets. He described the locals 'enjoying their pipes and supper, listening to the merry strains of Strauss and Lanner, while their families, the gay light-hearted daughters of the Danube, are whirling in the waltz or gallope'.[2]

When his six months were up, the wandering medical student set off on a tour of European cities, visiting hospitals and making valuable contacts. In Berlin, Johan Friedrich Dieffenbach, a pioneer of plastic surgery, allowed him to observe his methods. Moving on to Brussels he stayed for a short spell with Charles Laver, his friend from student days in Dublin, who was living there at the time. He read proofs of Laver's *Charles O'Malley* and the pair went off to tour the site of the battlefield of Waterloo and later dined with an army officer and his charming daughters. William described the military man as being 'a portly Peninsular officer' and 'the "Major Monsoon" of *O'Malley*'. The evening ended with the officer getting very drunk and becoming maudlin; what became of the daughters that evening is not revealed.

Returning to Dublin, the young doctor was equipped with enough knowledge and experience to embark successfully upon his chosen career as a surgeon specialising in the eye and ear. William Wilde set up practice at 15 Westland Row where his mother and sister Margaret kept house for him. The practice was an immediate success and soon he had to think about expanding. From a dentist friend, a Mr Grimshaw, he acquired the lease of a stable at 11 Molesworth Street, which he renovated, installing suitable instruments and fixtures. William had learned a lot while abroad and was now in a position to introduce some innovation to the treatment of the eye and ear. For example, he was the first to introduce into Ireland the speculum for inspection of the ear canal having observed its use in Vienna.[3] The poor of Dublin came in large numbers for treatment and they in turn told their masters and mistresses about this young and skilful doctor. Soon the converted stable was not sufficient and William had to think about expanding once again.

In 1844 William reopened the old St Marks Hospital off Great Brunswick Street as an Ophthalmic Hospital and Dispensary for Diseases of the Eye and Ear. He managed to fund the project through a skilful combination of public and private monies, including his own. He also established a monthly subscription from patients. The hospital soon earned itself a fine reputation, becoming the only hospital in the United Kingdom teaching aural surgery. Postgraduates flocked to it, particularly from America. William worked night and day, attending to both inpatients and outpatients, performing operations and also teaching his students. To add even further to his workload, the busy doctor accepted an invitation to join his old teachers, Cusack, Graves, Stokes, Hamilton and Fleming on the staff at Park Street School where he lectured on the eye and ear.

Amazingly, William continued to find time for his non-medical interests. In 1843 he addressed the King and Queen's College of Physicians in St Patrick Dun's Hospital on the subject of ethnology of the Irish people. He classified the various kinds of skull found in different types of prehistoric burials, describing three forms in particular. He then tried to match the skulls to the various ethnic groupings he found mentioned in an old Irish manuscript of Mac Fhirbhisigh, probably the *Book of Lecan* that had been recently transcribed for the Royal Irish Academy by George Petrie. But this time William was on the wrong path. The Firbolgs, the Tuatha de Danann and the other tribes or ethnic groups described in the ancient manuscripts are mythological rather than historical races and William came to some unfortunate conclusions about the skulls and their origin. He would always have difficulty in differentiating between historical facts and mere legend and later in life would make a similar error, believing that the mythical Battle of Moytura, which the ancient annals so graphically describe, was a real event. Not only that, but he came to believe the battle was actually fought through the fields around his newly built lodge in Ballymagibbon. He went so far as to call his new second home Moytura House after the great mythical encounter between the forces of light and the forces of darkness.

William Wilde sometimes blundered and occasionally reached outlandish assumptions, but he nevertheless had an extremely accurate mind, well ordered and with an enormous flair for classification. He also had a great gift for observation and believed the ability to observe was an essential quality for good medical practice. 'Destitute of this qualification the physician ... seldom rises to eminence; he may practice creditably, nay, usefully, but he possesses not the talisman of his art.'[4] William's writings and lectures brought him to the attention of Lord Elliot, the Chief Secretary for Ireland, who recognised his abilities as a gatherer of facts and figures. Together with Captain Thomas Larcom of the Ordnance Survey, Lord Elliot offered William the position of Medical Commissioner for Ireland for the 1841 census. He accepted the post, a position he held for the rest of his life, and threw himself into the task with his customary energy to produce a first report of outstanding merit. William's work on the 1841 census mostly involved an analysis of the data already collected by the time he came to the job. 'His report on the tables of death ran to 205 tables and 78 foolscap pages of close-written letterpress.'[5] He also included a classification of ninety-four diseases, matching their medical terms with their colloquial equivalents in both English and Gaelic. The analysis of the various diseases causing death in Ireland included fevers such as smallpox, measles and 'scarlatina'. Cholera was the most fatal epidemic disease while 'consumption' (tuberculosis or TB) accounted for 135,590 deaths. Cancer was very prevalent; William believed it was on the increase.

The 1851 census, dealing with a country recently devastated by the Famine, was a much more ambitious undertaking and ran to 10 foolscap volumes of 4,553 pages. William himself wrote 710 pages and compiled tables of statistics on mental and physical handicaps. His report, completed in May 1856 after eighteen months of work, also included a curious history of illness in the world from the earliest times down to the mid-nineteenth century. According to his biographer Terence de Vere White, the census report produced by William was worthy of Sir Thomas Browne and should be filed beside that noted seventeenth-century author's *Urn Burials* and not with the dry-as-dust statistics. After some wrangling, he received a fee of over £2,000.

This part-time post required a fair degree of ingenuity as the gathering of social data was viewed with suspicion and an element of hostility in those volatile days. The English Parliament might view Ireland as being part of the United Kingdom but a large portion of the population, mostly native Irish Catholics, were opposed to the Act of Union. Ireland was a nation divided along religious, class and political lines. Unionists supported the link with Great Britain but nationalists wanted, at a minimum, a parliament of their own in Dublin. Catholics who had been excluded from the levers of power were demanding 'Emancipation'. The landowning class, mostly Protestant and unionist, were often now resident in London leaving their estates to be run by local agents who were in many cases more ruthless in their dealings with the tenantry. The atmosphere in the countryside was often hostile towards officialdom and this meant that officers of the state going around asking questions might not always find a welcome. The first attempt at collecting data in Ireland during the years 1813 to 1815 had been less than successful and the censuses of 1821 and then 1831 were not much better. The 1841 census saw an improvement but the 1851 census, with William fully involved in the medical side, was deemed to have been a great success and an example to the rest of the world.

William's career continued to advance. In 1845 he became a Fellow of the Royal College of Surgeons and later that same year he took up the editorship of the *Dublin Journal of Medical Science*, a serious medical publication where important topics of the day were discussed. William had been a regular contributor and, on taking charge, he immediately implemented changes, increasing its size and circulation and altering its name to the *Dublin Quarterly Journal of Medical Science*. In the process he made an enemy. Arthur Jacob, a surgeon and professional rival, lost his position as assistant editor at the journal and believed that William Wilde was responsible. Jacob had actually lost his position before the new editor took over but this did not lessen his hostility towards Wilde.

Dr Arthur Jacob was twenty-five years older than Wilde and the son and grandson of surgeons. He had an international reputation and held a number of senior positions in Dublin. He did not take kindly to this brash young surgeon, an upstart, newly arrived on the scene from somewhere down the country. Jacob felt that William Wilde was lacking in tact and was in far too much of a hurry. Jacob could be harsh and had a brusque manner; he lived a frugal life, eschewing all personal honours or the mildest of festivities. He was almost the polar opposite of William and accused the young doctor of abusing his connections and apparent high standing with the authorities in the Castle to attract patients and position. He attacked William for using the title 'Assistant Commissioner' for his census work, declaring it did not officially exist and that Wilde had invented the title to inflate his own importance. That the Castle tolerated his use of this title was a further outrage. It was a case of the old versus the new and Dr Arthur Jacob was to remain an enemy, sniping at his talented rival on every available occasion. Eventually, Jacob would be presented with the perfect opportunity for target practice.

William always needed to be working on some new project and it was at this point, having completed his first census report, that he decided to take a look at his notes and reflections from the time he spent studying in Austria with a view to publishing a book on that country. The result was *Austria, its Literary, Scientific and Medical Institutions*, published in 1845 by William Curry, the same Dublin publishers who took his *Narrative of a Voyage*. It was another great success, containing a vivid description of Vienna at a time when little was known of the internal workings of the Austrian Empire. His next undertaking was a study of Dean Swift's medical history with a view to determining his mental state and the reasons for his ill health and death. He had received a query from a Dr William Mackenzie, an oculist from Glasgow, regarding an account of a large swelling around the Dean's eye towards the end of his life that caused him severe pain. Dr Mackenzie was wondering if this inflammation could have been the source of the Dean's 'madness'. Dr Mackenzie was probably expecting a letter in reply but the query set William off on an in-depth study, resulting in a series of essays that were eventually published in book form by Hodges and Smith in 1849 as *The Closing Years of Dean Swift's Life*. William managed to get possession of Swift's death mask for close examination and unearthed some previously unavailable documents. Nevertheless, his findings contained many unwarranted assumptions and conclusions. Dr Mackenzie more than likely never asked his Dublin-based colleague another question after receiving an answer to his Swift query in the form of a full book.

If the Swift project was less than successful for William, it did at least have an interesting aside. The Dean's death mask went missing, only to turn up almost forty years later when Willie Wilde, William's eldest son, sold it in 1885. William said at the time of the book's publication that the mask had been accidentally destroyed in Trinity College's museum. Had he mislaid it? Or was he tempted to keep it in his study with the urns from Egypt and the skulls he had snatched from the Field of Blood?

8

Hard Times

William's medical practice continued to expand but amazingly, given his huge workload, he still found time for antiquarian research. He confined his investigations to more accessible locations near Dublin, including the sites of the great tumulus (or barrow) of Knockmaree in the Phoenix Park and Newgrange, Dowth and Knowth in the Boyne Valley. The arrival of the railway in the 1850s eventually made travel easier and William was able to answer the call of his beloved west more often, but for now he would have to make do with visits to the countryside nearer the city.

He liked to wander along the banks of the River Boyne and its tributary the Blackwater, examining the ruins and putting the hunting and fishing skills he had learned as a child from Dick Blake and Paddy Welsh to use. He published articles in the *Dublin University Magazine* on the many interesting sites he came across there and, in keeping with his by now well established pattern, developed these articles and notes into a book, *The Beauties of the Boyne and Blackwater*, published in 1846 by James McGlashan. A letter from William to McGlashan in Dublin, written the week before publication, provides an insight into his frantic work rate.

> Dear MacGlashan,
>
> . . . Will you like a good man poke up the printers and don't leave all the abuse to me for I have enough to do

without it. Indeed I cannot complain of them. They are doing for Gill's people wonders, but I want them to do more. I want them to do Miracles, which I am doing at present. If I don't live to see the book finished write my Elegy – Killed by a book – Slain by a Book-seller – Squeezed to Death in a - Printing Press – made a Pye of, or anything literary of that description.

I send Sig I. Revise it for the printers at once
W. R. Wilde.

William was by now also enjoying his place in the social life of the city and he attended dinner parties with the best of Dublin's literary and professional society. As well as his medical colleagues and his literary associates he had many other friends, such as George Petrie and his staff in the Ordnance Survey office. He also knew the great Gaelic scholars of the day such as Eugene O'Curry and John O'Donovan and counted the wayward poet James Clarence Mangan and the lawyer Isaac Butt among his circle. All of these men met often for drinks in the 'snuggeries' around Great Charles Street or at the many uproarious supper parties where lavish feasting and hard drinking took place. Charles Laver, his old friend from medical school, was back in Dublin for a time working as editor of the *Dublin University Magazine*. Joseph Sheridan Le Fanu, the writer who succeeded Laver as editor in 1843, was also in this circle. Le Fanu went on to make a name for himself as a writer of gothic novels dealing with the occult and the supernatural, including a story of lesbian vampirism, *Carmilla*. This was read by a young Bram Stoker and influenced him greatly when he came to write *Dracula*. Today Le Fanu is probably best known for the macabre novel *Uncle Silas* and the collection of stories *In a Glass Darkly*. Young Oscar would have been very familiar with Le Fanu's work as he lived near the Wildes on Merrion Square.

About this time the artist Fredrick William Burton and Wilde became rivals for the hand of the beautiful actress Helen Faucit. However, she rejected both and married a third suitor, Sir Theodore

Martin. Oscar would experience a similar rejection many years later when the beautiful aspiring actress Florence Balcombe chose to marry his friend Bram Stoker instead. Stoker, at the time, was the newly appointed business manager of the Lyceum Theatre where Florence eventually made her stage debut.

A number of convivial dining clubs were formed in Dublin during the 1840s and 1850s and William was invited to join many of them. This was a period when many of the country's rural folk and poorer classes were experiencing hardships on an unprecedented scale. William was aware of the situation for the country's poor, both urban and rural, from his work with the census. He was also a man of the west, brought up among the fields of Roscommon and Mayo, with their wretched mud cabins and families who existed solely on the potato. He knew about the great number of landless farm labourers living hand-to-mouth, hiring out their labour in return for a small potato patch on which they could grow their single crop. What if the potato should fail?

William Wilde also understood the bigger picture, the bankrupt landlords or those 'absentees' who never visited their estates. He knew about the lack of investment in rural Ireland and the absence of capital and enterprise. William wrote about the lot of the native Irish peasant, saying they were 'ground down by the pauper absentee or his tyrannical agent; bullied by the petty sessions magistrates; alternatively insulted or cajoled by the minister of the day, mis-represented as Whig and Tory prevailed; bullied by the Brownes and Baresfords today, worshiping O'Connell tomorrow; vilified by the London press'.[1] The O'Connell he refers to was, of course, the Catholic barrister and Irish political leader Daniel O'Connell. Today, Dublin's main street bears his name. O'Connell was known as the 'Liberator' for his successful Catholic emancipation campaign, but by the early 1840s his influence was in decline. His campaign to repeal the Act of Union and restore the Irish Parliament was a failure; his series of 'Monster Meetings', where vast crowds of supporters gathered in carefully selected places of national significance, ended in the loss of his credibility. In October 1843, in the face of threats from the British authorities, O'Connell called off what was supposed to be the climax of his 'Monster Meeting' campaign, a huge gathering at Clontarf, near Dublin, chosen for its place in history as the scene of a great victory by the native Irish over the Vikings in 1014. O'Connell did not believe in violence as a political weapon and this perceived climbdown marked the beginning of the end of his position as the people's leader.

Younger, more radical members of O'Connell's organisation, the Repeal Association, began to question his leadership. Some were even prepared to use physical force to make Ireland 'a nation once again'.[2] These so-called Young Irelanders – middle-class and literary-minded nationalists – established themselves as a powerful cohort in the repeal movement. In 1842 three of the Young Irelanders, Thomas Davis, Charles Gavan Duffy and John Blake Dillon, established a newspaper to further the ideal of 'national independence' for Ireland. They called it the *Nation* and it attracted as contributors such talented and idealistic young men as the poet James Clarence Mangan and the fiery John Mitchel. The *Nation* became hugely popular both at home in Ireland and with Irish emigrants in America. It also attracted the attention of a young Dublin girl of privileged background from a solid Protestant-unionist family. Her name was Jane Elgee. But politics and idealism would, for a time, become tangential in the face of the major national catastrophe that was about to occur.

On 11 September 1845 the *Freeman's Journal* published a report on a disease affecting the potato crop: 'We regret to have to state that we have had communications from more then one well informed correspondent announcing the fact of what is called "cholera" in potatoes in Ireland, especially in the north. In one instance the party had been digging potatoes – the finest he had ever seen – from a particular field, and a particular ridge of that field up to Monday last; and on digging in the same ridge on Tuesday he found the tubers all blasted, and unfit for the use of man or beast.' Potato blight had arrived in Ireland and the Famine of 1845–52 had begun. It was to produce horrors that would reverberate through the national psyche down the decades even to the present day. The *Nation* was to the fore in describing the terrible conditions and the feeble response from the English government. The stirring voice of a poet was also heard adding her cry to the lamentations and to the ever more militant calls for action. This was the voice of Jane Elgee, soon to be known throughout a troubled land as Speranza of the *Nation*.

It may be difficult to understand how a country like Ireland could actually have a famine. After all, there was plenty of food being produced, but one needs money to buy food and a large number of landless farm workers simply had no money at all. They lived almost exclusively on potatoes grown on the little patches of land they were allowed use in return for labour, so when the potato blight struck, the effects were rapid and widespread. Overnight, green fields were left black and withered with the tubers rotting in the ground. Each winter the fungus lay dormant only to revive and infect the new crop in the spring. By February 1846 the blight had spread to every county in Ireland and three quarters of the country's potato crop was destroyed. Disease came with the hunger and soon typhus and dysentery were registered in twenty-five out of the thirty-two counties.

The prevailing political principle of the day was that government should interfere to the absolute minimum with the market forces of supply and demand. To do so, they believed, would endanger the natural flow to the market. The foremost guardian of this principle was Charles Trevelyan, permanent Head of the Treasury, who believed that the Famine was 'the judgement of God sent . . . to teach the Irish a lesson'. The Prime Minister Sir Robert Peel was a little more willing to bend the harsh economic rules and Indian corn was imported and a scheme of public works sanctioned. However, bureaucracy ensured long delays in implementing the various schemes and the distribution of food among the needy was slow. Exports of farm produce also remained high and what food remained in Ireland was simply too expensive for the Irish poor to buy.

At least a million people died of starvation and related diseases during the course of the Famine. Typhus ravaged the workhouses and hospitals while bodies rotted where they fell on the roads or in the fields. The *Nation* chronicled the disaster, claiming, for example, that Galway's jail was more of a pestilent hospital then a prison, with 115 inmates dying within two weeks in February 1847. The prison chaplain was reported as having seen 'living persons lying on the same bed with a corpse, whose fetid condition renders it dangerous to approach'.

William Wilde, in his official capacity as Medical Commissioner for the census, followed the Famine closely. As editor of the *Dublin Quarterly Journal of Medical Science* he also addressed a questionnaire to country doctors. Amongst the responses he received was a frightening account from a Dr Crumpe, medical officer to the jail at Tralee:

> In this horrid den those labouring under local disease, those ill from fever, those dying, and the dead from fever and from dysentery, were promiscuously stretched together. So insufferable was the atmosphere of the place, so morbidly fetid and laden with noxious miasma, notwithstanding constant fumigation with chloride of lime, that on the door being opened I was uniformly seized, on entering, with most violent retching . . . So foul was the atmosphere, so cadaverous was the smell that I could not make post-mortem examinations, nor was there any accommodation to do so, though the bodies were numerous, and often no claimants for them.

William Wilde's report on the medical aspects of the Famine ran through four numbers of the *Journal*, each separate part containing about sixty pages.

The causes of blight were not understood at the time and nobody knew how to treat it. Some of the official suggestions for dealing with an outbreak included the use of well-ventilated pits, exposure to air, kiln drying and covering the potatoes with ashes. William tried to take a broad and logical view, tracing its origin to a period just after the cholera epidemic of 1832 that had forced him back to Mayo. At that time there was a fatal epidemic among pigs, followed by foot-and-mouth in cattle, next in sheep and then domestic fowl began to die mysteriously. His was a fair attempt to understand the calamity in terms of previous outbreaks but, like everybody else, he could offer no effective cure for the rotting crops. The failure of the potato crop was in fact caused by the deadly fungus

Phytophthora infestans, which destroys the leaf and stem and turns the potato to a rotting pulp.

As officials pondered and recorded, news from the country told of disaster. An inspector of roads near Clifden had buried 140 bodies found scattered along the highway. On 19 December 1847 the Poor Law Inspector at Galway reported that 'no less then eleven boats, loaded with destitute persons had put into Galway harbour from Connemara'. These were people who had been evicted from the estate of Christian St George. The workhouses were full all over the country and those with any strength were making for the ports and new lives in America. In January of 1848 about 3,000 starving beggars roamed the streets of Galway; some of the children were 'mere animated skeletons . . . screaming for food'. It was the same in most parts of the country. Yet the professional classes and those with money went unaffected. Dublin society carried on with its dinner parties and Castle balls.

William was a prominent member of this Dublin society. However, that the horrors of the Famine loomed large in his mind is clear from the opening pages of his 1852 book *Irish Popular Superstitions*:

> The great convulsion which society of all grades here has lately experienced, the failure of the potato crop, pestilence, famine, and a most unparalleled extent of emigration, together with bankrupt landlords, pauperising poor-laws, grinding officials and decimating workhouses, have broken up the very foundations of social intercourse, have swept away the established theory of political economists, and uprooted many of our long-cherished opinions. In some places all the domestic usages of life have been outraged; the tenderest bonds of kindred have been severed, some of the noblest and holiest feelings of human nature have been blotted from the heart, and many of the finest, yet firmest links which united the various classes in the community have been rudely burst asunder. Even the ceremonial of religion has been neglected and

the very rites of sepulchre . . . have been neglected or forgotten; the dead body has rotted where it fell, or formed a scanty meal for the famished dogs of the vicinity, or has been thrown, without prayer or mourning, into the adjoining ditch . . . The fire on the peasants hearth was quenched, and its comforts banished . . . while the remnant of the hardiest and most stalwart of the people crawl about, listless spectres, unable or unwilling to rise out of their despair . . . Take care, landlords, gentlemen and governors of Ireland. The clearing system, if not carried too far, has been, at least, carried on too rapidly. Had you improved the condition of the peasantry, or even attempted to do so, some twenty years ago, you might not have to support them in the poor-house now, nor receive their dying malediction.

William was right. That 'dying malediction' was to have serious consequences for the ruling classes in Ireland and the cry 'remember Skibbereen', the scene in Munster of much suffering during the Famine, reverberates down to this very day.

9

Rebel Poet

On 21 February 1846 the *Nation*, organ of the Young Ireland movement, published a poem called 'The Holy War'. It was a translation from the German of a work calling for a hero to lead the people who were gaining in pride. The covering letter to the editor, Charles Gavan Duffy, enclosing the poem was signed 'John Fanshawe Ellis'. The poem itself was signed 'Speranza', the Italian for hope. Other contributions followed from the mysterious 'Mr Ellis', prose as well as poetry, all written in the same passionate, melodramatic style and all expressing strong nationalistic sentiments.

Impressed by the fiery contributions, Duffy invited 'John Fanshawe Ellis' to come to the newspaper's office. The mysterious contributor was reluctant to meet face to face but Duffy persisted. Years later, when he came to write his memoirs, he recalled the events surrounding his first meeting with 'Speranza', which took place in the summer of 1846:

> I was greatly struck by the first contribution, and requested Mr John Fanshawe Ellis to call at the *Nation* office. Mr Ellis pleaded that there were difficulties which rendered this course impracticable, and invited me to visit him in Leeson Street. I did so immediately, not without a secret suspicion of the transformation I was about to witness. A smiling parlour-maid, when I enquired for Mr Ellis,

showed me into a drawing-room, where I found only Mr George Smith, publisher of the [Dublin] University [Magazine]. 'What!' I cried; 'my loyal friend, are you the new volcano of sedition?' Mr. Smith only answered by vanishing into a back drawing-room and returning with a tall girl on his arm, whose stately carriage and figure, flashing brown eyes and features cast in an heroic mould, seemed fit for the genius of poetry, or the spirit of revolution. He presented me to Miss Jane Francesca Elgee, in lieu of Mr John Fanshawe Ellis. Miss Elgee . . . had probably heard nothing of Irish nationality among her ordinary associates, but as the strong and generous are apt to do, had worked out convictions for herself.

Jane's family were strong unionists and two of her uncles were officers in the British army. Captain John Elgee was paymaster of the 67th Regiment and William Elgee was a Major in the artillery. So how did it come about that Jane Elgee would decide to secretly contribute poems and articles of a seditious nature to the country's leading nationalist organ? There are varying accounts of Jane's conversion to nationalism. Oscar's unreliable version, which he told to an audience in San Francisco during his lecture tour of America in 1882, described his mother watching the funeral of Thomas Davis in 1845 pass below the window of 'her lordly home' in Dublin. She wondered who had died, obviously somebody much loved by the people, 'and learned it was the funeral of one Thomas Davis, a poet of whom till then she had never heard. That evening she bought and read his poems and knew for the first time the meaning of the word country.'[1] Jane was more than likely twenty-two at the time of Davis' death. She had taken up residence along with her mother at 34 Leeson Street in 1834, not exactly the 'lordly home' of Oscar's imagination. W. B. Yeats, in a speech on the centenary of Thomas Davis' birth, gave another account of the day, with Jane asking a shopkeeper about the deceased and being so 'struck to find so many people honouring a poet . . . that she turned nationalist and wrote those energetic rhymes my generation read in its youth'.[2]

Thomas Davis was a handsome, idealistic lawyer, the intellectual driving force behind the Young Ireland movement and the chief writer for the *Nation*. He was to the fore of Irish nationalist thinking and remains a major figure in the story of the development and promotion of an Irish identity. Davis, a Protestant, preached the unity of Catholic and Protestant and defined Irishness, not in terms of bloodline, but as the willingness to be a part of the Irish nation. He believed in Ireland's independence and his death at the age of just thirty from scarlet fever was a major loss. Today the poet and writer is probably best remembered among the general population as being the author of the famous Irish rebel song 'A Nation Once Again'.

Jane's own explanation for her conversion to Irish nationalism is a simple one. She was a girl who loved reading and would have been familiar with works such as Maria Edgeworth's *The Absentee* and William Carleton's *Dear Colleen Bawn* as well as Maturin's *The Wild Irish Boy* and other such novels about the evils of the English landlords and the plight of the downtrodden native Irish. Jane claimed she happened by accident on a collection of writings published by the *Nation*. 'I read it eagerly and my patriotism was kindled . . . Since I caught the National spirit, all the literature of Irish wrongs and sufferings had an enthralling interest for me; then it was that I discovered I could write poetry.'[3]

Speranza's melodramatic style of writing, full of rhyme and thumping rhythms, can sound out of place today but her rousing work caught the tempestuous sentiment of her own time. Surprisingly, for a woman of her social background and a city dweller, she was able to reflect the turbulent emotions that were intensifying throughout rural Ireland as conditions worsened. Perhaps her Wexford connections helped in this regard. Speranza soon became a national figure, widely read and quoted by readers of the *Nation* both at home and in America. Years later, Oscar, while on a speaking tour in the United States, was initially surprised to find that his mother was still so widely remembered and so highly regarded by the Irish emigrant community there. He realised it was very useful for him to be identified as the Irish-born son of the great Speranza and did not hesitate to play the Irish card in his talks.

Jane's prose and poems conveyed pity and outrage at the terrible sufferings of the native Irish poor and some were straightforward battle cries. Her most famous poems were written between 1846 and 1848, during the worst of the terrible Famine years. In 'The Voice of the Poor', Jane writes:

> Before us die our brothers of starvation;
> Around are cries of famine and despair.
> Where is hope for us, or comfort, or salvation –
> Where – oh! where?
> If the angels ever hearken, downward bending,
> They are weeping, we are sure,
> At the litanies of human groans ascending
> From the crushed hearts of the poor.

Eventually, despite using two noms de plume, Jane's family discovered her literary activities and there was consternation. 'One day my uncle came into my room and found the *Nation* on my table. Then he accused me of contributing to it, declaring the while that such a seditious paper was fit only for the fire.'[4] Her family's opposition did not stop the spirited young lady from continuing to contribute to the *Nation* but she decided to keep using the name Speranza. Jane was now being drawn more deeply into the Young Ireland movement. She admired the intellectualism and idealism of these young men and, of course, she revelled in all the attention and admiration that came her way as 'Speranza of the *Nation*'. There was also a strong social side to the movement with weekly suppers hosted by the paper as well as regular dinners, dances and excursions, all of which Jane would have enjoyed. The young poet liked to send little scented notes sealed with wax to her editor Duffy and Jane admired others of the group. She was particularly attracted to Thomas Francis Meagher, whom she thought to be handsome and daring with the most beautiful mouth, teeth and smile she had ever seen. She even wrote a poem called 'The Young Patriot Leader' based on this dashing rebel. It was an exhilarating time for a girl in her early twenties who had suddenly become a national figure and was surrounded by so many handsome and idealistic young men. But the Young Ireland movement was about much more than end-of-week parties. It was becoming a very significant political organisation and the eyes of the English establishment based in Dublin Castle were watching with growing disquiet. Soon they would pounce and Jane would find herself caught up in a series of alarming events.

As reports of the Famine flooded in from all parts of the country, the content of the *Nation* grew more and more inflammatory. John Mitchel, the fiery son of an Ulster Presbyterian minister, resigned from the *Nation* where he had been leader writer because he wanted to set up an even more radical organ, the *United Irishman*. 'Let the man among you who has no gun sell his garment and buy one,' he cried. Speranza too was sounding increasingly bellicose:

> We'll conquer! We'll conquer! No tears for the slain,
> God's angels will smile on their death-hour of pain.
> On, on in your masses dense, resolute, strong
> To war against treason, oppression, and wrong

Events were becoming increasingly disquieting and the Young Irelanders were now all in danger of arrest for treason. Jane was relatively safe being a woman and of sound Protestant stock. She continued to intensify her confrontational tone: 'If a government stands in the path of that people, and refuses those demands . . . that government must be overthrown . . . The country, therefore, is now in the position which O'Connell himself avowed would justify armed resistance to tyranny, and an armed enforcement of the people's rights.'[5]

William Wilde would not have agreed with these sentiments. While he admired the romanticism and idealism of the Young Irelanders, any idea of a violent insurrection against the Crown would be an abomination as far as he was concerned. William knew many of the Young Irelanders such as William Smith O'Brien and Charles Gavan Duffy personally from the Council of the Celtic Society of which he was also a member. But the aim of the Celtic Society was the promotion of the history, literature and antiquities of Ireland, not

the furtherance of sedition. William Wilde, in his role as member of
the Royal Irish Academy, attended the funeral of Thomas Davis and
it is a reflection of the complexities of Irish politics that William, a
supporter of the link with Britain, was later invited to head a
committee formed to seek ways to commemorate the writer and
scholar whose ideology inspired the Young Ireland movement. The
marble figure of Thomas Davis by the sculptor John Hogan that
today stands in Dublin's City Hall was commissioned by William as
part of this project.

On 15 July 1848 the government finally swooped. A dozen
policemen arrested Charles Gavan Duffy and took him off to jail on
a charge of treason-felony. The offices of the *Nation* were raided but
Duffy's cousin and sister-in-law Margaret Callan took over the
editorship and kept the paper going, defiantly publishing a militant
poem from Speranza in the next issue. On 29 July 1848, with Duffy
in prison, Jane wrote the paper's leader, 'Jacta Alea Est' (The Die is
Cast), a call to arms of the most warlike kind. 'Now, indeed, were the
men of Ireland cowards if this moment for retribution, combat, and
victory, were to pass by unemployed.' The government immediately
seized the issue and suppressed the paper. Next, the Habeas Corpus
Act was suspended and those Young Irelanders still free had to decide
between action and arrest. William Smith O'Brien decided on action
and led a small band of men and women against a party of Royal
Irish Constabulary that had moved on the village of Ballingarry in
County Tipperary to execute a warrant against him. Smith O'Brien
was a gentlemanly figure, educated at Harrow and Cambridge, and
had served as an MP at Westminster for a number of years. He was
wholly unsuited to the role of military leader that had fallen to him.

The 'rising' began when the police arrived to arrest William
Smith O'Brien and found the village of Ballingarry barricaded. Sub-
Inspector Thomas Trant and some forty-six constables were chased
and took refuge in a grey-stone farmhouse 2 miles outside the town
that they set about fortifying with pieces of furniture. Stones and
some shots were fired at the house and the Constabulary replied with
a volley into the crowd who then dived for shelter behind the
surrounding walls. There followed an hour of intermittent fire until

another force of police arrived and raised the siege. Smith O'Brien and his aides made off into the countryside but two of the besiegers lay dead and several were wounded. Smith O'Brien was arrested a week later at nearby Thurles railway station as he stood on the platform waiting to catch the regular train to his home town of Limerick. This skirmish became known as the Battle of the Widow McCormack's Cabbage Patch. In terms of an insurrection it was pathetic, but shots had been fired in anger at the British Empire and this was enough to keep alive the tradition of violent rebellion.

Smith O'Brien, Meagher and the other leaders joined Duffy in jail where they were well treated and allowed to associate with each other. State trials followed and death sentences were handed down but these were soon commuted to penal servitude for life in Van Diemen's Land (Tasmania). Mitchel had been arrested at an even earlier stage and would join his fellow convicts in Van Diemen's Land. Meagher and Mitchel later escaped from the penal colony and made their way to America where the seeds of the Fenian movement took root.[6] Smith O'Brien was eventually pardoned in 1856 and allowed to return to Ireland. Charles Gavan Duffy was tried six times during 1848 and into 1849 and each time his trial collapsed on points of law or lack of evidence. Jane's leader 'Jacta Alea Est' was cited as one of the proofs of seditious libel. Jane went to the Solicitor General and denounced herself as the author but the case nonetheless went ahead. Gavan Duffy's defence barrister, Isaac Butt, told the court he had a letter from the authoress of the leader in question assuring him that his client never saw the article before it was published.

A story gained credence of the plucky Speranza shouting out her own guilt from the body of the court in a heroic but futile attempt to save her editor. But no such outburst ever took place. At the time Speranza was, in her own words, 'in quite alarm lest I should have to appear as a witness, however I wrote a letter acknowledging the authorship and the court said they must believe me'.[7] The authorities were eventually forced to abandon the prosecution and on 10 April 1849 Charles Gavan Duffy walked free. The *Nation* was relaunched on 1 September 1849 but the old enthusiasm was no longer there, the heart had gone out of the Young Ireland movement. There is a letter in the National Library of Ireland written by Jane to the Irish author William Carleton where she states: 'I am very uneasy about him [Duffy], but that Ballingarry killed us all. I have never laughed joyously since.' Charles Gavan Duffy grew ever more disillusioned and emigrated to Australia in 1855. There he entered politics becoming Prime Minister of the state of Victoria in 1871. Some years after, the one-time agitator was offered and accepted a knighthood from the Queen.

In just two years Jane Francesca Elgee had risen from obscurity to become a national celebrity who would be remembered for years to come by the ordinary folk for her rousing poems during Ireland's darkest days and for her 'brave intervention' in the Duffy trial. She thoroughly enjoyed her fame and never doubted that she had talent, but the demise of the Young Ireland movement left Jane without direction, vowing after the Duffy trials to 'never write sedition again. The responsibility is more awful than I imagined or thought of.'[8] As Dublin began to settle down after the tumult of rebellion, Jane became involved in the usual round of balls, occasional riding parties and evenings at the theatre. She was now a favourite in Dublin society and was once again living a comfortable if more mundane life with her mother at Leeson Street. She liked to sleep late, a habit that stayed with her for life and another practice she passed on to Oscar. Jane enjoyed dressing up and attending the grand gatherings at Dublin Castle, the heart of the British Empire in Ireland, completely ignoring any hint of inconsistency in the bellicose Speranza being present at Castle functions. She did, however, take note of the Viceroy of Ireland, Lord Aberdeen, smiling 'very archly as he bent to kiss my cheek, which is the ceremony of presentation. I smiled too and thought of Jacta Alea Est.'[9]

Jane was always acutely aware of her position in society and would have regarded it as her right to be in attendance at the best social gatherings. She could be haughty, but she also had a highly developed sense of the ridiculous, something that rarely found its way into her published works but is very obvious in the many private letters she liked to write to friends and later to Oscar. Oscar's public posing had much the same measured portentousness as his mother's, albeit tempered with a dash more irony. Mother and son were very much alike. If there was pride, there was kindness. If they both took themselves very seriously, and they did, they were also keenly aware of the fragility of the world.

Jane was a gifted linguist and after the excitement of the Young Ireland era put this talent to work. She began translating a German terror-tale by William Meinhold called *Sidonia the Sorceress* but found it tedious compared with her previous work as Speranza. Nevertheless, Jane would go on to carve out a fine reputation as a translator of both fiction and non-fiction. *Sidonia the Sorceress* was a surprising choice being a rather grisly gothic romance featuring a cruel femme fatale who enjoyed harming little creatures and torturing young men. Sidonia was eventually found guilty of witchcraft and executed after a trial that saw her stoutly defend her actions. Jane's translation, which was published by The Parlour Press in 1848, later found wider recognition when it was taken up by the literary wing of the Pre-Raphaelite Brotherhood. It inspired a number of paintings, including two by Edward Bourne-Jones, and became one of Dante Gabriel Rossetti's favourite books. Rossetti used his own girlfriend, Fanny Cornforth, as a model for his painting of Sidonia.

Oscar loved the book, which was based on the strange life of a real Pomeranian noblewoman who lived in the early seventeenth century, and read it eagerly as a child. It contains a scene describing a portrait of Sidonia hanging on the wall of the Count von Brok's castle. She is beautiful, dressed in azure and with her golden hair in a golden net, but behind her lurks another portrait of Sidonia with the terrifying features of the sorceress. Could this be a foreshadowing of *The Picture of Dorian Gray*? Many years later and living in much-altered circumstances, Jane would be very grateful to receive a cheque for £25 when a new edition of *Sidonia the Sorceress* was published by William Morris. Indeed, the book by William Meinhold as translated by Lady Wilde remains in print to this day.

Jane also began a long-lasting correspondence with an unknown male friend in Scotland around the time she was writing as Speranza. In the aftermath of the failed Young Ireland rebellion she described to him how 'excitement is my genius. I have none without it and Dublin is bleak of the divine inspirer as a Polar icefield – I should like to range through life – this orthodox creeping is too tame for me – ah, this wild rebellious ambitious nature of mine.'[10] The Wildes through the generations could never be described as 'orthodox creepers'. Their individuality saw to that. In another letter, written in 1850, she expresses her views on love: 'Why, I would grow jealous of sun, moon and stars had I a lover – I would not let him love midnight or the moon, nor seem conscious they existed. I must be his Universe, terrestrial and celestial . . . in love I like to feel myself a slave – the difficulty is to find anyone capable of ruling me. I love them when I feel their power.'[11]

Just such a man was about to enter her life.

10

William and Jane

The first meeting between William Wilde and Jane Elgee went unrecorded. They shared many interests and acquaintances and their paths could have crossed at any number of events. They both enjoyed the theatre and literature and liked to keep abreast of events of the day. Perhaps they met at one of the many social gatherings associated with the Young Ireland movement or maybe at a Royal Irish Academy ball. In a letter to her Scots friend Jane does mention attending 'a full dress dancing affair' held in the Academy's fine rooms. In any event, their paths did cross and Jane, as a writer and poet, would have been different from all the other young ladies in Dublin's society. As she wrote herself: 'Clever ladies are rare in Dublin . . . Beauty is the grand characteristic of the Dublin Belles, so in that department I leave them undisturbed in possession of their domain and am content with undisputed sovereignty in mine.'[1] Perhaps that is what attracted the busy doctor to her in the first place.

In the issue of the revived *Nation* dated 15 September 1849 there appeared an admiring review of a newly published book, *Beauties of the Boyne and Blackwater* by Dr William Wilde. It was one of Jane's first tasks after starting work on the relaunched paper: 'Few men indeed could be more fitted than the accomplished author to render such subjects popular by their mode of treatment, combining as he does profound and varied erudition, and the subtle acuteness of a practised critic, with vivacity, feeling and the most genial sympathies.'

William, for his part, had quoted one of her poems in the book while describing a monument on the banks of the River Boyne. They were at least aware of each other's existence at this point.

As for Jane's relationships, there is no evidence to suggest that she was amorously involved with any of the men in the Young Ireland movement or others in the circle at that time even though there were plenty of opportunities for romance. Despite the developing crisis, the *Nation* had continued to host their social evenings and Charles Gavan Duffy recalls in his memoirs *Four Years of Irish History* that 'There was much wooing and some marrying in that day.' The heady cocktail of rebellion, danger, literature and politics contained all the potential for romance and Jane did admire Duffy, believing he had the most cultivated mind in Dublin. She wrote to him regularly, flirtatiously sending him those little scented notes sealed with wax while he lent Jane books such as Thomas Carlyle's biography of Cromwell and Philip James Bailey's narrative poem *Festus*, but that was the extent of it.

In a letter to her Scots friend Jane described the Young Irelander Thomas Francis Meagher as 'handsome, daring, reckless of consequences, wild, bright, flashing eyes, glowing colour and the most beautiful mouth, teeth and smile I ever beheld'. Her poem 'The Young Patriot Leader' is based on Meagher and he was just the sort of fellow to turn any girl's head. But, when the government's axe fell, he was arrested, tried and sentenced to penal servitude for life in Van Diemen's Land. Jane attended his trial in Dublin where they had a brief opportunity to meet before he was taken away.

Jane had a tendency to conduct her relationships with men by letter. At one stage she corresponded regularly with the author William Carleton and wrote to her friend in Scotland saying that 'My greatest friend is now Carleton the author, he is the most excitable, passionate, poetical enthusiast you can imagine.' She then had to write and reassure this mysterious Scot that there was nothing of a romantic nature in their relationship and that Carleton was a family man of fifty, married with 'all his love as a man … given to his wife'. Jane appears to have been attracted to men on an intellectual level and they responded in the same way.

So who was this man in Scotland with whom she corresponded for so many years? Unfortunately, none of his letters have survived but from the fifty letters written by Jane it would appear that he worked in some kind of financial institution – Jane called it a 'counting house' – and also wrote reviews under the name of 'Gurth'. The letters show a certain level of intimacy and they have that easy tone of one confident in the sympathies of the reader. They probably met in 1847 when Jane was away from Dublin for a few months and visited Scotland as part of her travels. The letters reveal a well-read, opinionated woman full of spirit and humour who was willing at times to be self-deprecatory. She also comes across as being surprisingly conservative in her politics, despite her Speranza persona, believing in the established class system and with little time for the ideals of democracy. The ruling class had, in her opinion, a duty and right to rule but to do so wisely and humanely.

If Jane was eager for something more than a long-distance relationship with her friend in Scotland her hopes were dashed when, in 1850, he wrote telling of his intentions to marry. Jane's written reply is rather acerbic: 'Who is the sublime Semiramis who has led you captive . . . do forgive me if I am not very enthusiastic.'[2] But his marriage did not end their long-distance relationship and the pair continued to write to each other regularly for many more years.

Jane was by now working on a translation of Alphonse de Lamartine's *Pictures of the First French Revolution*. It was paid work but once again she found it much less exhilarating than writing for a rebellion. On completion she took herself off to rural Monaghan to be close to nature for a while, an uncharacteristic act as Jane was never very interested in the glories of the countryside. Soon she was writing to her friend in Scotland, pleading with him to send her some reading material. Monaghan, she declared, had no books, libraries, papers or periodicals to brighten its 'murky darkness'. Jane was a city girl and would remain so. Back in Dublin and still living with her mother in Leeson Street, Jane wrote once more to her Scots friend telling of the regular evening parties that carried on late into the night. She does not appear to have been enjoying them very much, however, and complained that the late nights left her unfit for thought the next day. On the other hand, she found the occasional riding parties, which often lasted for up to four hours, very exhilarating.

Overall, Jane would appear to have been uncharacteristically gloomy at this point in her life. Her Speranza 'era' had passed and an anticlimactic low had set in after the high drama of the government crackdown. While she found some days enchanting, especially the rainy ones, other days were depressing and lonely and she 'would be glad for the society of a cat'. Then, in 1851, Jane's life was thrown into turmoil when her mother died. The will left the property divided between Jane and her sister, Emily, but there was a problem. In those days it was considered unacceptable for a young woman to live alone and it would be very awkward all around for the nationalist Jane to move in with her unionist relatives.

What could she do?

An announcement, which appeared in *Saunders' Newsletter* of 13 November 1851, shows how the situation was resolved:

> Married on the 12th inst. At St Peter's Church by the Reverend John M. Wilde, A.M., Incumbent of Trinity Church, Northwich, William R. Wilde, Esq., F.R.C.S., to Jane Francesca, youngest daughter of the late Charles Elgee, Esq., and grand-daughter of the late Archdeacon Elgee, of Wexford.

Dr William Wilde and 'Speranza' had both met their match.

Part 3

Marriage

'Alas! the Fates are cruel / Behold Speranza making gruel.'

Lady Jane Wilde

11

A Well-Matched Pair

Even though both the bride and groom had many friends and enjoyed socialising, the wedding of Dr William Wilde and Miss Jane Elgee was a quiet affair, probably because the bride was still in official mourning for her mother. Jane's uncle, John Elgee, was there and wrote to her sister, Emily, with an account of the wedding:

> Everything went off remarkably well, the carriage called for me this morning a little after eight . . . as soon as Wilde came I drove to Leeson Street for Jane and found her ready, so that no time was lost and at nine precisely we entered the church – a brother of the Dr who is a clergyman residing in Cheshire was the chief priest – William 'assisting' – We fairly stole a march on the Town, no one was expecting the affair till tomorrow, and so nobody was present save ourselves and the old hangers on of the church . . . Jane looked and comported herself admirably – she wore a very rich dress of Limerick lace with a very rich lace veil, a white wreath in her hair etc. – by ten we were at breakfast at the Glebe and by eleven Jane had resumed her mourning and had driven for Kingstown.[1]

In another revealing letter to Emily, he wrote how 'she [Jane] likes him, which I think a great point – she respects him another – his intellectual and literary standing is superior to hers which is also very material, had she married a man of inferior mind he would have dwindled down into insignificance or their struggle for superiority would have been terrific'. There are also signs of conflict between the two sisters, for while praising Jane for having 'some heart' and 'good impulses', nevertheless 'the love of self is the prominent feature of her character – as to caring for either of us, I don't believe that our fortunes cost her a thought – however, I don't want to see open war between you and them'. Jane's individualism, her nationalist views and writings and her refusal to be influenced by her pro-English relations would have all contributed to any other unknown family tensions.

Jane once told her friend in Scotland that 'When I meet a Baronet of £5,000 a year with the Athenian's soul and your good heart – why, I'll fall in love with him.' William Wilde certainly comes close to being Jane's 'Baronet' – a wealthy doctor with a wide reputation as an author and a scholar combined with a streak of sentimentality would certainly come near enough to her heart's desires. If they were not physically well-matched, William being slight of frame and unkempt whereas Jane was big-boned and much taller, they were well matched intellectually. Both were brilliant, ambitious and proud, with William exuding dynamism and self-confidence and Jane flamboyant but with a great soul. The new bride summed up her emotions in a letter to her friend in Scotland: 'I love and suffer – this is all I am conscious of now and thus at last my great soul is prisoned within a woman's destiny – nothing interests me beyond the desire to make him happy – for this I could kill myself.'[2]

How the pair met, the length of their engagement, the nature of the wooing all went unrecorded. The one available reference to the courting couple is contained in a letter written in 1921 by Jack B. Yeats to his son, the poet William, and is little more than tittle-tattle. The old artist is reflecting on the Wildes and wondering what Jane really thought of her husband, given the reputation he had earned as a womaniser and the subsequent revelations at the sensational trial of the early 1860s.[3] But Yeats at this time was an old man recalling scraps of gossip from long ago and it is impossible to say if his recall got it right.

In truth, Jane needed to be tolerant of her husband but was at all times loyal and unquestioning even to the end. As well as having a son, Henry Wilson, during his last year as a medical student, William fathered two daughters, Emily, born in 1847, and Mary, born in 1849, before his marriage to Jane. They were adopted and taken on as wards by William's kindly brother, the Reverend Ralph Wilde. The identity of the mother, or perhaps mothers, is unknown but Jack Yeats mentions in his chatty letter that the woman who gave birth to William Wilde's two illegitimate daughters kept a 'black oak shop' in Dublin. Little more is known about her identity, although Oscar does mention a mysterious lady dressed in black who came and sat in silence by William's sickbed during his final days.

Jane is silent on the subject of her husband's illegitimate children and always maintained discretion. It can only be assumed that she was aware of Henry Wilson and, indeed, of the two toddler girls before she agreed to marry. She never once expresses any concern about the possibility of her husband having a continuing relationship with the mother of his daughters or with any other woman for that matter. Later, when a young woman levels certain accusations against Sir William and it all ends up in a blaze of publicity in the public courts, Jane refuses to believe the allegations, insisting instead that the woman was mad.

William Wilde and his new wife returned from their honeymoon on 1 December 1851 and began married life at 21 Westland Row, a three-story Georgian terraced townhouse that today is part of the nearby Trinity College, Dublin complex. William had moved up the road from his original home at number 15 when his mother Emily died in 1846. The newly wedded couple had many friends and could now enjoy having them visit regularly for convivial evenings and supper. Their guests would have included the barrister and poet Samuel Ferguson, his wife Mary, who was a member of the Guinness brewing family, John Gilbert, a young archaeologist and historian, the writer Charles Laver whenever he was in Dublin, the lawyer Isaac Butt, defender of Charles Gavan Duffy, John Hogan the sculptor, Dr William Stokes, who was by now President of the Royal Irish Academy, George Petrie and the publisher McGlashan.

Jane soon realised that she would not be seeing as much of her busy husband as perhaps she would have liked. As well as the daily routine at the hospital William might also be preparing for a talk or writing an article. On Saturday afternoons during the winter he liked to attend meetings of the Pathological Society in the medical school in Trinity College where the famous doctors of the day told of illnesses they had come across and laid out specimens for the other medical men to examine. William also had to attend the regular meetings of the many clubs and associations he had joined, including the prestigious Royal Irish Academy where he was a member since June 1839. Then there was the arduous task of putting together his 600-page conspectus for the census of 1851 as well as his many private projects such as compiling the manuscript for *Irish Popular Superstitions*, which he eventually published in 1852 and dedicated 'To Speranza'.

Jane as a newly married woman may have regularly found herself alone but this was nothing new. She had often been on her own in Leeson Street where she had worked translating books. Jane was always very proud of her husband and his achievements and would never have questioned him or interfered in his routine. Her stance on the role of women in society, like a good number of her opinions, was almost contradictory. In many ways she was a feminist, believing that women had to break free from a position where they 'still weep and toil, as they had ever done, that man, the lord of the world, may find existence made easier and pleasanter by the ceaseless devotion and patient self-sacrifice of the inferior, at least, the weaker sex'.[4] She also deplored the fact that 'husband-worship'[5] was the main subject being taught to women and believed strongly in 'equal rights, equal culture, and equal honours for men and women'.[6] Nevertheless, she could at the same time hold the view that women should know their place in a marriage, particularly when the husband was 'a man of genius'. In an essay called 'Genius and Marriage', Jane writes that married women can have 'grievous faults' that 'a literary husband and a man of genius' would find 'very irritating'. She supplied an anecdote about Lady Byron to support her point: 'Lady Byron was entirely deficient in this subtle tact that can guide and sooth the wayward, turbulent and terrible temperament of genius. "Am I in your way, Byron?" she asked one day, entering the poet's study while he was at immortal work. "Damnably!" was the answer of the poet-husband. And she deserved it. She had no tact, no fine instincts. She ought to have known intuitively that she was in the way, and effaced herself.'[7] Sir Charles Cameron, in his occasionally inaccurate *Reminiscences*, recalls that Jane communicated with her husband by way of written notes. Perhaps it was her way of displaying that 'subtle tact' she believed Lady Byron lacked.

Jane had married an exceptional man and she herself was no ordinary woman. She would later write of her husband: 'There was probably no man of his generation more versed in our national literature, in all that concerned the land and the people, the arts, architecture, topography, statistics, and even the legends of the country.'[8] The couple would share triumphs and later experience deep tragedy but their marriage was basically a happy one, founded on mutual respect and affection. Of course difficulties existed as they do in every marriage, William's occasionally morose temperament being but one example, but Jane's ability to soar above the mundane allowed her to appear oblivious to any possible shortcomings in her industrious husband. As for their children, Willie, Oscar and Isola, they experienced much love and care from their extraordinary parents. They all had happy childhoods in a bohemian family that was experiencing increasing levels of affluence as William's career continued to prosper. There were servants and governesses to tend to the domestic chores but Jane, perhaps surprisingly, was a good mother and a constant presence in her children's lives.

The first months of the marriage between the doctor and his poet bride passed contentedly. Jane was settling well into her role as a wife with a household of her own to organise when, in early spring, she discovered she had some good news to break to her busy husband. Jane, who had now turned thirty, found herself expecting their first child. On 26 September 1852 she gave birth to a baby boy. He was given four names, William Charles Kingsbury Wills Wilde: William after his father, Charles after Jane's father, Kingsbury as the family surname of Jane's mother and Wills after the family of playwright W. G. Wills who were known to the Wildes. The inclusion of the name Wills needs further examination. Ralph Wilde had, for some unknown reason, given the name Wills to his son Thomas who had in turn passed it on to William, calling him William Robert Wills Wilde. When Ralph Wilde was Mount Sandford's agent in Roscommon, a William Wills, half-brother to the writer W. G. Wills' father, married a co-heiress of Lord Mount Sandford and came to live in Castlerea House. The Wills family became substantial landowners in the area. Ralph might have given his son the name Wills out of respect for the family who were his social superiors or maybe there was some very tentative connection through his wife's people, the O'Flynns. Perhaps Ralph felt that the name Wilde needed to be buttressed by aligning it to a name with superior social standing in the area. Whatever the association, the Wildes were proud of the Wills name and continued to use it although proof of any kinship seems to be lacking. The Wildes had a talent for social climbing and probably saw some benefits in being linked, however loosely, to the name Wills. For a short period a young Oscar went so far as to hyphenate Wills-Wilde. It is yet another coincidence that the judge who sent Oscar to prison also bore the name Wills.

A letter to her friend in Scotland reveals Jane's struggles to reconcile her new-found mothering instincts with the high ideals of Speranza. She wrote:

> Was there a woman's nature in me after all? Oh Patriotism, oh Glory, Freedom, Conquest, the rush, the strife, the battle and the Crown, ye Eidolons of my youth, where are you? Was I nobler then? Perhaps, but the present is the truer life. A mere woman, nothing more. Such I am now. The other was an abnormal state . . . I never read now; as someone said seeing me over little saucepans in the nursery, 'Alas! The Fates are cruel / Behold Speranza making gruel!' Yes, my friend, to this complexion have I come at last. Well, I will rear Him a Hero perhaps and President of a future Irish Republic. Chi sa? I have not fulfilled my destiny yet. Gruel and the nursery cannot end me.[9]

But Jane was a loving mother, doting on her first-born son as she would on Oscar and later on her beloved daughter Isola. In the same letter to Scotland she wrote: 'I scarcely know myself, I who have lived in lofty abstractions, who loved objects only for the ideas they incarnated, how is it I am enthralled by these tiny hands?' William was also a caring father. Even though his bustling life was lived at an intense pace he always made an effort to include his children in his world. The Wilde household would be the scene of many children's parties where birthdays and achievements would always be celebrated. There would be many holidays in the west of Ireland and at the seaside closer to Dublin.

Despite the making of gruel, Jane continued with her literary work. In 1852 she published her fourth translation, *The Glacier Land*, an account by Alexander Dumas of his travels in Switzerland. Many years later and in dire need of income she would attempt to write about her own travels in Sweden in the same style. William was also working on an important book on aural surgery. It was published in 1853 as *Practical Observations on Aural Surgery and the Nature and Treatment of Diseases of the Ear* and it sealed his reputation as a leading member of the medical profession in Ireland and also in Europe. 'I have laboured, and I trust not in vain to expose error and establish truth; to lay down just principles for an accurate diagnosis of Diseases of the Ear; to rescue their treatment from empiricism, and found it upon the well established laws of modern pathology, practical surgery and reasonable therapeutics ... In an art but just emerging from the mists of quackery.'[10] It became the first textbook of importance on the subject and was used for many years at home and abroad. But that same year also brought the death of William's old medical teacher and friend, Dr Graves. William felt deeply the loss of the man who had cared for him when the fever struck after his final exams and who had recommended him to Meiklam for that great trip to the Holy Land.

William grew increasingly cantankerous and irritable at this time. He resigned abruptly from the Royal Irish Academy before returning a year later and was given to bouts of depression. Jane was beginning to feel the strain of living with her dynamic but temperamental husband, describing to her Scots correspondent how 'My husband so brilliant to the world envelopes himself . . . in a black pall and is grave, stern, mournful and silent as the grave itself . . . when I ask him what could make him happy he answers death and yet the next hour if any excitement arouses him he will throw himself into the rush of life as if life were eternal here. His whole existence is one of unceasing mental activity.'[11]

If Jane's husband had a tendency to be morose in private, his public standing, already high, was about to rise even higher. William Wilde gained the first of his many public honours in 1853 when he was appointed Surgeon Oculist in Ordinary to the Queen in Ireland. Unlike the census position, this was a prestigious title that required no work but was a reflection of his distinguished reputation. In theory it meant that William would be the person called upon to attend to the Queen should she ever be in Ireland and find herself in need of an oculist. It was meaningless but impressive, and William appreciated titles and honours. In the following year, 1854, his next book, *On the Physical, Moral and Social Condition of the Deaf and Dumb*, was published. He also wrote a detailed two-part article on 'The Food of the Irish' for the *Dublin University Magazine*. Jane was also busy contributing a biographical sketch of her cousin Robert McClure to the June issue of the magazine. Robert John le Mesurier McClure was an explorer of the Artic and while on the ship *Inventor* he became associated with the discovery of the Northwest Passage.

William, as usual, was driving himself hard, often to the point of collapse from exhaustion, but success brought prosperity. He loved the west of Ireland and the arrival of the railway line into Galway on 1 August 1851 meant that William could now travel into the west more often and with ease. His wish was to be able to establish some kind of base there. When the opportunity arose he was in a position to lease 9 acres of remote land together with the rights to angle for salmon and trout from Lieutenant General Alexander Thomson of Salruck, Connemara. The lease is dated 23 December 1853 and is registered in the Registry of Deeds. Here, on a small peninsula called Illaunroe near Killary Harbour, William built a modest two-storey hunting lodge, his first property in the west of Ireland. Illaunroe can still be found today on the banks of Lough Fee. Charming and intact, it remains hidden from sight behind pine trees and high shrubbery on its little promontory in a remote valley to the right off the Leenane-to-Clifden road. Facilities must have been basic here in William's time but the atmosphere, even today, is one of total peace and tranquillity as the grey waters of Lough Fee lap around the house and the great craggy mountains of Connemara rise up all about. It was to become the perfect hideaway for the busy Dublin-based doctor, and so great was Wilde's love of Illaunroe and the west that his friends were known to refer to him in jest as the 'Wilde man of Connemara'.[12]

12

Merrion Square

On 16 October 1854 Jane Wilde gave birth to a second son. She and William called him Oscar Fingal O'Flahertie Wills Wilde. The names Oscar and Fingal came from Irish legend and reflected Jane's growing interest at the time in old Irish mythology. Oscar was the grandson of Fionn, the leader of the ancient band of warriors known as the Fianna.[1] An Ossianic Society had been founded in Dublin that same year to promote the study of ancient Gaelic folklore and the poet Samuel Ferguson, a regular diner at the Wildes' home in Westland Row, was inspired by the stories of Fionn and his warriors and wrote poems about the legendary hero Oscar and also about Fingal, 'the fair-haired stranger'. The name O'Flahertie came from William's tentative connections through the Fynns with the ancient native Gaelic clan whose territory comprised of vast tracts of land in Connemara. The name Wills also continued to be used.

Jane wrote to Scotland: 'A Joan of Arc was never meant for marriage, and so here I am, bound heart and soul to the home hearth by the tiny hands of my little Willie and as if these sweet hands were not enough, behold me – me, Speranza – also rocking a cradle at this present writing in which lies my second son – a babe of one month old on the 16th of this month and as large and fine and handsome and healthy as if he were three months. He is to be called Oscar Fingal Wilde. Is not that grand, misty and Ossianic?' Then Jane strikes a darker tone in her letter as if some strange premonition had crossed her mind: 'Yes, I ought to be happy. God has lavished blessings on me. If I am sad it is because the apprehension of the unknown future sometimes comes over me. Life has such infinite possibilities of woe.'[2] These were strange thoughts for a new mother of a healthy baby to express but, according to Oscar in *De Profundis*, Jane had a strong belief in the inevitability of tragedy. Jane was nevertheless enchanted with her two children, and her life at this time was pleasant even if her overworked husband could be difficult on occasions. Writing to Scotland again she reflects upon her new responsibility: 'If I can but make them wise and good it seems to me that is all can be done in this brief moment-life of hours.' This would become her life's work and Jane would remain an ever-present figure in the lives of her two sons, encouraging, cajoling, praising or admonishing.

The Wildes were now in a position to employ plenty of staff to help with the domestic chores and Jane continued to enjoy society, attending banquets and other social occasions with her husband. The well-known couple were now receiving invitations to dine with the country's high society including the Lord Lieutenant of Ireland, Lord Carlisle. 'Speranza' declared that the bachelor Viceroy was a good conversationalist. At a dinner party given by Colonel and Mrs Larcom in April 1855 Jane met Sir William Rowan Hamilton, the famous astronomer and mathematician. Although he was a friend of her husband's through the Royal Irish Academy this was Jane's first time to meet the eminent scholar and she surprised him with an invitation to be godfather to Oscar. He politely declined but they went on to become good friends, exchanging many letters over a lengthy period. Jane visited him at the famous Dunsink Observatory dome and he introduced her to the poet Aubrey de Vere who praised her poems. Writing to his friend Professor Augustus de Morgan, Hamilton told him he had met a 'very odd and original lady . . . she asked me to be a godfather, perhaps because I was so to a grandson of Wordsworth the Poet . . . However, I declined . . . she is quite a genius, and thoroughly aware of it.'[3]

William, meanwhile, continued to keep up his frantic work rate and was now suffering regularly from severe asthma and recurrent bronchial attacks. In the summer of 1855 he was taken seriously ill and for three weeks his life was in danger. 'I look with terror on all that can ruffle the calm happiness of the home life,' Jane wrote to Scotland. When he had recovered sufficiently to travel he took his wife and two children off to recuperate at his new hunting lodge on Illaunroe and stayed there for two weeks. Jane, who was never very fond of the countryside, found the place 'grand, desolate and bleak'. There were 'lofty mountains, rude and bare, interminable bays, no trees and no people. They died of the famine or emigrated. The roofless cabins everywhere made me sick with helpless despair and rage.'[4]

Jane was finding it increasingly difficult to turn her mind to writing and poetry was definitely out of the question as the burden of domesticity took its toll on her creativity. She was also concerned for her busy and often morose husband who was driving himself steadily into illness. This worry, coupled with the care of two toddlers, was beginning to weigh heavily upon her normally buoyant spirits. But the doctor's wife was soon to get a much-needed boost. She was about to become mistress of one of Dublin's most impressive Georgian townhouses with an address to match. William was growing ever more successful and wealthy and the Wilde family was now in a position to leave their terraced house on Westland Row and move upmarket to 1 Merrion Square North,[5] a fitting 'mansion' for Speranza and her husband. Today the red-brick house with its beautiful first-floor drawing room still dominates that corner of the elegant square designed and built in the eighteenth century for the country's aristocracy. Jane was able to employ six servants as well as a German governess and a French *bonne* to help with her growing family and the orderly running of their splendid new home with its Turkish carpets, marble-columned mantelpieces and solid walnut and mahogany furniture.[6]

This was the most desirable location in Dublin city. Thirty years later fellow Irishman George Bernard Shaw had occasion to describe Oscar as being 'a snob to the marrow of his being, having been brought up in Merrion Square, Dublin'.[7] Here the doctor and his flamboyant wife joined many other notable Merrion Square residents such as the eminent physicians Robert Graves at number 4 and

William Stokes who lived at number 5, Lord Justice Fitzgibbon at number 10 and the author Sheridan Le Fanu at number 18. Le Fanu found himself living on the exclusive square only because he had married the original owner's daughter. Le Fanu's house is now number 70 and houses the offices of the Irish Arts Council. The Wildes' house is today part of the American College and has been fully restored.

Jane was delighted with her new home: 'This move is very much to my fancy as we have got fine rooms and the best situation in Dublin.'[8] William at last could have a proper library for his large collection of medical and antiquarian books and Jane, an extremely well-read woman, had her own library full of ancient and modern classics. Number 1 Merrion Square was to be the scene of many lively and lavish dinner parties and it was here that 'Speranza' established her celebrated Saturday afternoon salons, attracting the great and the good from the world of the arts as well as politicians, academics and anybody of interest who might be visiting Dublin at the time. The large reception rooms on the first floor proved to be ideal for hosting large, informal gatherings and people crushed in on Saturday afternoons to enjoy lively conversation, recitations and musical performances.

It is no surprise that Oscar later thrived on social gatherings, having had the privilege of listening to the best conversationalists of the age as a child. Their close neighbour William Stokes, Professor of Medicine at Trinity College, was a wonderful and witty conversationalist who loved to entertain dinner guests with dazzling talk full of paradox and humour. Stokes' conversational skills were greatly admired by a young student, John Pentland Mahaffy, who was to become one of the century's great speakers. The influence of William Stokes on Mahaffy can be seen in the book *The Principles of the Art of Conversation*, which Mahaffy went on to publish in 1887. Oscar in turn was hugely influenced at Trinity College by John Mahaffy, who by then had become Professor of Ancient History, describing him as his 'first and greatest teacher'.

William Stokes had a son, Whitley, who was a Celtic scholar. His translations of ancient Celtic manuscripts would have an impact on the Celtic Revival, which in turn had an influence on Oscar.

Dante Gabriel Rossetti and other Pre-Raphaelites were friendly with Whitley Stokes and aware of his work in the area of Celtic studies. Later, Matthew Arnold would write an important work, *On the Study of Celtic Literature*, which influenced the aesthetic movement in its espousal of beauty over Victorian utilitarianism. Oscar would become for a time the personification of the aesthetic philosophy. Stokes' daughter Margaret was an illustrator of books and another neighbour on Merrion Square. Her beautiful illustrations in Samuel Ferguson's major work *The Cromlech on Howth* are based on natural landscapes and on The Book of Kells. Oscar developed a love for beautifully illustrated books and even as a schoolboy he always made an effort to locate an attractive edition of a textbook.

Life continued pleasantly at 1 Merrion Square and by the following summer the eminent doctor's wife was pregnant for the third time. On 2 April 1857 Isola Francesca Emily Wilde was born and the entire family was overjoyed. The name Isola comes from the Gaelic Isult, Francesca from Jane's adopted second name or possibly from Dante Alighieri's Francesca da Rimini in *The Divine Comedy* while Emily was a traditional Elgee name. Jane had always desired a baby girl and now her wish had been granted. A ridiculous story that surprisingly continues to persevere to this day purports to 'account for' Oscar's homosexuality by pointing an accusing finger at Jane for treating him as if he was a girl 'in every detail of dress, habit and companions' for ten years in order to satisfy her desire for a daughter.[9] This, of course, is nonsense. Oscar was not yet two when Jane fell pregnant for the third time so she had not long to wait.

A posed photograph exists of Oscar as a young child wearing a dress with lace trim and with his hair in ringlets, but this proves nothing as it was not uncommon in Victorian times for adoring mothers to dress their little boys occasionally in fancy girl's clothes. The rumour blaming Jane for Oscar's homosexuality can be traced to two sources. Robert Sherard in his 1906 biography *The Life of Oscar Wilde*, the first biography of Oscar to appear, makes reference to Jane dressing Oscar in girl's clothes and to the fact that she liked to drape him in jewels. But this was innocuous fun. Jane herself loved to wear large jewels and ornaments, bedecking her ample chest in brooches and stones. Oscar too would always have a taste for ostentatious jewellery. The other source was Luther Munday's gossipy book *A Chronicle of Friendships* published in 1912 where he claims that Lady Wilde was heard telling guests at a party that she had treated Oscar for ten years as if he had been her daughter because of her strong desire to have a baby girl. Munday confidently claimed that this treatment had turned Oscar into 'a neurotic woman'. Munday knew Oscar in London, having managed a number of the city's clubs. Among his many other activities, this 'man about town' had looked after the affairs of actors Sir Herbert Beerbohm Tree and Sir Charles Wyndham. Munday's book was popular when it appeared but is unreliable and was written at a time when anything to do with homosexuality or Oscar Wilde was viewed with severe hostility.

Following Isola's birth, William continued to cram his life with activity. For the past year he had been involved in an enormous project, the cataloguing of the many artefacts in the museum of the Royal Irish Academy, a task that brought with it the added irritant of conflict with some of his closest colleagues in the Academy. This huge undertaking would consolidate his reputation as an outstanding antiquarian and be a contributing factor in his knighthood. But the workload was enormous, even for Wilde: 'Had I known the amount of physical and mental labour which I was to go through when I undertook the catalogue, I would not have considered it just to myself to have done it; for I may fairly say, that it has been done at the risk of my life.'[10]

The Royal Irish Academy[11] was experiencing a high period in its existence at this time. Members included eminent scholars such as William Rowan Hamilton, the mathematician and scientist, and his friend the scholar Samuel Haughton. Other members included George Petrie, the artist and antiquarian, John O'Donovan, a famous scholar of Irish antiquity and the first historic topographer, and his equally eminent in-law Eugene O'Curry. Sir Thomas Larcom, a high-ranking government official and former Director of the Irish Ordnance Survey, was also a member. In 1855 the Academy began preparations to host the visit of the British Association for the Advancement of Science. It was agreed that the great wealth of antiquities and artefacts in their museum should be suitably displayed and explained for the distinguished visitors but there were two serious problems. No proper descriptive catalogue existed and the articles were in disarray. The collection had been lent to the Dublin Exhibition of 1851 and returned to the Academy's house minus many of its numbers. A committee was set up under the direction of George Petrie with the aim of organising the artefacts and preparing a catalogue. The British Association, the most important archaeological organisation in Europe, was due to arrive in the summer of 1857 so the Academy had less then two years to get organised.

Progress in compiling the catalogue was painfully slow. There were many problems and not a little bickering. Exasperated, Wilde offered to take on the whole task himself. Not without some opposition, the work was taken out of the hands of Petrie and his committee and entrusted to Wilde, together with £250 expenses. He set about the job with characteristic dynamism. Scrapping the work of Petrie's committee, he started again from scratch and adopted a new approach. William decided to classify the objects on the basis of their nature and use, irrespective of age. Attempting to date the objects was too slow and time was of the essence. There were objections to this method from Petrie and his coadjutors who believed in the importance of establishing chronological succession. Wilde was able to progress the project along his own lines for a time. He had drawings and wood engravings prepared, preferring this method to photography, and managed to do a good deal of other valuable work before the objectors gained support. As the pressure to complete the huge task increased, many clashes occurred between Wilde and his fellow members. Eventually, realising that he would be unable to complete the full catalogue in time for the British Association's visit, Wilde decided to concentrate on what he called 'Part 1' – articles of stone, earthenware and vegetable materials. This left all the gold and bronze items and animal materials to be catalogued at a later date. The many coins and silver and iron objects were also put aside for another time. On 24 August 1857, two days before the British Association's visit, Wilde laid Part 1 of the catalogue before an extraordinary meeting of the Royal Irish Academy. It had taken him just six months and was recognised at once as being an extraordinary feat.

The visit of the British Association was a great success both scientifically and socially. When the formal part of the programme was completed in Dublin, Wilde, as President of the Ethnological Section, organised an excursion to Galway and the Aran Islands. No fewer than seventy members took part in the trip, including Samuel Ferguson, Petrie, Stokes and Professor Eugene O'Curry. The French Consul was present and the English party included Professor Simpson of Edinburgh, a noted Celtic scholar, Norton Shaw of London and C. C. Babington, FRS of St John's College, Cambridge, who later published an account of the tour. The party left for Galway by train on 3 September 1857. The Trinity House yacht *Vesta* was waiting at the pier in Galway to take the group across the bay to Inishmore, the largest of the three Aran Islands. Even today Aran is a magical place, resting on the very western edge of Europe. The islands are rich in historical and ancient monuments and the visitors got down to business straight away, examining the ruins that lay within walking distance of the little pier. Next day they wandered about the main island, with Petrie or Wilde holding forth for the benefit of their guests.

On a previous visit to Aran, Wilde had gathered together fragments of a beautifully sculptured cross he found scattered among the ruins of the 'Seven Churches'. A local man named Martin O'Flaherty was given the title of 'guardian of the ruins'. Wilde was delighted to meet his old Aran friend again and to find that he had performed his 'duty' well, even constructing a low stone wall around the cross. The most spectacular archaeological site on the island is Dún Aengus, a semicircular prehistoric stone fort built on the edge of a high cliff with a sheer drop to the Atlantic at its back. The innermost wall is 18 feet high and from 8 to 12 feet thick with an internal platform walk. There are two outer walls and then *chevaux-de-frise* made of large stones set irregularly into the ground. It is a truly impressive and mysterious monument, made more so by the wild grandeur of its setting on the very periphery of Europe. To this day little is known about its builders, its origins or indeed its purpose.

When the exhausted party of antiquarians eventually reached this citadel after their day spent exploring the island, they found to their great surprise a grand feast spread out before them in the open air. William had selected Dún Aengus to be the setting for their celebratory dinner and here among the ancient ruins, just feet away from a frightening drop to the swelling waters of the Atlantic, the antiquarians sat to dine. What the curious locals made of this strange assembly is anybody's guess. They watched from the ramparts as the famous scholars from faraway places made speeches and drank many toasts in the gathering twilight. The minutes record a proposal to publish a book on the antiquities of Aran that would 'serve as a lasting memorial of our appreciation of the services of Mr Wilde, as director of this expedition'. The strange banquet ended with some bagpipe music and a lively Irish jig. The entire undertaking was deemed a great success.

13

The Swedish Connection

In July 1857, just three months after the birth of baby Isola, two unfamiliar visitors arrived at the door of 1 Merrion Square. One was a distinguished-looking gentleman in his late middle years; his companion was a young woman not yet thirty. They had letters of introduction to the Wildes and were surprised when a servant told them 'it was not yet light in his mistress' apartment' even though it was one o'clock in the afternoon. Jane liked to stay in bed late, a lifelong habit, and Oscar in his turn was not an early riser. They were shown to William's study and he soon arrived with 'a small boy in his arm and holds another by the hand. His eyes rest on them with content. They are soon sent away to play, whereupon he gives us his undivided attention.'[1] This is a wonderful peek at a young Oscar and Willie with their father.

The female visitor noted William's 'noble and independent personality' and also the fact that he stooped, brought on, she thought, not from age but from the burden of work. Thick, grey-streaked hair fell on to a broad forehead and his bustling manner gave the impression of one who did not like to waste valuable time. The visitors introduced themselves as Baron Robert von Kraemer, the Governor of Uppsala in Sweden, and his daughter, Lotten. Thus began an important association that would eventually lead to further honours for William and long-lasting friendships for Jane who was to become enchanted with Sweden, visiting the country on at least four occasions and eventually managing to learn the language.

The von Kraemers dined with the Wildes and some friends on their first night in Dublin and were invited to return. Lotten, then aged twenty-nine, was a poet, essayist and editor of a Swedish magazine called *Our Time*. She and Jane found they had much in common. Lotten had endowed a scholarship for women at the University of Uppsala and, like Jane, was interested in improving the position of Swedish women. Jane was greatly impressed by Lotten, by the descriptions of her weekly receptions and by her being at the centre of a vibrant literary circle in Sweden. Lotten also admired Jane, 'with her classic pure features and with a Junoesque figure and bearing . . . The fire in her gaze betrays the famous poetess whose lofty songs are so beloved in her homeland. One is tempted to say, as of the beauty Deugala, to whom Ossian sang; "She believed in nobility, on the highest / In her heart proud dreams reside."'[2]

Through Lotten, Jane became friends with Rosalie Olivecrona who lived in Stockholm and was married to the Chief Justice. Rosalie edited a journal for the home called *Tidskrift för Hemmet*, which she and her sister had founded. It was devoted to the aim of furthering the intellectual and social position of Swedish women. Jane was delighted to hear that in many ways the women in Sweden fared much better than in Ireland. Although not a person of constant views, Jane, in her own way, was a feminist of sorts and pleased to have met two literary women of like mind, something she could not have done in Dublin. Lotten and Rosalie became important confidantes and Jane would correspond with them for some twenty-five years. Taken together with her letters to her male friend in Scotland, a picture emerges of a complex and contradictory woman who could be both extremely sensible and completely impractical or even fantastical in the same paragraph. It is obvious from these letters that Jane had ambitions to be a writer of repute but often laments the fact that she can be distracted. Her interests are seen to be wide-ranging and include politics, books and women's rights. But Jane's major topic is her family: her husband, her sons and her baby girl, Isola. The letters reveal a woman who is a loving, proud mother and a caring wife. She is most definitely the mother and maker of Oscar insofar as anyone can 'make' an Oscar Wilde.

Jane took her children down to Enniskerry, County Wicklow, for a six-week holiday during the summer of 1858 and then left for England with the aim of hiring a nanny or governess. She was a doting mother and told her Scottish friend in a letter that 'their quick kiss and warm hug at parting fill me with remorse for going away at all from them and I long to have Willie's pretty graceful head resting again on my shoulder while I read *The Lady Clare* to him from Tennyson or the scene in *Hiawatha*, two favourites of his'.[3] Jane encouraged her children's interest in literature and liked to steer her sons towards certain authors and away from others. Dickens was far too commonplace. Instead the works of Disraeli were favoured and in poetry Keats and Shelley were championed. Later, Oscar liked to read Balzac and declared 'the death of Lucian de Rubempre is the great drama of my life', referring to the tragic hero in Balzac's *The Splendors and Miseries of Courtesans* who after many intrigues hangs himself in his prison cell. His quip (referring to the main character in Dickens' *The Old Curiosity Shop*) about needing 'a heart of stone to read the death of Little Nell without laughing' is one of his most famous quotations.

The Wildes' first visit to Sweden took place in the autumn of 1858, a year after the arrival of Lotten and her father at Merrion Square. The trip was part of a major tour of northern Europe, encompassing among other cities Berlin, Copenhagen and Stockholm, with William studying the contents and arrangements of the principal museums. William's fame went before him and the Dublin doctor and his intriguing wife received great attention wherever they travelled. In Berlin, William was made an honorary member of the Antiquarian Society; in Stockholm the medical men held a public dinner with the Wildes as chief guests. The ancient University of Uppsala bestowed an honorary degree upon their Irish visitor and Viceroy Baron von Kraemer entertained William and Jane publicly in the grand surroundings of his castle. Memories of those glittering occasions would sustain Jane in her darker days many years later. Jane was greatly impressed by the festivities and the grand setting. She loved everything about Scandinavia and filled her notebook with sharp observations on the people and their costumes. She described sailing through the fiords of Norway and along the Göta Canal in Sweden admiring the beautiful pine forests and the enchanting wooded islands of the Baltic. She also enjoyed hearing the local legends told to her by Lotten as they sat in the regal castle, which was then home to the von Kraemer family. Years later, in much-altered circumstances, Jane would plunder these notes to write *Driftwood from Scandinavia*, for which she would be more than grateful to receive fifty guineas.

Back home in Dublin, William was shocked to learn that the Academy had decided to stop all work on the catalogue. Scholar Martin Haverty, the recorder of events at Dún Aengus during the Aran visit and author of *A History of Ireland*, describes in a letter to John Gilbert, the Academy's Secretary, a casual meeting with William: 'He seemed a good deal annoyed about the proceedings in the Academy, and I think justly. He has been badly treated.' In a further letter Haverty remarked 'I am afraid that our friend, Dr Wilde, has been too hasty with the Academy. His nature is too impulsive, if it could be helped.'[4] The Academy was divided on the issue of William's methods and those who believed that a proper chronological order should be established before proceeding any further had managed to carry the day. William believed that a catalogue based on the nature or use of the artefacts would at least be possible to complete whereas discussions regarding age would drag on forever. A subscription was started amongst Academy members in the face of some very strong opposition but sufficient funds were collected for William to complete Part 2, which was published in 1860, along his own lines, with Part 3 following in 1862.

William, partly due to his tenacious nature, was brilliant at the tedious work of cataloguing. His ability to observe and then go on to describe eloquently what he had observed was second to none. Wilde's fame as an archaeologist rests principally on these three catalogues. Despite the bitter quarrels, William was elected Vice-President of the Academy on completion of the huge task and presented with a hundred copies of his catalogues. A decade later, in 1873, he received the Cunningham Medal, the Royal Irish Academy's highest award. However, his bustling, no-nonsense nature had ruffled some influential feathers and he was never to achieve the Presidency.

William was now in prosperous circumstances and his personal reputation was at an all-time high. Many famous people came to visit him and to examine the museum, including the ill-fated Emperor Maximilian I of Mexico and his wife, the Empress Charlotte. William himself conducted the Prince of Wales, later King Edward VII, over the Academy's museum and was surprised by the Prince's sound knowledge of Celtic antiquities. Charles Laver, on one of his regular visits back to Ireland, commented that William and his friends had become puffed up with self-importance due to all this intercourse with notables. There certainly was a lot of high living. Robert Sherard, Oscar Wilde's first biographer, rather prudishly condemned William Wilde for consorting with companions who were boozy and for the bohemian atmosphere of opulence at 1 Merrion Square where late suppers, deep drinking and careless talk constituted, according to Sherard, a danger to their children. But Sherard was being overly severe. The Wilde household had always been the scene of a great many gatherings where conversation sparkled and all the great scholars, writers and wits of the day gathered at William's dining table or in Jane's drawing room. This could only have been of benefit to his children. Oscar recalled seeing the man he called 'the earliest hero of my childhood', the Young Ireland leader William Smith O'Brien, dining at Merrion Square. He also remembered meeting John Mitchel, Jane's old colleague from the Young Ireland days. There were also many parties for the children to mark birthdays or achievements. Oscar described his father in later years as a man of the greatest social charm and intellectual superiority and, like his son a generation later, he was a man who liked to dominate the conversation at table.

There were family holidays to the seaside at Sandymount or Bray and the Wildes were regular visitors to a farmhouse named Crone at Glencree, County Wicklow. But the favourite place of all at this point was their west of Ireland hunting lodge on Illaunroe, or as young Oscar liked to call it, 'the little purple island', where the children learnt to fish and hunt. Years later, Oscar would tell his own children fantastic stories of the 'great melancholy carp' living at the bottom of the lake. Oscar and Willie always spent a large part of their school holidays in the west, boating and fishing on Lough Fee or Lough

Corrib and helping their father explore the ancient sites later set out so well by William in *Lough Corrib, its Shores and Islands*. Oscar always spoke happily about his childhood, even about potentially dangerous incidents. He recalled one evening when he and Willie were having a bath in front of the fire in the nursery while their nightshirts were warming on a fender. The nurse had only left the room when Oscar noticed one of the nightshirts was about to catch fire. When the flames appeared he clapped his hands with delight. Willie, however, immediately called for the nurse who appeared and quenched the flames, 'whereupon Oscar cried with rage at the spoiling of the pageant and the end of the fun'.[5] He also spoke of owning a toy bear that he loved dearly but gave to Willie when his brother asked for it. Whenever the pair quarrelled, Oscar would ask for his bear to be returned.

There is an account by the then chaplain of the newly opened Glencree Reformatory, a Reverend L. C. Prideaux Fox, of Jane, on holiday nearby, bringing her children to his Catholic chapel when Oscar was about eight or nine. Reverend Fox maintained she asked him to instruct the two boys and after a few weeks he baptised them, it being their mother's wish. He recorded his version of events in an article called 'People I Have Met', which appeared in *Donahoe's Magazine*, where he states 'it was not long before she asked me to instruct two of her children, one of them being that future erratic genius, Oscar Wilde. After a few weeks I baptised these two children, Lady Wilde herself being present on the occasion. At her request I called on their father and told him what I had done, his sole remark being that he did not care what they were so long as they became as good as their mother.'[6] There is no official record of this act, but private baptisms often went unregistered. Jane, at times, did show an interest in Catholicism, a preoccupation she passed on to Oscar who, years later, claimed to have a vague recollection of having been baptised a Catholic.

Jane was the granddaughter of the Protestant Archdeacon of Wexford but she had her own views on religion. According to Oscar, his mother believed that 'the people' needed dogma but 'she rejects all forms of superstition and dogma, particularly any notion of priest and sacrament standing between her and God. She has a very strong faith in that aspect of God we call the Holy Ghost – the divine intelligence of which we on earth partake.'[7] Jane was instinctively drawing a distinction between the high-minded intelligentsia and the common flock, and she was most definitely not to be numbered among the common flock.

Portrait of William Wilde drawn on stone by J. H. Lynch from a
daguerreotype by L. Gluckman. Lithographer: J. H. Lynch

National Library of Ireland

Portrait of a young William Wilde.

National Library of Ireland

Ballymagibbon House near Cong, the Mayo home of the Fynn family.
As a boy William Wilde regularly came to stay here, his mother being the
daughter of John and Elizabeth Fynn. William's grandfather John Fynn
died in 1779.

William Wilde, portrait by Thomas Herbert Maguire, 1847.

National Library of Ireland

Jane Wilde wearing a tiara, from
The Irish Fireside,
2 September 1885.

National Library of Ireland

Illaunroe: on this remote peninsula on Lough Fee near Little Killary, Connemara, William Wilde built his first hunting lodge in the west.

Illaunroe lodge today.

Aughnanure Castle, near Oughterard, County Galway, a stronghold of the O'Flaherty Clan. Oscar's parents believed the Wildes were connected to this native Irish clan through the Fynns of Cong.

No. 1 Merrion Square, the Dublin home of Sir William Wilde and Lady Jane Wilde and their family.

Oscar Wilde as a child, wearing a girl's dress, from a miniature belonging to
Robert Ross. The hand-tinted original belongs to Merlin Holland.

Oscar Wilde in Dublin in the 1860s.

Reproduced with permission of the William Andrews Clark Memorial Library,
University of California, Los Angeles.

Moytura House, near Cong, County Mayo: Sir William Wilde's retreat
in the west, built in 1865.

'In Memoriam' stone in the garden of Moytura House.

Stone circle near Cong, County Mayo, one of many such sites in the area which inspired Sir William Wilde.

14

Moytura

Those were lively days in the city for members of the professional classes. On St Patrick's Day 1859 2,000 people attended a ball given by the Lord Lieutenant of Ireland at Dublin Castle. In a letter to her Swedish friend Lotten von Kraemer, Jane describes the event: 'Everyone wears shamrock mixed with the artificial trimmings of the dress on that night – and all the ladies wear white feathers and lappets or tulle veils – my dress was three skirts of white silk ruched round with white satin ribbon and looped up with bouquets of gold flowers and green shamrock – a wreath of the same for the hair, plumes of feathers and white tulle veil bordered with gold'.[1] That same year William and Jane visited Sweden for the second time and were overwhelmed once more by the attentions they received. Jane wrote to thank Lotten for her hospitality and described their unforgettable experiences, the 'enchanting country with its noble historical associations, its queenly capital throned on her seven hills and robed in her mantle of pine forests and your graceful people'.

Two years later, in 1861, Dublin was again the host city for the annual meeting of the Association for the Promotion of Social Science and Jane's Swedish friend Rosalie, the magazine editor, and her husband, Professor Olivecrona, attended. A reception was held at Dublin Castle for 1,800 guests while Jane and William kept open house at their Merrion Square residence for the Swedish contingent. In October the Wildes were once again back in Sweden for a short visit but this was to be the last time they would be entertained by the von Kraemers in the beautiful castle of Uppsala as the Baron retired from his position as Viceroy the following year. In the spring of 1862, King Charles XV of Sweden bestowed upon William Wilde the Order of the Polar Star. Baron von Kraemer, no doubt, had the ear of the King and put in a good word for his friend from Ireland before he left office.

William's friends and wits saw possibilities in this latest Swedish distinction for the esteemed doctor. The minutes for the Medico-Philosophical Society, of which William was a long-standing member, for 2 April 1862 state: 'it was resolved that the congratulations of the Society be offered to Mr Wilde on the acquirement of this very distinguished honour and that henceforward at every meeting of the Society he shall be addressed as Chevalier Wilde'. Indeed, they would refer to him as Chevalier Wilde for the rest of his life, even though the Swedish Order carried no official title rights. A committee was formed, as the minutes show, to 'arrange the Chevalier in a proper and becoming position, and have his photograph taken'.[2] William Wilde's friends were obviously enjoying this opportunity to poke some fun at a colleague who could at times be a trifle haughty.

That same year, the World Exhibition opened in London. The Association for the Promotion of Social Science held their annual meeting there to coincide with the exhibition but William, only recently returned from the trip to Sweden, was not feeling well enough to attend. Instead he brought his family west to Connemara for a recuperative month. The three children, Willie, Oscar and Isola, had whooping cough and, in a letter to Rosalie, Jane admits to having passed a miserable time with them. Even today, the lodge at Illaunroe is remote and looks rather basic. It certainly would have lacked the creature comforts of Merrion Square and Jane was a woman who liked her creature comforts.

During the autumn and winter of 1862 Jane was working on a translation of a German philosophical romance called *The First Temptation or Eritis Sicut Deus* by Marie Schwab, published the following year to mixed reviews. The plot tells of an aesthete who turned aesthetics into a religion of beauty and died tragically. Jane was delighted when she heard that her translation had reached Sweden and she hoped it might be reviewed in Rosalie Olivecrona's magazine. Oscar would, of course, have read his mother's translation and later was to become closely identified with aestheticism in Oxford. There is evidence that aesthetics had captured his interest even as a student in Dublin. A reference in 'The Suggestion Book of the Philosophical Society' at Trinity College, Dublin, for 1874 pokes fun at Oscar for his developing aestheticism.

The winter of 1862 was a particularly sickly time. A Swedish friend Professor Siegfried lunched with the Wildes on Christmas Day but died two weeks later from what was termed a 'brain fever', probably meningitis. Oscar was also ill that Christmas and was confined to his bed for five weeks. William, however, continued to prosper. As well as collecting honours and titles he was, at this time, also collecting property. He built four houses overlooking the sea at Bray, a resort town just south of Dublin. Jane took one of these and furnished it for family holidays, the other three were rented for £120 each per annum. The 'Chevalier' and his family appeared to be doing very well, and a letter of Jane's to Lotten soon told how 'He is now going to build a residence on his new property in the County Mayo on the shores of Lough Corrib.'[3]

Wilde had secured a base in the west when he purchased Illaunroe. This was very remote, however, and he was pleased when he managed to acquire part of the ancestral estates of his mother's family, the Fynns of Ballymagibbon, near Cong in County Mayo. The Fynns were, to some extent, a mentally unstable family. John Fynn was a man with a reputation for being tyrannical, perhaps even unbalanced, with a penchant for carrying out impromptu baptisms in a nearby pond on any Papist willing to be 'saved'. When John Fynn, known as the Dipper, died, some of the property passed to William's aunt, Miss Fynn, who was mentally unwell and soon had to be officially declared insane. William was involved in the certification process but there is no suggestion that her condition did not warrant being certified. The 620 acres she had inherited from John Fynn were sold for her benefit in the Landed Estate Court; William purchased 170 of these acres in an area west of Cong along the northern shores of Lough Corrib. There he found a wretched tenantry, too many of them to make a living from the amount of land at their disposal. William, who was not known for his tact, nevertheless managed to employ some dexterity in this case and with the help of the local Catholic clergy was eventually able to remove a number of tenants without it costing him too much money. The others he rehoused in comfortable cottages and with a generous measure of tenant rights. The little estate would never offer up much in the way of rental income, especially in the turbulent Land War years to come, but it provided a perfect base for William in his beloved west of Ireland.

William chose the site for his new house with care, a ridge overlooking the Corrib with the majestic peaks of the Maumturk Mountains rising in the distance across the lake. There he built Moytura House, a two-storey gabled lodge, beautifully proportioned with dormer windows and a commanding view. He called it after the ancient Battle of Moytura, which he believed was fought through that exact locality. Today, historians tell us that the Battle of Moytura belongs in the realm of myth rather than reality. The legend involves the dark forces of the Firbolgs fighting the magical warriors of the Tuatha De Danann and William was convinced he had found the actual location of the bloody conflict. If a battle of some nature did take place in the dim and misty prehistorical past, then, according to the annals, it was more than likely fought over territory way off to the north near Sligo. William, however, had no difficulty imagining great warriors fighting that heroic battle and erecting huge burial mounds to honour their fallen heroes in the actual fields around his new house. After all, were not the mounds and monuments still extant? The proof as far as he was concerned could be seen in the many ancient sites he knew were scattered on his very doorstep between Cong and Cross. He was to spend the following years in a detailed exploration of all the local ruins in an effort to provide concrete evidence in support of his claim. He would later write a paper on the subject of the Battle of Moytura and it would form a large and colourful section in his book on the locality, *Lough Corrib, its Shores and Islands*.

Moytura House made a comfortable second family home with its Connemara and Kilkenny marble fireplaces in the downstairs rooms, a walled kitchen garden to the side and a rose garden with a sundial out front. Here in the silence, peace and solitude of the west, William and his family spent much of their holiday time. As the years progressed and events took their toll, the failing doctor was to spend more and more of his time at his Moytura haven. Terence de Vere White, William Wilde's biographer, writes that 'If Wilde was difficult or hasty in Dublin, he seemed to have been a happy man in the west . . . Here, beyond doubt, is where Wilde's heart lay. Here the passion for the past which fired his imagination in Palestine, which produced the mammoth Census and the no less prodigious catalogue of antiquities in the museum, joined with all the associations of childhood, to make every stone familiar, every sod nostalgic, every stream evocative.'[4]

William knew the people of Cong and they knew him. He had been fair and tactful with his tenants when he took over from the Fynns. To the local tenantry, he was the great doctor down from Dublin, a scholar and healer from the big world beyond their horizons. Some folk still remembered him as a boy tramping the fields of his grandparents' estate or as a youth helping out during the cholera epidemic. Others would have met him out on the lake fishing or boating. Now Sir William's flag flew from the stone tower he built beside Moytura House. It was here he liked to sit, looking south over grey Lough Corrib or north across the green fields to the many cairns, caves, stone circles and other antiquities that still dot the locality today. Moytura was furnished in 1864 and Jane was anxious that her Swedish friend Lotten would come over for a visit and see their new retreat and the 'grand wild scenery and the lovely dark eyes of the half-Spanish peasant girls . . . You may do just as you like in our house, read when you like and take breakfast in bed . . . I never come down out of my room till 1 or 2 o/c – then we can go out and drive and enjoy ourselves – and always a pleasant friend worth talking to drops in to dine.'[5]

The unpublished memoirs of a Dr Conor Maguire of Claremorris give a very interesting account of William Wilde at Moytura in the 1860s:

During these holidays he drove about the neighbourhood in a small pony phaeton. The harness mainly consisted of hemp ropes and the reins more usually rope instead of leather. My father was Dispensary doctor in Cong for a good many years about this time. He also took a great interest in archaeology. I remember once my father sent word to Sir William about his discovery of a cairn or what was the remains of a cairn at Ballykine in which there was a skeleton. When Sir William got the message he sent a note to my father who was attending a Dispensary at Cross. 'Dear Maguire, Brush off the patients as quick as possible and come along to see the cairn.' Both went off as soon as they could and when they reached the spot Sir William produced an old-fashioned travel bag and packed the skull and all the other bones he could find into the bag and took them away with him for the museum in Dublin. Sir Arthur Guinness, the landlord, afterwards Lord Ardilaun, heard of the find a few days after and wrote a sharp note to Sir William, pointing out that he should not have removed the skeleton without permission.

Maguire was about thirteen or fourteen years old at the time he knew the Wildes and would often visit Moytura with his father. He recalled Jane as a 'very charming lady' and William's 'long white hair down to the collar of his coat and his long white whiskers and the funny old caubeen, a soft hat, and a piece of twine tied round it to keep it on his head'. Contradicting T. G. Wilson, Wilde's biographer, who believed that William could speak the Irish language, Maguire described how Wilde would 'often take me with him as interpreter with Irish-speaking farmers when he was investigating old forts or any archaeological remains.' Maguire remembered the Wildes' children too:

Sir William had two sons, William and Oscar, and one daughter. The daughter died very young and he erected a little pillar stone near the house with the simple

inscription In Memoriam. Oscar seldom came to Moytura
and when I met him he always seemed to me very dull
company. I suppose he looked on all the people about as
a brainless ignorant lot, not worth talking to, whose souls
never rose above the weather, the crops, fishing or
shooting. Whereas his thoughts were centred on Greek
poetry. He had a long solemn face and rarely ever smiled.
I am sure he did not know how to laugh. Willie Wilde was
entirely different. He was gay and jolly, smoked and drank.
A friend of mine said once about a mutual acquaintance
– 'Oh, he is a foine eater and a nice drinker'. Willie was a
big man, he was over six feet and well built. He was fond
of music and played quite nicely and sang to his own
accompaniment. He died when a fairly young man – I
suppose about forty-five. He was the eldest son and
inherited the little property of Moytura and came every
half year to collect the few pounds rent for the grazing of
the farm.'[6]

This was written after Oscar's fall from grace, when few had a good
word to say about him.

15

Schooldays ·

In Feburary 1864 the Wildes sent their two sons, Willie and Oscar, to board at Portora Royal School, Enniskillen, about 100 miles northwest of Dublin. Oscar had not yet turned ten years of age. Portora was a prestigious school catering for the sons of colonial officials, clergy, members of the professions and the landed gentry. The school prepared pupils for Trinity College, Dublin, and was presumptuously called 'the Eton of Ireland' by its headmaster, the Reverend William Steele. Perhaps William's decision to send his sons there was influenced by his friendship with William Wakeman who taught art at the school. Better known as 'Bully Wakeman' to his students, he had worked with William as an illustrator on his Royal Irish Academy catalogues and on *The Beauties of the Boyne and Blackwater*. He would later contribute to *Lough Corrib, its Shores and Islands*. Wakeman remained friends with the Wildes and went on to write a book on Lough Erne that was published in 1870 and dedicated to Speranza.

In a letter to her friend Lotten von Kraemer in Sweden written the previous April, Jane revealed that the idea of sending the boys away to boarding school was being considered. 'My eldest boy is nearly eleven – very clever and very high spirited . . . and tho' he obeys me he will scarcely obey a governess. I feel it would be a risk to leave him. But we think of sending both boys to a boarding school soon.' The fees were sixty guineas a year with an additional one guinea a quarter for drawing lessons. Oscar would spend seven years at the school and eventually win a Royal scholarship to Trinity College, one of only two awarded that particular year. For this achievement Oscar had his name inscribed in gilt letters on an Honours Board in the school. After his imprisonment in 1895 the name of Oscar Wilde was erased from the board but it has since been regilded. Portora continues to thrive today and boasts some other famous past pupils, including Samuel Beckett.

The school terms were long with only two breaks, one from about 21 June to 10 August and the other at Christmas from around 21 December to 28 January. The school accommodated approximately 100 boarders and 50 day boys divided into the Lower School, for those between ten and twelve, and the Upper School for the more senior pupils. Even though the students were mostly from the Protestant Ascendancy classes, the headmaster, a tolerant man with liberal views, opened the school to the sons of Catholic parents and at one stage proposed the establishment of a new boarding house on the grounds especially for Catholic students. Oscar appears to have settled in well at Portora. He was a prizeman in the Junior School in 1866 and so was exempt from the annual examinations. Willie also settled well and became a popular 'character' often ridiculed for his tendency to boast. Willie's nickname was 'Blue Blood' because he claimed the colour of his unwashed neck came not from dirt but from the blue blood of the Wilde family. Oscar was known as 'Grey Crow', a name he disliked, but he in turn had the knack of providing humorous if apt nicknames for his fellow students and they tended to stick.

The school grounds, over 60 acres, ran along the banks of Lough Erne and so bathing and fishing were popular pastimes as was skating in the winter. Collecting birds' eggs was also a popular hobby among the pupils and Oscar liked to take a boat out on Lough Erne to hunt for birds' eggs on the wooded islands. Devenish Island, with it ancient monastic ruins and round tower, was a regular destination for the rowers. Willie liked to play the piano and sometimes entertained the junior pupils. Oscar, not being musical or sporty, was known more for his appreciation of beautiful books and liked to have well-produced editions of the texts while the others were pleased to make do with the standard copy. Oscar also displayed an extraordinary ability to read at high speed. He could read a page at a glance and often conducted a conversation as he quickly turned the pages. Frequently, for a wager, he would read a lengthy novel in an hour and then be able to answer questions, relay the plot and quote pertinent passages of dialogue. He liked English novels and poetry but disliked maths and the sciences and would neglect texts and sections of the course he found boring, such as grammar and textual criticism. Like his mother, Oscar had a liking for languages and the literary aspects of classical studies. In his penultimate year he won the Carpenter Greek Testament Prize. The following year he was awarded the Royal scholarship. Oscar's academic successes, without any obvious serious effort, surprised some pupils at Portora who regarded him as a skimmer. He would go on to surprise his fellow students in Trinity and later in Oxford.

A number of students at Portora later recorded their memories of Oscar. Louis Claude Purser, the son of Benjamin Purser who taught history and geography at the school, remembered a boy who 'was somewhat reserved and distant in his manner, but not at all morose or supercilious. He had rather a quick temper, but it was not very marked.'[1] He also said that Oscar had 'a real love for intellectual things, especially if there was a breath of poetry in them'. Purser was awarded a Royal scholarship the same year as Oscar and eventually became Trinity's Professor of Latin. It was there that Robert Sherard found him when he came to Dublin after Oscar's death researching his biography. Louis Purser had many good things to say about his boyhood friend and particularly remembered the skill he displayed in the *viva voce* when he won the Gold Medal for classical Greek. Another school companion, Edward Sullivan, remembered Oscar as having 'no very special chums while at school . . . Willie Wilde was never very familiar with him, treating him always, in those days, as a younger brother.'[2]

The school had extensive grounds but in winter the boys liked to gather around a stove in an entrance area known as the Stone Hall because of its flagged floor. It was here that Oscar and Willie were often to be found entertaining a group of fellow scholars by telling stories, with Willie being the boys' favourite. Oscar had a romantic imagination and could transform mundane events into epic dramas. He once knocked over a disabled bystander while escaping from a boyish prank committed in the town but in the telling of the tale the poor disabled individual was transformed into an angry giant that Oscar had to overcome through acts demanding enormous courage. And it was here that he spoke of his wish to be remembered for his part in some famous court case that would be known as 'Regina Versus Wilde'.

A letter from Oscar in Portora to his mother dated September 1868 has survived. Oscar is thanking his 'Darling Mama' for sending a hamper containing food and items of clothing. 'The hamper came today, and I never got such a jolly surprise, many thanks for it, it was more than kind of you to think of it.'[3] These are the earliest written words that exist from the pen of Oscar Wilde. All the items arrived safely, he tells his mother, except for the blancmange that was a little sour. The letter is of great interest. Already the fourteen-year-old is exhibiting many of the characteristics he would later cultivate. He displays an impish humour and a taste for the unorthodox view when he asks his nationalist mother if she had written to her staunchly unionist sister 'Aunt Warren on green notepaper'. He goes on to complain that the 'flannel shirts you sent in the hamper are both Willie's, mine are one quite scarlet and the other lilac but it is too hot to wear them yet'.[4] Oscar was even then cultivating the taste for individualism in his style of dress that he would further develop at university. The letter also includes a playful drawing of two actors in Elizabethan costume dancing delightedly about a hamper while a third looks on in tears because he must do without.

His relationship with his mother is obviously warm and loving. She is 'Darling Mama' and later 'dear Mamma'. He sends his 'love to Papa' who was also keeping in touch with his sons. Oscar writes: 'You may imagine my delight this morning when I got Papa's letter saying he had sent a hamper.' Both parents are getting praised for the appreciated delivery. He shows interest in her literary affairs when he asks to see a copy of the *National Review*, which had recently published a new poem by Jane called 'To Ireland', and complains that she has not told him 'anything about the publisher in Glasgow, what does he say?' Jane, at the time, was in discussions with Cameron & Ferguson about a new edition of her poems. The collection was eventually published three years later. Oscar's lack of interest in games is borne out in the letter when he says how he 'went down to the horrid regatta on Thursday last'. He does, however, show some enthusiasm for a recent school victory in cricket. They had 'played the officers of the 27th Regiment now stationed in Enniskillen, a few days ago and beat them hollow by about seventy runs'.

With Oscar and Willie off in boarding school, Merrion Square was a quieter home but Jane still had Isola for company. Perhaps because she had a little more time on her hands Jane managed to write two poems, which were published in *Duffy's Hibernian Magazine*. They were in the old Speranza mode, one on the theme of poverty and the other a call for someone to lead Ireland out of its difficulties. Jane was inspired to take up the pen once more as Speranza because of the growing unrest in the countryside. Unemployment was on the rise and the Fenian Brotherhood, founded in America in 1858 with the aim of ending British rule in Ireland, was beginning to gain strength. But time had dampened the fiery rebellious spirit of Speranza and the poems received some criticism, something unheard of in the days of Young Ireland. Even the Fenian organ, the *Irish People,* had harsh words for her latest poems: 'Speranza's "Who Will Show Us Any Good" is even more difficult to make out than her verses usually are', the newspaper complained, 'and we scarcely know whether we rightly understand its meaning.'[5]

Undeterred, Jane decided to push ahead and publish a full collection of her earlier work. Called *Poems by Speranza*, published by James Duffy in 1864, the frontispiece read:

Dedicated to My Sons, Willie and Oscar Wilde
I made them indeed,
Speak plain the word COUNTRY. I taught them, no doubt,
That a country's a thing men should die for at need![6]

This dedication was replaced with her poem 'To Ireland' when the Glasgow publishers came to produce later editions in 1871 and 1883. The collection got mixed reviews. The *Freeman's Journal* praised it highly and the *Dublin Review*, while recognising her 'extraordinary influence', criticised her thumping technique. The *Irish People* was again disparaging of her work. Speranza had been above criticism back in the 1840s but times had changed.

William, meanwhile, was spending a good deal of time at Moytura, often travelling over alone. When the boys were visiting they liked to spend their time boating, hunting or fishing. They might occasionally row across Lough Mask to see George Moore, the son of George Henry Moore, Sir William's friend and frequent guest at Moytura. Other times they helped their father explore the ruins and monuments in the locality, often sketching what they saw. Willie was particularly skilful and a small number of his drawings would be used in William's classic book *Lough Corrib, its Shores and Islands*. William credits his son 'Master Wilde' with the illustration of the stone fortress on Hag's Castle in Lough Mask. In the sketch a man can be seen sitting on a rock beneath the crumbling stone walls of the fort. He is wearing a hat and appears to be making notes on a sheet of paper while a young boy crosses the shore beside him. It is not too much to assume that this drawing by young Willie shows his father at work with his younger brother, Oscar, assisting nearby. William delighted in his peaceful retreat on the shores of Lough Corrib. He would soon need just such a haven where he could come to lick his wounds as the fates were lining up to deliver a series of mighty blows on the Wilde family.

Part 4

Trials

'Whatever is in him, he gives to this wretched woman, whom he has thrust into your society, into your home, to shame you before everyone.'

Lady Windermere's Fan

16

The Pamphlet

William Wilde received his knighthood on 28 January 1864. It was the last act in a long afternoon of pomp and pageantry in the magnificent Throne Room of Dublin Castle. When William's name was called, the distinguished assembly of lords and ladies watched as the slight, middle-aged doctor with long greying hair, a fuzz of side-whiskers and beard made his way to the right of the chair of state. His Excellency, the Earl of Carlisle, Lord Lieutenant of Ireland, then spoke. 'Mr Wilde, I propose to confer upon you the honour of Knighthood, not so much in consideration of your high professional reputation which is European, as to mark my sense of the service you have rendered to statistical science, especially in connection with the Irish Census.'[1] Having knelt, his Excellency laid the sword upon his shoulder and said 'Arise Sir William Wilde.'

The gathering then adjourned. They would reassemble later in the evening for the Lord Lieutenant's first Drawing-room of the season, when Dublin Castle, the symbol and centre of the British Empire's rule in Ireland, would be a blaze of twinkling light. The season's first Drawing-room was always one of the most splendid occasions in the city's social calendar, with the Castle's corridors echoing to the chatter of debutantes and the rustle of pompous-looking matrons while men of high rank and station mingled with the guests in the great Throne Room. Outside at the gates, bedraggled crowds always gathered to watch the stream of carriages pass through, hoping to catch a glimpse of the fine ladies in silks and satins and their dashing escorts in splendid uniforms or formal dress. The following day the papers were positively gushing. It was, according to *Saunders' Newsletter*, 'the most imposing and brilliant ceremony of the kind which has taken place for many years back. The array of rank and fashion assembled in the Castle recalled the memories of the Irish Court before the Union . . . the occasion was rendered still more agreeable when, unexpectedly, his Excellency availed himself of the opportunity afforded by the presence of so brilliant an assemblage to confer the distinction of knighthood upon one of the most eminent members of the medical profession and the scientific associations of Ireland.' The account went on to describe the ladies' dresses in great detail, including a Lady Fitzgerald who wore a 'train and corsage of the very richest (rose de chien) moiré antique, lined with white gros de Naples'. Lady Wilde wore 'a train and corsage of richest white satin, trimmed handsomely in scarlet velvet and gold cord, jupe, richest white, satin with bouillonnes of tulle, satin ruches and a magnificent tunic of real Brussels lace lappets; ornaments, diamonds'.[2]

The new knight and his wife – how she revelled in her new title Lady Wilde – were congratulated on all sides and their many friends were equally delighted. There followed a hectic round of social engagements. Writing to her Swedish friend Rosalie Olivecrona in the summer of 1864, Jane tells of her busy social life, with 'so many dinners and invitations following on our receiving the title to congratulate us that we have lived in a whirl of dissipation'.[3]

In February, *Saunders' Newsletter* published an 'Epigram on a Recent Dubbing in Dublin':

> The news of your knighthood was welcomed with cheers;
> Oh! eminent aurist, 'twas good for our ears.
> The *Gazette* that records it, wherever it flies,
> To thy friends through the world, will be good for their eyes;
> Thus Carlisle, judiciously dubbing thee, Will,
> In honouring thy merit hath rivalled thy skill.
>
> SAMUEL LOVER

This congratulatory verse drew the following reply from someone signing themselves 'Sam Weller':

> To Samuel Lover, Esq.,
>
> My Dear Sam – Apropos of the memorable event which you have chronicled in the above lines. I beg to send you the following bit of a doggrel; and if you do not at once procure its insertion in the paper in which your epigram appeared, I shall be coerced, when we next meet, to confer upon yourself the signal (dis) honor of a sound d(r)ubbing. – Ever yours, fraternally,
>
> Sam Weller

The letter was accompanied by a verse seeming to disparage Sir William's achievement in being knighted. But who was this mysterious 'Sam Weller'? Certainly, there appeared to be an individual in the city who was not very happy with William Wilde's elevation to the rank of 'belted knight'.

In April 1864, a few months after he received his knighthood, Sir William was scheduled to give a lecture on 'Ireland Past and Present: the Land and the People' at the Metropolitan Hall. It was one of a series given by men of distinction under the auspices of the Young Men's Christian Association. Attending lectures was a popular activity among the educated classes of the time and fashionable Dublin did indeed flock to the event. As the carriages drew up and the crowd entering the hall mingled with the sightseers on the footpath, a small boy ran through the assembly ringing a handbell, drawing attention to four other boys who were selling a pamphlet entitled *Florence Boyle Price: or a Warning, by Speranza*. They held large placards advertising the booklet emblazoned with the words 'Sir William Wilde and Speranza'. On further flysheets were printed seventeen letters written by Sir William Wilde, all of a very private nature. The newsboys called out 'Sir William Wilde's letters! Sir William Wilde's letters!' and thrust them into the hands of everybody willing to take one. There was no shortage of takers. Further commotion ensued when friends of Sir William, upon realising the scurrilous and harmful nature of the printed matter, attempted to seize the pamphlets and the placards.

The pamphlet told the tale of a high-spirited girl, Florence Boyle Price, who was seduced by her doctor in his consulting rooms while she was under the influence of chloroform. The doctor was referred to as 'Dr Quilp'. 'Mrs Quilp', meanwhile, was 'an odd sort of undomestic woman' who 'spent the greater portion of her life in bed, and except on state occasions, she was never visible to visitors'. Sir William and his wife were easily recognisable.

The controversial pamphlet sets the scene in the doctor's room:

> The patients have been seen, prescribed for, and dismissed – all, save one, an intimate friend, whose throat requires to be touched with caustic. The trifling operation has been performed – another is deemed advisable – an appointment is made for her to come the following day – she rises to say good-bye, but she is detained! The doctor asks her is she 'afraid' of him. She answers – 'No; why should I be afraid of you?' 'You look pale,' he says: 'here,' and he places a handsome scent-bottle close to her face – she grasps it, and, pouring out some of the liquid, says: 'I will put it to my temples' . . . The bottle contained a strong solution of chloroform; the vapour filled the room rapidly; and the handkerchief on which the liquid had fallen was snatched violently, and flung into the fire by the medical man, whom we may now call Quilp . . . Florence – for it is she – rushes to the door, but is interrupted by the detected Quilp, who, flinging himself on his knees, attempts a passionate outburst of love, despair and remorse; but the horror-stricken Florence implores to be released from this dangerous place. She dreads to give alarm, knowing the irreparable disgrace, the everlasting ruin it will entail.

The pamphlet continues:

> Some days later a letter from Quilp arrived, which read as follows – 'Forgive – I am miserable and very ill – utterly

sleepless. Remorse and illness are doing their work. For God's sake see me and say you forgive before I die!' Florence knew that Quilp was sometimes at death's door with asthmatic and gouty attacks, and she could not help feeling concern for the unhappy man, now that he was stricken down with pain of both body and mind . . . She thought it too much sternness to refuse a death-bed request. She went; she hastened, as she thought, to the dying man; she was ushered into the study where she was surprised to find Quilp seated. He threw an agonised look at her as she entered. Neither spoke for a moment. Florence stood at the table by his side. He spoke first – 'See my drawn features – my sunken eyes – my haggard face. Florence, have pity; oh forgive and forget.' 'I forgive,' she replied. 'You do not say that from your heart,' he said. 'You hate me! I always knew it, but I –' 'Hush,' she said, 'or I leave you. I forgive, I must forget – forget I ever knew you. I esteemed you above all others; here our acquaintance ends. Farewell for ever!' She left the house, as she thought, never to enter it again. Little she dreamed she would again enter it, and leave it again under very different auspices.

But return she would, after a bit of subterfuge from the doctor:

Quilp's study again. Florence, with flashing eyes and scornful tone, indignantly flings a book on the table. 'How dare you sir,' she says, 'tell me you want my "intellect strengthened by reading" when it is such a book as that you presume to offer me. Better far say you wish my heart to be corrupted! Think you I have never heard of Goethe's *Elective Affinities*? Yes, too often have I heard it condemned by competent judges to be ignorant of its immoral tendency. Impious unbeliever, I now leave you to the mercy of the God you say does not exist except in man's intellect. Never approach me again. I am no longer the credulous simpleton of old; your subterfuges will not mislead me, attempt them not again; disguise your handwriting, put false addresses on your letters to me, to deceive me into opening them if you will; "forewarned is forearmed". You tried all this before, it will not succeed again. I never will recognise you on this earth; we are strangers from this hour, my –"Florence, Florence,' exclaimed Quilp, 'I am no longer a suppliant for mercy from the passionless, unnatural woman that I have loved for years in silence, because I dared not strive to win her, but whom I determined to conquer. Florence, you would give your life to do me a service – do not repel me; you are true as the magnet, notwithstanding all your threats; you will never divulge what has occurred.' Florence thunders to him to open the door or she will raise an alarm.

But Quilp now believes he has the upper hand:

'I will turn the tables on you now – you are now in my power. If you breathe a syllable of the chloroform, you blast yourself by revealing it, for you should never have entered my doors after the attempt – my cleverness got you back. I am not in your power quite so much as you think, but if the devotion of a lifetime can –' The crisis had come; the hypocrite unmasked himself, and there was no longer to be a spark of compassion for him. Florence recovered her presence of mind in a moment. She left the house and wrote the following note; 'Miss Price's compliments to Mrs Quilp, and requests she will make it her convenience to be at her town residence as soon as possible. Miss Price considers it necessary to inform Mrs Quilp, in her husband's presence, of the immorality and the brutality to which she has been subjected by Dr Quilp, in his own house.'

The letter was duly posted and delivered but Quilp intercepted it:

After some days Florence learned that her letter had never reached its destination. About the same time a rumour reached her that Quilp was artfully circulating a report that she was mad, and had suddenly and unaccountably taken a dislike to him, and indeed that he feared that she would become dangerous. Here was a master stroke of the too-clever Quilp! Mrs Quilp returned to town, when Florence called and sent up her card, requesting to see Mrs Quilp. Quilp (who was in the hall when she entered) darted upstairs to his wife. The result need scarcely be told; Mrs Quilp refused to see her visitor. Florence was thoroughly roused at this indignity, her blood boiled at the audacious affront; but this was not all she had to endure upon that memorable day. Mr Quilp came racing down the stairs, proclaiming to Florence, in exulting tones: 'Mrs Quilp will not see you; she does not want your acquaintance; you may write to her if you wish!' 'For you to intercept the letter,' thought Florence . . . Over the scene that ensued, I draw a temporary veil; suffice to say, that the false-hearted coward Quilp so far forgot himself in the presence of others as to exhibit himself in his true character of ruffian and bully!! The foregoing is merely an outline of events that took place many years ago; the details, many of which are painful, but important, are reserved for future publication . . . 'Hope' being the English for Speranza, I have assumed that name for its appropriateness, hoping this warning will be of use to more than 'SPERANZA'.

A copy of the pamphlet was dropped into 1 Merrion Square after the lecture and a number of doggerel rhymes and articles appeared in *Saunders' Newsletter* and the *Dublin Weekly Advertiser*. A few days after the lecture, Jane took the children off to Bray in County Wicklow to escape the distress of the strange and unsettling events.

17

Miss Travers

The person behind the pamphlet and the organiser of the sale and distribution of the fliers on the night of the lecture was a girl called Mary Josephine Travers, the daughter of Dr Robert Travers, Professor of Medical Jurisprudence at Trinity College. Miss Travers and William Wilde had been involved in a relationship, the exact nature of which is unclear, over a number of years.

Wilde first met Miss Mary Travers in July 1854 when she arrived, chaperoned by her mother, for a consultation over a hearing problem having been referred by Dr Stokes. She was then nineteen, slim and attractive, with dark hair and a volatile temperament. Her parents did not live together. Professor Travers had been appointed physician to the South Dublin Cholera Hospital that same year and had taken to residing in his rooms at the hospital. Mary lived with her mother but they did not get on very well. She had two older brothers in Australia while her two younger sisters and another brother lived with her at Williamstown, a Dublin suburb. By autumn the young lady's treatment was over. But the patient and her doctor formed what was later called 'an acquaintanceship' when William asked Dr Travers if Mary, who had certain literary talent, could correct some of his manuscripts. William soon began to offer advice to the girl on reading matter and on how she should spend her spare time. If Wilde's interest in Miss Travers was initially paternal, perhaps it later developed into something more intimate. It is certainly obvious that some form of relationship did exist; the nature of the letters written by Wilde are a testimony to that.

William took Mary Travers openly about Dublin. He presented her with a season ticket to the Dublin Exhibition of 1859 and went there in her company on numerous occasions. With Jane, he took her to the meeting of the British Association when it was held in Dublin. She also joined William and his children on outings and excursions. On realising that the girl had to survive on an allowance of just £16 a year from her father, William began advancing her money for clothes and other necessities, which she endeavoured to pay back. He wrote to her while on his tour of the northern cities of Europe, telling of his 'charming journey . . . fine weather, interesting people, splendid countries, a glorious reception everywhere; public entertainments in Stockholm, and any amount of adventures, all of which I will tell you when we meet'.[1]

As the friendship deepened, Miss Travers was invited to 1 Merrion Square. Jane was initially kind to her, having her to dinner on occasions, including Christmas Day 1861. She sometimes called around to take the children off for short outings, perhaps bringing them across the road to play in the railed-off gardens accessible only to residents of the Square. Could these restricted gardens have been in Oscar's mind years later when he came to write *The Selfish Giant*?

The original letters written by William to Mary Travers no longer exist. However, the excerpts from his letters to her printed on the fly-sheets 'give the impression of being from a person in the throes of first love'.[2] In one letter he invites her to a party: 'Mrs Wilde and I hope you will come in at nine o'clock tomorrow evening, Friday.' He then curiously adds 'Do this to please me.' In another, he appears to be trying to patch things up after a tiff of some kind: 'Don't throw over your truest friend, one you may never meet again: don't be as rash in one way as he is in the other.' A further letter interestingly states: 'Nevertheless, if it is a farewell for paternal intercourse, say how I can serve you. You would not look back after putting in the letter. God forgive you.' Other letters show him begging for forgiveness, asking her not to write a cross letter and even resigned to the fact that she will injure him in some way and have satisfaction from doing so.

William's tone is curious, more like a lovesick adolescent than an eminent medical man. He is, without doubt, compromised by these letters, but they do not prove or indicate at what level of intimacy the relationship operated. The letters and William's behaviour bear all the hallmarks of that age-old infatuation that can overcome a man of middle years when he becomes bewitched by the charms of a much younger woman. The similarity between these letters and Oscar's letters to his lover, Lord Alfred Douglas, a generation later is striking. Indeed, the entire Travers affair has the feel of a minor yet terrible dress rehearsal for Oscar's ruin. It is another example of the uncanny foreshadowing that haunts the story of the Wildes.

Miss Travers continued to call around to Merrion Square, and although Jane never gave any indication of believing her husband was unfaithful, the situation was undoubtedly growing tense. William tried to put an end to the relationship in March 1862 when he gave Miss Travers the price of a ticket to Australia. She crossed to Liverpool but changed her mind and returned to Dublin. Two months later she again travelled as far as Liverpool with the intention of joining her brothers in Australia but once more returned to Dublin. Mary Travers finally ran foul of Jane in June 1862 when she entered her Merrion Square bedroom uninvited. Jane spoke harshly to her and the young lady took offence. Feeling rejected, Miss Travers began a campaign of harassment and revenge. If Jane and William wanted to snub her they would pay. She would expose her relationship with Wilde to Dublin's society and thereby inflict embarrassment on the haughty Jane Wilde and damage the great doctor's standing and perhaps even his career. It has been suggested that the unsettling behaviour of Mary Travers and the accompanying pressures may have been a factor in William and Jane deciding to send the two boys away from Dublin to Portora School as boarders.

In the autumn of 1862 Mary Travers turned up at William's study on a number of occasions, sometimes for the purpose of demanding money. On a day in early October they quarrelled over money and she left the study only to return again. Once more they had words and she left. This time she returned in an agitated state clutching a bottle of laudanum, a preparation of alcohol and opium common in Victorian times as a cure-all. She poured it into a wine glass and drank the full bottle in front of him. William, in a panic, believing she wanted revenge by having people suppose that he poisoned her, rushed her off to the nearest apothecary's for an antidote and followed after to make sure she took the emetic. Alarmed by this erratic behaviour, William told Miss Travers that she was mad but this only added further fuel to her burning rage. A few days later she wrote to him complaining of a corn on her foot and seeking his attention to remove it, adding the strange warning: 'I will keep your nose to the grindstone while your wife is away, and when she returns I will see her.'[3]

Later that same month she again visited William. He examined a mark on her neck, an old burn from childhood. Miss Travers later claimed that during this visit William pressed his knuckles against her throat very forcibly. When she told him she was suffocating, he replied that he would suffocate her, that he could not help it. Miss Travers went on later to claim that she passed out and in that interval of unconsciousness was sexually violated. If so, she failed to report it to anybody. Instead, Miss Travers continued her obsessive campaign, sending William venomous rhymes through his letterbox:

> The oculist cured,
> I give you my word
> With his own bottle, too, I have dosed him.
> I have sent him a drink,
> That will set him to think,
> Until his own blushes will roast him.

Another rhyme, sent to William after his knighthood, refers to his illegitimate children, his 'breed'. Wilde was very sensitive on this subject:

> Your progeny is quite a pest
> To those who hate such 'critters';
> Some sport I'll have, or I'm blest
> I'll fry the Wilde breed in the West;
> Then you can call them Fritters.

The name is not equivocal,
They dare not by their mother call,
Nor by their father, though he's Sir,
A gouty knight, a mangy cur;
He does not dare to call them Frits –
How much he'd wish that I'd say Quits.

Why did Wilde, a distinguished medical man, put up with such irrational behaviour? Was he emotionally entangled with 'Moll' Travers or in some way compromised? In August 1863 she went even further in her erratic actions. Bizarrely, she had her own death notice printed up in the form of a newspaper cutting, sending one copy to Jane who was away in Bray and one to William who had taken off to Cong where Moytura House was nearing completion. The notice read: 'July 21st, suddenly at the residence of her father, Williamstown, Mary Josephine, eldest daughter of Robert Travers MA, MDFRQUIP.' She included a drawing of a small coffin beneath the printed words. Jane became alarmed because it could be interpreted as a threat.

Mary Travers called on Jane at Merrion Square on 13 August but Jane refused to see her. Miss Travers, however, remained in the hall downstairs for two hours, seated on a marble table, forcing Lady Wilde to eventually descend and pass her without recognition. Miss Travers spoke to Willie, who was with his mother, but Jane enjoined him not to reply. 'This improving scene was watched by young Mr Hogan, son of a famous sculptor, who was also present on the occasion of the bedroom scene.'[4] Enraged by the snubbing, Miss Travers determined to carry on tormenting the Wildes, writing the pamphlet *Florence Boyle Price: or the Warning by Speranza*, a fictionalised account of incidents that occurred between Mary Travers and William and Jane Wilde. She had 1,000 copies printed. Some were distributed by post to Wilde's friends and patients, others were dropped through letterboxes or scattered around Dublin. And yet Sir William took no steps to put an end to her nonsense.

In January 1864, soon after Wilde's knighthood, Mary Travers published a verse under the name of 'Sam Weller':

'The Late Dubbing in Dublin Castle'

The other day, with great surprise,
I saw it in the paper,
Great W. W. rose a knight
By touch of Carlisle's rapier.
The doctors have it their own way,
Though neither wise nor witty,
Not long ago 'Grey' got his tip
For watering our city.
Then why should not another man
'Gainst fickle fortune fight, sir,
And try by art of surgery
To be a belted knight, sir,
For deeds of blood and slaughter?
But now a man may win a name
By bottles of eye water.
The deaf can hear – the blind can see,
These are his triumphs great, sir.
The only wonder really is
They were discovered so late, sir.
Backed by our honest Dublin Press
By friendly puff and pars, sir.
Publicity he sought and found –
Oh! don't he bless his stars, sir?
For, perched upon a niche of fame,
Dame Fortune opes her store, sir,
And all with admiration gaze
On him for evermore, sir.

Her campaign against Wilde then reached its crescendo that night outside the Metropolitan Hall, organising with military precision the distribution of the pamphlet outside the doors by five hired newsboys. Mary Travers watched the ensuing commotion from a cab discreetly positioned across the street.

Lady Wilde, for such was now her title, left Dublin for their house in Bray a few days after the debacle at the Metropolitan Hall, but if she thought she could escape from the furore she was mistaken. Miss Travers followed Jane to Bray. She again hired local boys to distribute the pamphlet to every house on Lady Wilde's street. Copies were also delivered to the Wilde's house. Jane had an altercation with a boy who came to her door selling the pamphlets. Soon another boy arrived with four pamphlets and a placard. Again a squabble arose. Jane snatched the placard and kept one pamphlet without paying for it. When little Isola came to her mother enquiring about the events, Jane lost her temper and on 6 May fired off a letter of complaint to Mary Travers' father:

> Sir – You may not be aware of the disreputable conduct of your daughter at Bray, where she consorts with all the low newsboys in the place, employing them to disseminate offensive placards in which she makes it appear that she has had an intrigue with Sir William Wilde. If she chooses to disgrace herself that is not my affair; but as her object in insulting me is the hope of extorting money, for which she has several times applied to Sir William Wilde, with threats of more annoyance if not given, I think it right to inform you that no threat or additional insult shall ever extort money for her from our hands. The wages of disgrace she has so loosely treated for and demanded shall never be given her.
>
> Jane F. Wilde

Jane had been provoked beyond endurance. She posted the letter herself in Bray. It was an understandable reaction but unwise in the extreme.

Meanwhile, Mary Travers had a summons issued against Sir William and his wife for illegally retaining a pamphlet and placard offered for sale in Bray. She did not as yet know about the letter sent to her father. The case concerning the pamphlet and placard was heard at the Petty Sessions at Bray on the 14 May. When Mary Travers discovered the letter sent by Jane to her father she immediately recognised it to be a valuable weapon. Jane was served with a writ for libel. Robert H. Irvine, solicitor for Miss Mary Josephine Travers, charged that the letter reflected upon his client's character and chastity and was seeking damages of £2,000.

18

Reputation in the Dock

The lawsuit could have been settled out of court. Given the nature of the evidence that was sure to be heard, perhaps it would have been the wiser option. But Jane would not countenance such surrender. The case came up for hearing on Monday 12 December 1864 before Lord Chief Justice Monahan and a special city jury. Miss Travers had employed an impressive legal team led by Serjeant Richard Armstrong, a skilled cross-examiner, and Isaac Butt, QC, a long-standing acquaintance of Sir William's, with Mr Heron, QC and two juniors, Mr Hamill and Mr Quinn. Serjeant Sullivan, Mr Sidney, QC and Mr Morris represented the Wildes with Mr John Curran and Mr Purcell. It was going to be an expensive suit. The case caused a sensation in Dublin. Sir William had been knighted less than a year before and Speranza, now Lady Wilde, was still remembered and beloved of the Irish people for her inspiring poems in the *Nation*. Crowds thronged the Four Courts for the six days of the case and the papers were full with news of the trial.

Serjeant Armstrong opened, telling how his client had been sent to Dr Wilde for treatment ten years before. He had cured her but would accept no fee. A friendship had developed and the pair exchanged voluminous correspondence. Wilde sent her books, tickets for functions, accompanied her on outings to dances and the theatre. He had also given her money when she needed it and bought her clothes and bonnets. He described how Wilde treated her ailments, including a scar on her neck, which he examined while his patient knelt on a cushion by his chair. The events of her visit in October 1862, when William allegedly sexually assaulted or raped her, were then briefly explored. Serjeant Armstrong said he would leave it to the plaintiff herself to tell what happened on the day. He then uttered his famous line: 'she went in a maid – that out a maid never departed more', misquoting awkwardly Ophelia from *Hamlet*.

On the second day Isaac Butt cross-examined the plaintiff, bringing her through her version of events as they occurred on the day of the alleged sexual assault. Miss Travers set the background, saying that she had always paid back the money Wilde had given her. She told the court that Dr Wilde had, on a previous occasion, taken her in his arms and embraced her while she was in her usual kneeling position before him, declaring that he would not let her go until she called him William. This had caused a rift in their relationship but he had coaxed her back by being penitent and attentive. On the day in question Miss Travers said that Lady Wilde and the children were away. Wilde showed her into his study and began to examine her throat. He removed her bonnet and fastened his hand somewhat roughly between a ribbon she had tied around her neck and her throat. She told him she was suffocating but he said he could not help it. She passed out and could not recollect anything more until he was dashing water on her face. When asked if she had lost consciousness, she replied that she had. When she had somewhat recovered, Wilde took her upstairs to a bedroom to rest. He gave her a little wine to drink. After some time she left the house but could not remember if Wilde had accompanied her. She was too dazed to know what she or anybody else was doing.

Then Mr Butt asked her the straight question: 'Are you able to state whether in that interval of unconsciousness you have described, your person was violated?' 'Yes,' replied Miss Travers. 'Was it?' Mr Butt again asked. 'Yes,' said Miss Travers.[1] The case was then adjourned for the day.

As the suit progressed more details of their relationship became public. The people crowding into the court were greatly amused as story after story emerged of the quarrels between the young patient and her doctor, of her determination to annoy him and how Jane became angry when William escorted Mary Travers to a ceremony in the Castle even though he had told his wife he was not going to attend. Evidence was also given of the bizarre suicide attempt with the laudanum.

Serjeant Sullivan, senior counsel for the Wildes, exposed numerous discrepancies and contradictions in Mary Travers' evidence, including that she did not know the exact date of the alleged assault. He also revealed the fact the she was in the habit of taking laudanum. Everything she had done was motivated by a strong enmity for Dr Wilde. A picture emerged of a discarded mistress acting in a vengeful manner rather than an innocent wronged. It was revealed that Miss Travers had published, as an act of revenge, an extremely negative review of Lady Wilde's latest translation from the German of a book called *The First Temptation*. The defence later suggested that it was a chapter in this book that actually inspired Mary Travers to claim that Wilde had violated her.

Lady Wilde was called and appeared in the witness box dressed in black. Her brother had recently died in America. Isaac Butt, who knew Lady Wilde and Sir William well, attempted to create the impression that Lady Wilde was cold and lacked compassion because she showed no concern when Miss Travers wrote to her telling of her suicide attempt. He also tried to throw a shadow over her morals by reading translated passages from *The First Temptation*. Jane's legal team counteracted these attempts by describing Miss Travers as excitable, furious, uncontrollable and vindictive, whereas Lady Wilde was beyond impeachment and should never have been dragged into court. She had not intended to imply immoral relations when she wrote to Miss Travers' father saying his daughter 'consorted' with the 'low newsboys' of Bray. Neither did Lady Wilde believe that her husband had illicit intercourse with Miss Travers. Sir William himself did not appear in court, denying Miss Travers of the satisfaction of watching him squirm. But he was not spared the humiliation of having his numerous histrionic episodes made public.

Summing up for Miss Travers, Isaac Butt made full use of Sir William's decision not to appear. He said Wilde owed it to the jury to leave no doubt in their minds, and that he owed it to his profession, to his wife, to morality and to public justice that his oath be pledged that the story was untrue. But William was not the one on trial. In question was the existence of libel. Be that as it may, as far as a great many people were concerned, Sir William Wilde was the one really in the dock.

Summing up for the jury, Lord Chief Justice Monahan wondered how a woman could have been forcibly outraged as Miss Travers alleged, with servants and patients passing to and fro in the hall outside the consulting room. Also troubling him was the delay in reporting the alleged attack. A woman forcibly violated usually tells her story at once. Miss Travers continued having dealings with Dr Wilde for a long time after – if an attack had taken place would not the relationship be discontinued? However, the correspondence between William Wilde and Miss Travers was of a very extraordinary character to take place between a middle-aged married man and an attractive young woman. William was helped by the Lord Chief Justice's comments that if the action had been taken for rape or criminal assault the case would have been thrown out of court because of the girl's failure to report the occurrence to her father or anybody else and by the fact that she continued to go to balls with him.

The jury retired but were recalled to let the Chief Justice explain a point of law. They then called for coals for their fire after ninety minutes. Before the coals arrived, however, they were back out with a verdict. The jury found for the plaintiff, Miss Mary Travers. The letter, they said, was libellous. Nevertheless, they went on to allow her only a paltry one farthing in damages. However, the burden of costs – in excess of £2,000 – fell to the Wildes. It may have saved the Wildes some money, and a lot of personal embarrassment, had they settled with Mary Travers in the first place. Had Oscar or his mother remembered the lesson of this trial, it may have saved Oscar from his terrible ruin too.

Although the press coverage was extensive, the content could have been a lot worse for the Wildes. Almost all of the newspapers and medical magazines came out in support of Sir William. According to the *Lancet*:

Sir Wm. Wilde has to congratulate himself that he has passed through a trying ordeal supported by the sympathies of the entire mass of his professional brethren in this city; that he has been acquitted of a charge as disgraceful as it was unexpected, without even having to stoop to the painful necessity of contradicting it upon oath in the witness-box, by the expressed opinion of one of the ablest of our judges, by the verdict of a most intelligent special jury, by the unanimous opinion of his fellow citizens, and by, what I am sure he will not value least, that of every member of his own profession.

William had not been charged with anything, yet he was seen to have been acquitted of a vile accusation. The *Medical Times and Gazette* was interesting on the matter:

Genius has its penalties as well as its privileges; and its necessarily more erratic and irregular walk must subject it to collisions unknown in the humdrum existence of commonplace mortals. Persons whose imagination is of great development, are, as is well known, liable to form friendships of a most enthusiastic and exaggerated cast; and if the parties be of the opposite sex it is perfectly possible that either of them may put too warm an interpretation on what really are outpourings of genius, through indiscreet and unconventional friendship. To anyone who knows the hysteric temperament, there is not only no evidence for, but plenty of it against, the probability of the plaintiff's story.

This insightful article could equally have been applied a generation later when Oscar's 'indiscreet and unconventional' friendships were the cause of him having to serve two years in prison.

The *Caledonian Mercury* said 'The unhappy girl, though the daughter of a respectable man, has done herself irreparable damage by her vulgar and vindictive attack upon an eminent medical man and his not less eminent and respected partner in life – the "Speranza" of other days.' The *London Standard* called Miss Travers' conduct 'scandalous, unwomanly, vulgar and degrading'. But not every voice was supportive, with *The Times* of London accusing Sir William of being 'guilty, at any rate, of so much indiscretion'. There was also one commentator who was without any doubt delighted to take advantage of the whole episode. The *Dublin Medical Press*, owned and edited by Sir William's great rival, the oculist and anatomist Arthur Jacob, used the trial to attack Wilde:

> If there is one unanimous opinion which pervades all minds, it is that Sir William Wilde has not satisfactorily refuted the charge of which he stands accused, of having taken advantage of that confidence which ought to be sacred for an immoral purpose. True it is that the nature of the legal process did not render legal denial absolutely essential to the defence . . . but, nevertheless, there were demands on Sir Wm. He owed it to his profession . . . he owed it to the public . . . he owed it to Her Majesty's Representative, who had conferred an unusual mark of distinction on him, to purge himself of the suspicion which this moment lies heavy on his name.

Arthur Jacob had been a long time waiting in the tall grass. Now William had provided his old enemy with sufficient fodder to feed his deep animosity.

William also had to endure the many rhymes and street ballads holding him to ridicule. One piece of doggerel sung by Trinity College students began:

> An eminent oculist lives in the Square,
> His skill is unrivalled, his talent is rare,
> And if you will listen I'll certainly try
> To tell how he opened Miss Travers's eye

In this Miss Travers had some measure of satisfaction, but William's colleagues, and Dublin society generally, did not ostracise the Wildes.

There followed a full round of social engagements including a Lord Mayor's ball with 3,000 guests in attendance. The Medico-Philosophical Society also had a series of dinners with plenty of cheer. Nevertheless, William's reputation had been tarnished and it was a hard personal blow. Even if the rape of Miss Travers with its convenient blackout at the crucial moment was a fabrication bred out of malice or hysteria, it still leaves the letters, the presents and the failure to report the girl's bizarre actions. William put up with a lot of harassment and it is very difficult to explain away what appears to be the infatuation of a middle-aged married man for a young woman who first came to him as a patient.

The damaging story had not yet gone away; there was to be one final twist. Miss Travers sued *Saunders' Newsletter* over a report on the trial. Isaac Butt again took her case and it came to court in June 1865. The paper had written: 'It is not possible to believe the infamous story she concocted as to Sir W. Wilde.' Mary Travers demanded damages of £2,000 for implying she had committed perjury. This time the jury took all of twenty-five minutes to decide against her. After this disappointment, Miss Mary Josephine Travers disappeared from the scene. Her final years were spent at Kingston College, an almshouse or retirement home for Protestants in Mitchelstown, County Cork. She died on 13 or 18 March 1919 and her grave is in the adjoining churchyard. In November 1876, twelve years after the Travers case, Isaac Butt applied for membership of the Royal Irish Academy. His application was denied.

19

Repercussions

Biographers disagree about the effect the entire sorry business had on Sir William. T. G. Wilson believed Wilde never really recovered from the 'terrible blow'. 'From that date forward he seems to have degenerated. His originality disappeared. He lost interest in his profession, became dirtier, uglier, more abrupt and intolerant of others. He was not the same physically upright, energetic man he had been. He appears to have burnt himself out, to have shrunk, mentally and physically. Temporary flashes of the old fire only served to heighten the contrast.'[1] Terence de Vere White, on the other hand, in his work *The Parents of Oscar Wilde*, points out that Wilde had been escaping off to his beloved Corrib country for a number of years prior to the court case. He appeared to have lost enthusiasm for medicine but not for his antiquarian activities, to have tired of society and scientific inquiry but not tired of life. He bases this belief partly on the vigour and enthusiasm of the opening paragraph of *Lough Corrib, its Shores and Islands*, first published in 1867, with its famous opening cry: 'Westward ho! Let us Rise with the sun, and be off to the land of the West.'

Sir William must surely have felt the stress of the growing harassment from Miss Travers. The very public denouement must also have caused him great distress, even if he did bring much of it down upon his own head. Sir William's biographer de Vere White also managed to explain the mistaken yet widely held belief that Miss Travers bore Wilde a son. This idea of a son came from a misprint in an account of the trial carried by *Saunders' Newsletter* referring to a letter handwritten by Miss Travers to William concerning the loan of money. The paper reported her promise to take up 'from you my son as quickly as I possibly can'. This naturally led people to believe that a son had been born to William and Miss Travers. By consulting other newspaper reports of the trial Terence de Vere White detected a serious error. The full sentence should have read: 'The return I offer to make for the loan of your money is to remove myself from under the obligation by taking up from you my iou as quickly as I possibly can.' The word 'son' replaced 'iou' in the report in *Saunders' Newsletter*. On the basis of this one report, Sir William's earlier biographer T. G. Wilson naturally concluded that Wilde had a sexual affair with Miss Travers and that they had a son. This 'desperately serious error has been used as evidence of Wilde's profligacy' ever since.[2]

And what of Sir William's wife, how did Lady Wilde view the proceedings? Her thinking on the case can be seen in two letters she wrote to her friend Rosalie Olivecrona in Sweden. The first was written on New Year's Day 1865:

My Dear Madame Olivecrona,

You know of course by this of the disagreeable Law affair in which we have been involved. I send you a few extracts from the various papers. Please ask Professor Olivecrona to show them to Baron Dubben and Magnus Ritzens.

The simple solution to the affair is this – This Miss Travers is mad – All the family are mad too. She was very destitute and haunted our house to borrow money and we were very kind to her and we pitied her – but suddenly she took a dislike to me amounting to hatred – and the endeavour to ruin my peace of mind assumed a series of anonymous attacks. Then she issued vile publications in the name of Speranza, accusing my husband. I wrote to her father about them, and she took an action for libel against me. It was very annoying, but of course no one believed her story. All Dublin has called on us to offer their sympathy, and all the medical Profession here and in London have sent letters expressing their entire disbelief of the (in fact) impossible charge. Sir Wm. will not be injured by it, and the best proof is that his professional hours never were so occupied as now. We were more anxious about our dear foreign friends who could only hear through the English papers which are generally very sneering on Irish matters. But happily all is over now and our enemy has been signally defeated in her efforts to injure us.

I have a book of poems out. I shall try to send them to you. Thanks for two magazines, but your translation of 'The Exodus' has not arrived yet. Pray tell our dear friends the Broems all about our late troubles, and the cause of them. I hope you will write to me soon and say where Lotten is now. Give our best love to her. And with affectionate regards.

Rosalie replied, enclosing a copy of Jane's poem 'The Exodus' in translation. Jane was delighted to read her poem in Swedish and wrote back thanking Rosalie for her 'kind note' and for taking the time to reply at all. Miss Travers was still on Jane's mind when she wrote her reply. The girl had just then taken her action against the newspaper *Saunders' Newsletter*. Jane put all the trouble down to madness on Mary Travers' part and her envy of Jane's literary reputation. Turning to a more pleasant subject Jane promised to send her Swedish friend a copy of her newly published collection of poems and to also send one to Lotten von Kraemer. 'They have sold greatly in Ireland, but are not suited to English taste you may suppose. Oh what an incubus this English Government is on our country.' Speranza's youthful spark of rebellion had not yet been fully doused by age and troubles. She finished by telling her Swedish friend that 'Sir William is quite well and sends his regards.'

With the court case out of the way Sir William, together with his loyal ally John Gilbert, began work on Part 4 of the catalogue for the

Royal Irish Academy's museum. His many friends rallied around, making sure he had plenty of cheer with dinners, balls and nights in the snuggeries. But William was not content to stay in Dublin and when the wave of social engagements died down he took himself off to Moytura, leaving Henry Wilson, Sir William's natural son who had joined his father's practice, to look after the patients.

Sir William's interest in medicine appears to have waned from this time on. He had bequeathed his hospital, St Marks, to the city and was now just a member of its board, which meant he was only required to attend occasional meetings. On top of that, he began neglecting his practice, preferring to spend as much time as he possibly could in the west of Ireland. But medicine was his main source of revenue and he was not yet in a position to retire. With his various households to run and his family still to be educated he needed to be generating a sizeable income. Sir William was not idle when he came to stay at Moytura House. He was working hard on researching material for his next book, *Lough Corrib, its Shores and Islands*, and preparing a paper on the Battle of Moytura. Then Sir William fell ill. Perhaps it was the strain of the Travers case finally catching up with him, coupled with his frantic work rate. Whatever the cause, the knight's loyal wife was deeply concerned.

While Lady Wilde kept a concerned eye on her flagging husband, the country began to experience political unrest once again as the 1860s progressed. Many wanted an Irish parliament reinstated in Dublin with powers to legislate at least for domestic matters. Other nationalists would only be content if Ireland's link with the British Empire was severed altogether. More than 20,000 people turned out in November 1861 to see the coffin of a former Young Irelander called Terence Bellew MacManus pass through the streets of Dublin, escorted by horsemen with black armbands. MacManus had been involved in the 1848 attack at Ballingarry with William Smith O'Brien and afterwards transported to Van Diemen's Land. He managed to escape to America in 1852 but failed to prosper there, dying in San Francisco at the age of fifty. It was decided that his body would be brought home to be buried in Glasnevin Cemetery, Dublin, as part of a great Fenian display of strength.

The Fenian Brotherhood was an Irish republican organisation founded in the United States in 1858 by the former Young Irelanders John O'Mahony and Michael Doheny. The organisation's Irish branch, called the Irish Republican Brotherhood (IRB) was established by another veteran of 1848, James Stephens. A flurry of recruitment in Ireland followed the funeral of MacManus with secret oaths being administered and drilling of civilians taking place by night in various parts of the country. A new song ran:

> Pay them back woe for woe,
> Give them back blow for blow,
> Out and make way for the bold Fenian men!

Lady Wilde had no interest in becoming involved in the Fenians having seen enough of sedition in the 1840s with the Young Irelanders. 'I am not a Fenian', she wrote to a Swedish friend, Mrs Perinetta, 'and I disapprove highly of their projects – it is a decidedly democratic movement and the gentry and aristocracy will suffer much from them – their object is to form a republic and heaven keep us from a Fenian republic!'

The Fenians and the IRB promised their followers that a great uprising would occur in Ireland in 1865 but the British authorities foiled their plans and James Stephens was captured. He later escaped to America. A further attempt at an uprising in 1867 in Ireland was a complete disaster. Meanwhile, a section of the Fenians in America made several shambolic attempts to invade Canada West (Southern Ontario), then a British dominion, with the unlikely notion of holding it hostage in return for a free Ireland. If the Fenian movement of the 1860s failed in its immediate objectives, its actions became part of the national story and helped pave the path, as the Young Irelanders had done before them, towards the eventual successful struggle for an independent Ireland in the early twentieth century.

Isaac Butt conducted the defence of the Fenian rebels in 1867, in the same way as he had defended the Young Irelanders almost twenty years before. Butt spoke publicly in support of an amnesty for the Fenian convicts and he moved from being the leader of the most extreme Orange party (unionist) in Dublin Corporation to become the leader of the Irish Party in Westminster (moderate nationalists). Eventually, he would head up a new national movement with the aim of establishing a parliament in Ireland for Ireland. It was known as the Home Rule party. Times were indeed changing. The idea that Ireland needed some level of self-government was growing even among Sir William Wilde's own class of Protestant professionals who, in the main, would have been staunch supporters of Ireland's membership of the United Kingdom. At one of Butt's political meetings Charles Laver advocated a Federal Parliament in Ireland. The poet Samuel Ferguson, meanwhile, was made chairman of a Protestant Repeal Association, which had the aim of repealing the Act of Union and thereby shared the principles of the Young Ireland movement of the 1840s.

Time, however, was running out for the Irish Protestant-unionist class, although few could have predicted that their world of privilege and position would collapse so rapidly. Fenianism in the 1860s followed by the political activities of nationalist leader Charles Stewart Parnell and then the failure of the Home Rule movement to secure a parliament in Dublin led eventually to the Easter Rising of 1916. The Rising did not succeed in its military aims but the execution of its leaders caused a huge swing in public opinion against England. The Irish War of Independence, from 1919 to 1921, was followed by a treaty between Ireland and England that saw the formation of the Irish Free State in twenty-six of the thirty-two counties on the island. Many of the old Anglo-Irish Protestant families left Ireland following independence, believing that the new state held no welcome for them.

The Protestant-unionist tradition was strongest in the north of the island. Unionists there managed to keep six of the counties in Ulster out of the Free State and maintain all links with the United Kingdom. This led to the establishment of Northern Ireland, which remains part of the United Kingdom to this day. The Irish nationalist population in Ulster found itself cut off from the rest of Ireland and in the minority on that small part of the island. The ensuing troubles in Northern Ireland between the two rival communities, which came to a head in the 1960s, have lasted down to the present and are only now being addressed in arrangements flowing from the Good Friday Agreement signed in 1998.

Like Ireland itself, Sir William's politics were complex. He was far from being a Fenian. Instead his patriotism found expression in his antiquarian work and in his interest in folklore and Irish culture. He was in favour of Ireland's links with the Crown and tried to articulate the complicated way the two islands are interconnected. Understanding identity in terms of race, culture, history, beliefs and aspirations was one of the major themes of his life. T. G. Wilson in his biography quotes a 'contemporary journal' that described Sir William Wilde as 'a Liberal-Unionist, with Nationalist proclivities'. In other words, stout English Durham blood mixed with that of the Gaelic clan known as 'The Ferocious O'Flahertys'.

Sir William's health continued to be a cause for concern throughout the 1860s and in the autumn of 1866 he fell ill once again. As soon as he was able to travel he again left Dublin to recuperate at Moytura. He wrote to his friend John Gilbert: 'Many thanks for your letter. I am better, and able to oversee workmen and take short antiquarian journeys, but nothing more . . . Did you hear that part of New Grange has fallen in?' Then came news that his colleague in the Royal Irish Academy, George Petrie, had died. They had been firm friends since their first archaeological investigations at Lagore, and even though they had numerous disagreements their quarrels were always short lived. Wilde felt the loss severely but the fates soon had much worse in store for the tiring doctor.

Part 5

Heartbreak

'Alas! I was entering into the shadow which now will never more be lifted.'

Lady Jane Wilde

20

The Radiant Angel

In the spring of 1867 Isola Francesca, William and Jane's beloved daughter who was not yet ten years of age, fell ill with a fever. She recovered somewhat and it was decided to send the little girl out of the city to her aunt's house in Edgeworthstown, County Longford, some 50 miles west of Dublin. William's only surviving sister, Margaret, was married there to the local rector, Reverend Noble. It was thought the fresh air of the countryside might do her some good. But Isola had a relapse at her aunt's house, probably meningitis. The Wildes were summoned but arrived only in time to see their much-loved daughter sink beyond hope and die. It was a devastating blow. Writing to Lotten von Kraemer 'in deep affliction', Lady Wilde tells of Isola's 'sudden effusion on the brain – we were summoned by telegraph – and only arrived to see her die – such sorrows are hard to bear. My heart seems broken. Still I feel I have to live for my sons and thank God they are as fine a pair of boys as one could desire.'

Lady Wilde continued:

> But Isola was the radiant angel of our home – and so bright and strong and joyous. We never dreamed the word death was meant for her. Yet I had an unaccountable sadness over me all last winter, a foreboding of evil – and I ever delayed writing to you till I felt in my heart more of an energy and life.

Alas! I was then entering into the shadow which now will never more be lifted . . . But for the glorious promise of scripture, 'the dead shall arise', I think I would sink down in utter despair.

Sir William is crushed by sorrow. Isola was his idol – still, he goes on with his life work and is even now writing a book to be published very shortly on 'Lough Corrib and its Islands', for the daily work must be done and the world will not stop in its career even tho' a fair child's grave lies in its path.[1]

The following obituary appeared in the Dublin papers:

WILDE – February 23 at Edgeworthstown Rectory, after a brief illness in the 10th year of her life, Isola, the beloved and only daughter of Sir William and Lady Wilde.

Oscar too was devastated by his young sister's sudden death. The local doctor remembered him as 'an affectionate, gentle, retiring, dreamy boy' who paid long and frequent visits to his little sister's grave in the local cemetery.[2] Oscar was only twelve at the time but never forgot Isola. Robert Sherard, who knew Oscar and published a biography of him in 1906, recalled him speaking often about Isola, his 'wondrous eyes' softening as he described her as being 'like a golden ray of sunshine dancing about our home'.[3] When Oscar died in the Hotel d'Alsace in Paris an envelope was found among his possessions with 'My Isola's hair' written on it.

Oscar's poem 'Requiescat' reflects the feelings of loss and sadness he felt at the time:

Tread lightly, she is near
Under the snow,
Speak gently, she can hear
The lilies grow.

All her bright golden hair
Tarnished with rust,
She that was young and fair
Fallen to dust.

Lily-like, white as snow,
She hardly knew
She was a woman, so
Sweetly she grew.

Coffin-board, heavy stone,
Lie on her breast,
I vex my heart alone,
She is at rest.

Peace, Peace, she cannot hear,
Lyre or sonnet,
All my life's buried here,
Heap earth upon it.

For years after, Lady Wilde refused all social invitations with the reply, 'I do not go out into evenings at present'. The once vivacious woman, so fond of socialising, no longer had the heart for it. She also decided, during the summer of 1867, to take the boys off to the Paris exhibition for a few weeks as a diversion from their sorrow. Jane wrote to Lotten afterwards, saying than Paris was a brilliant city and had cheered them all up somewhat. Nevertheless, she was, she said, unable to get back into writing mood 'and so nothing is left to me but the sorrow – the deep, eternal sorrow for ever and for ever like a sword through my heart'. Sir William, who coped as best he could by keeping to his regular routine of meeting with friends and working on his book, went down to Moytura alone, preferring the peace of his beloved lake country to the heat and bustle of the French capital. The terrible events of spring were still fresh in all their minds.

The British Medical Association met in Dublin in August but even the huge importance of Joseph Lister's groundbreaking paper 'On the Antiseptic Principle in the Practice of Surgery' did not fill Sir William with any enthusiasm. Instead, he took a party of Association members on a tour around the antiquities of the Boyne Valley. Henry Wilson was now doing most of the work in St Mark's, with Sir William continuing to show little interest in medicine or in his dwindling private practice. T. G. Wilson, Sir William's biographer, tells of an incident that occurred around this time when a little boy was brought to see the famous doctor with an eye problem that required lotion. Unable to locate an eyedropper, Wilde instead took a pen, dipped it in the lotion and flicked the droplets, cutting the eye in the process. The scar remained with the patient for life.

21

An Ancient Battle

In the autumn on 1867 Sir William Wilde's book *Lough Corrib, its Shores and Islands* was published in Dublin by McGlashan and Gill. It was an immediate success with a second edition following in 1872. The book is still read and enjoyed today and first editions are expensive collectors' items. The author's enthusiasm for his subject is obvious and infectious and the romanticism of the narrative brings a certain magic to the realities of the locality. The work was aimed at 'intelligent tourists, with eyes to see and hearts to admire the beauties of nature ... where your architectural or antiquarian tastes may be gratified, your historical knowledge increased by the legend or annals ... and the hitherto neglected resources of a portion of our island may be glanced at if not profoundly studied'. The vitality reflected in the book's opening sentence led one biographer to believe that Sir William, though bending under life's pressures, was not ready to give up on life just yet.

> Westward, ho! Let us rise with the sun, and be off to the land of the West – to the lakes and streams – the grassy glens and fern-clad gorges, the bluff hills and rugged mountains – now cloud-capped, then revealed in azure, or bronzed by evening's tints, as the light of day sinks into the bold swell of the Atlantic, and leaves his reflection in long level streaks of crimson, green, and orange, among

the greyish-purple robe of twilight, when the shadows of the headlands sink deep into the placid waters of the lake.

It is Sir William Wilde's finest published work.

Lough Corrib, its Shores and Islands contains a detailed study of the many ruined castles, monasteries and archaeological remains still to be seen around the lake today or on its principal islands. It also contains Sir William's misguided investigations into the Battle of Moytura, which he presented to the Royal Irish Academy in a detailed paper the year before publishing the book. Wilde believed that a great battle had been fought in ancient Ireland between the Firbolgs, a Belgic colony, small, swarthy and dark, and the Scandinavian Tuatha de Danann, a large, fair, sandy-haired people of superior knowledge and intelligence, which obtained for them the attributes of magical skill and necromancy. Wilde sets the scene for the battle:

> The Belgae having refused to divide the country with the invaders, the Dananns proceeded westward, and occupied the great plain of Memedh, or Magh-Ith, which stretches for about 12 miles from the hill of Knockma, in the county of Galway, through the fertile barony of Kilmain, in Mayo, to Slieve Belgadain, now called Benlevi, a short distance from the village of Cong, in the barony of Ross, and county of Galway . . . Eochy, son of Erc, King of Erin, advanced to the hill of Knockma with all his forces from Tara, in Meath, then the seat of government, to attack the Tuatha de Dananns, whose leader, Nuad, took up position on Benlevi, with his warriors, sages, Druids, bards, poets, and physicians . . . King Eochy, with his Firbolg host, descended into the plain of Moytura, and, passing westwards, was met by the heralds and ambassadors of Nuad, on that portion of it subsequently called Conmaicne Cuile Toladh, extending from the present village of Cross to the neck of land that divides Lough Mask and Corrib. They then . . . agreed upon a trial of skill

and manly prowess; and twenty-seven youths from each army engaged in a game of hurling ...This warlike pastime ended in the defeat and death of the thrice nine youths of the Dananns, over whom was erected the great carn or stone monument ...There it stands to this day, about 50 feet high, and 400 in circumference – an historic memorial as valid as that which commemorates the spot on the shore of Attica, where the Athenians fell beneath the long spears of the Persians on the field of Marathon. Next day, supposed to be the 11th of June, in the year of the world 3303, the battle commenced; it lasted four days, and it is said 100,000 men were engaged in it.

After four days of fighting a truce was called. The Firbolgs were reduced to 3,000 men but were allowed to retain Connaught although the Dananns held the rest of the country. It was not a good result for the Firbolgs and many of the warriors were supposed to have fled west to the Islands of Aran.

Sir William's principal source of information was an ancient manuscript written in Gaelic and transcribed in the fifteenth century by Cormac O'Cuirnin at a place called Moy-Enne, near Ballyshannon in present-day Donegal. Wilde got his hands on an English translation of this manuscript, which was provided to the Ordnance Survey and the Royal Irish Academy by Dr John O'Donovan. He then began the process of associating the descriptions of the places and events described in the manuscript with the ancient remains he found scattered through the fields between Cong and Knockma, a hill to the south near Tuam. Aiding and abetting Wilde in his examination of the ancient monuments was an ex-schoolteacher called Andy Hopkins. The two men, the local retired schoolmaster and the Dublin man of medicine, travelled about the immediate locality of Ballymagibbon, Nymphsfield and on as far as The Neale and Cross, recording and measuring the sites and matching them with the various battle scenes described in O'Cuirnin's manuscript. Hopkins was 'a versatile man of fertile fancy who was chockfull of local lore'. However, the names he 'transferred from O'Cuirnin's manuscript to the ancient monuments of this district, and which Sir William unquestioningly adopted, were never extant in the traditions or topography of Cong, nor have any of the personal names been known in this territory through the vanished generations of men'.[1]

The legend of the Battle of Moytura is an ancient one, 'referred to by Cormac Mac Cullinan, King and Bishop of Cashel, the most learned man of his age, when he wrote his celebrated Glossary, in the ninth century'.[2] From topography and place names used, the story is clearly not set around Cong at all but further north near Sligo. Most scholars now believe that the battle described in the annals never actually took place. Pre-Christian Irish history will not stand the test of modern historical criticism and legend cannot be mistaken for fact. Be that as it may, as far as Sir William was concerned, a great battle had been fought and the battlefield was the countryside around Cong. The evidence lay all about and he was going to prove it.

Armed with O'Donovan's translation of Cormac O'Cuirnin's fifteenth-century manuscript, Wilde got workmen to excavate a cairn that he believed marked the burial place of the young warrior who, according to the annals, saved the life of King Eochy. Deep in the cairn they came across as a small square chamber, 28 inches high and 37 inches wide. Here they found a small urn, 5½ inches high and 6 inches wide, containing the incinerated remains of human bones. He donated the urn to the museum of the Royal Irish Academy and saw the discovery as proof positive of his belief in the battle of Moytura and its historical location: 'Here, no doubt, the body of the loyal Fir Bolg youth was burned, and his ashes collected and preserved in this urn. Perhaps a more convincing proof of the authority of Irish or any other ancient history has never been afforded.'[3] Wilde prepared his account of the battle, correlating the results of his excavations and explorations with the incidents described in the manuscript. He then returned to Dublin and presented a paper, which later formed a key section in his book, to the Royal Irish Academy on his findings.

Although his account of the mythical battle is seriously flawed, *Lough Corrib, its Shores and Islands* remains an important work and a good read. It includes many interesting insights into the Ireland of William's own day and offers an opportunity to glimpse something of the mind and character of this remarkable man. Even today, it is still a useful handbook for anyone wishing to explore the ruins and sites and the reader can follow the footsteps taken by Sir William a century and a half ago as he circled the lake.

Sir William reveals a lot about himself in the book when he turns his attentions to the land question and the Irish experience. He reflects on the indolence of the landowning classes of the pre-Famine era as well as the effects of the Famine on the fabric of society and the fresh life and energy he sees emerging in the country with the arrival of 'new money':

> Debts accumulated as a result of reckless extravagance, contested elections, unsuccessful horse racing, Chancery suits transmitted for generations, bills of cost, interest on loans, and mortgages – the dowers of dowagers, and the jointures of grandmothers and aunts. All these kept the gentry poor; but they were tolerably loyal to the state, which sheltered them in a country where the King's writ did not run. The people were also poor and likewise ignorant, improvident, and uneducated, although far superior to the same class in the sister country; but they were disloyal – not so much on account of Protestantism, tithes, Catholic disabilities, the want of educational resources, or any other real or sentimental grievance, but because they had never been conquered by either force, justice, or kindness. However, what diplomacy and the sword could not effect for so many centuries, a single night of blight, followed by a few years' failure of the tuber introduced by Raleigh achieved. It cut off almost in a moment the food of an entire nation. The rent ceased; the mortgages were unpaid; the agents failed; the poor rates could not be collected. Pestilence followed the famine; the herds diminished; the workhouses buried such of the dead as had not fallen by the wayside; emigration helped off the

remaining living; the Incumbered Estates Court sold up the bankrupt landlords, as a sheriff's sale, and often at half the value of the land; the old properties changed hands; and, although hundreds of thousands were lost both to the owners and creditors, new blood was infused and new life and energy thrown into the country. And now, the old Abbey of Cong, and the adjoining estates, with many a mile westward of this famed locality, have been purchased with the produce of ability, honest industry, and successful commercial enterprise.[4]

This is an amazing lecture, a very interesting summing-up of the situation. It ends with praise for his new neighbour in Cong, the enterprising and extremely wealthy Sir Benjamin Guinness. Sir William is optimistic that the 'new blood' will bring the prosperity that the old landowning classes and native peasants were unable to produce.

Following the book's publication, Sir William invited his friends and colleagues in the Medico-Philosophical Society to visit him at Moytura House. The minutes of the society describe an enjoyable, light-hearted excursion. The merry group boarded the steamer *Lady Eglinton* in Galway and then cruised up the lake to Cong. Along the way they passed many of the ruins and islands described so vividly in Sir William's book. Upon arrival at Cong they were met by a fleet of carts, cars and wagons to take them the short distance to Moytura House. From out on the lake they could see the 'flag of the Chevalier' flying from the top of the tower in the grounds of Moytura. A flavour of proceedings can be gleaned from the fact that the minutes praise William's prudence in pinning the names of his guests to their pillows in case they suffered any 'obfuscation of intellect' and forgot where their beds were after sampling the produce of the local home distilleries. The society's meeting took place around the regular oval table brought from Dublin especially for the occasion. The following day Sir William took his friends on a tour of the locality, inspected some local antiquities, cast a line in Lough Mask and visited the demesne of Sir Benjamin Guinness. By all accounts this was a jolly event and a boost for Sir William's spirits.

Back in Dublin, 1 Merrion Square was a quieter place since the death of Isola. Lady Wilde did not go out. Instead her friends came to visit and eventually she was prevailed upon to reinstate her weekly receptions. Invitations were sent out saying: 'At Home, Saturday, 4 pm to 7pm. Conversazione.' Jane's Dublin salons were famous for attracting all kinds of celebrities and she proved a very capable hostess. The idea of hosting a salon had always attracted Jane, influenced perhaps by the stories she had heard in her youth about Lady Morgan. People from the world of literature, art, drama, medicine and academia came to these lively get-togethers, both residents of Dublin and others who might be passing through the city. The fine drawing room upstairs at Merrion Square was the ideal setting, with a table for wine and coffee placed in the corridor. Sometimes there was music or recitations with Jane, the perfect hostess, moving about the room, encouraging a performance here or rescuing a guest there who might be trapped by a bore.

She took her duties as a literary hostess seriously and came to be acknowledged as the leading hostess in Dublin. The salons were held by candlelight with the shutters closed and Jane liked to dress up in an elaborate manner. She was often seen in voluminous skirts or crimson silk gowns with flounces of Limerick lace topped off with exotic headgear. The flamboyant Lady Wilde with her large pieces of jewellery also tended to overdo the make-up, plastering her face in white powder. Years later she would attempt to recreate her salon in London, but by then circumstances had altered and the London gatherings never achieved the high standing of her Dublin salons. When Oscar rose to fame, many people attended Jane's 'At Homes' in London only in the hope of catching a glimpse of her celebrated son.

22

Sons and Daughters

Portora was the perfect environment for a gifted child like Oscar. According to Louis Claude Purser, the teacher's son and contemporary of Oscar's who went on to become Professor of Latin at Trinity College, Dublin, the school offered 'a far greater width of culture and diffusion of ideas then in any other school with which I have been acquainted; it was in that respect more like a college of a university than a middle-class school'.[1] Davis Coakley, author of *Oscar Wilde: The Importance of Being Irish*, believed 'Portora played a crucial role in Wilde's development and its importance in this respect has been greatly underestimated. It was an ideal environment for a child with an interest in culture, and it complemented the influence of his home.'[2]

To begin with, Willie was regarded as the better student. Oscar disliked maths and tended to focus only on the subjects and areas he found interesting, such as Classics and modern literature. Eventually, Oscar managed to outshine his elder brother, winning several prizes including a school prize for art from 'Bully' Wakeman, Sir William's art teacher friend. He was later awarded the school's Gold Medal for displaying his mastery of classical Greek. He also won the Carpenter Greek Testament Prize and then crowned his years at Portora by winning one of only two scholarships to Trinity College.

Willie left Portora for Trinity College in 1868. He became a prominent member of the university's Philosophical Society and went on to win a number of prizes including a Gold Medal for Ethics. Willie moved on from Trinity College in 1872 and crossed to London to study law at the Middle Temple. He eventually qualified as a barrister and was called to the Irish bar in 1875. Jane was delighted and proud of her eldest son and she anticipated a great future for him. In her plans he would have a thriving career as a barrister before entering Parliament where he could display his eloquence. He would also, of course, be happily married by this stage. Unfortunately for Willie, as well as for his ever-faithful mother, none of this would come to pass. His career in law was short-lived and unsuccessful despite initial support and encouragement from family and friends. Willie, unlike his industrious father, just did not like the idea of having to work for a living.

On 10 October 1871, at the age of sixteen, Oscar left Portora behind and joined his brother at Trinity College, the alma mater of Jonathan Swift, Oliver Goldsmith, Robert Emmet, Henry Grattan and Thomas Davis. He was beaten into second place in the entrance examinations by his friend from Portora, Louis Claude Purser, perhaps because he underperformed in mathematics. Trinity College was founded in 1592 by Queen Elizabeth I and in Oscar's time had about 11,000 registered students, approximately 90 per cent of whom were Protestants. Trinity still retains its beautiful campus of almost 40 acres in the very centre of Ireland's capital city. Oscar lived at home with his parents during his first year at Trinity College, Merrion Square being only a short walk from the university. The Register of Chambers, however, shows that Oscar was given rooms in the university in November 1871 and retained these rooms throughout the three years he spent studying there. The grimy accommodation – two bedrooms, a sitting room and a pantry – was on the first floor in the quadrangle known to all as Botany Bay and Oscar took up residency there with Willie in his second year.

Oscar was not diligent in attending lectures during his first year but still managed to excel in his examinations. At that time Trinity College had a strong Classical department where fluency of expression in the oral examinations was emphasised. Here the young man from Portora School came under the influence of Reverend John Pentland

Mahaffy, Professor of Ancient History. Mahaffy was an old friend of the Wilde family and Jane acknowledged that it was the Trinity professor who gave the first 'noble impulse to Oscar's intellect'.[3] Dr Mahaffy was renowned for his conversational skills and had wide interests that included Georgian architecture, antiques, wine and hunting. His many publications included the book *On the Art of Conversation* and another on the philosophy of Kant called *The Aesthetic and Analytic*. In 1874, the year Oscar moved to Oxford, Mahaffy published *Social Life in Greece from Homer to Meander* in which he acknowledged Oscar Wilde and another former pupil, H. B. Leech, for their assistance in making improvements and corrections to the manuscript. This book is interesting in that it addresses the question of homosexual practices in ancient Greece where the love between a man and a handsome youth was considered finer than heterosexual love. It was the first time a scholarly work had addressed this delicate area of classical studies. A second edition of Mahaffy's book was published the following year but with all references to homosexuality removed. The scholar obviously had second thoughts about the wisdom of such discussions in print. The generous acknowledgment of his former students' help was also missing.

Edward Carson, the man Wilde would later face across the floor of the Old Bailey in that famous clash between barrister and celebrity, entered Trinity College the same year as Oscar but did not take rooms. He would later deny that he was ever close to Oscar at Trinity College, although Oscar maintained they often took walks together with their arms draped about each other's shoulders in the innocent way of schoolfriends. An interesting footnote to the relationship between Oscar Wilde and fellow Dubliner Edward Carson was a letter that appeared in *The Irish Times* on 28 August 1954 from a solicitor by the name of Murroe Fitzgerald. He stated that in 1919 he prepared a claim for a woman who once had been nanny to both Edward Carson and the Wilde children while they were staying at Dungarvan, a seaside town in County Waterford. The nanny was fifteen years old in 1859 when, according to her account of events, the two boys played together on the seashore. Dublin-based actor and wit Micheál Mac Liammóir, whose tour-de-force in the 1960s was a one-man show called *The Importance of Being Oscar*, commented: 'Yes, that would explain it all. Oscar probably upset Edward's sandcastle.'[4]

Oscar got on well at Trinity College. On 29 April 1872, he came 'first of the firsts' in Classics and was awarded a diploma on vellum. By June of the following year, the bright young doctor's son was among the fifty students sitting the examination for a Foundation scholarship worth £20 per annum plus certain privileges. He came out on top and secured the prize. Oscar liked to bring his friends home to Merrion Square or invite them to his mother's receptions where they might meet a celebrity or two. Sherard, in his biography of Oscar, quotes him as once saying to a fellow student: 'Come home with me, I want to introduce you to my mother. We have founded a society for the suppression of virtue.' This is an early example of Oscar Wilde's desire to make an impression and not an indication that 1 Merrion Square was a hotbed of immorality. He loved sensation and would court it regardless of the personal cost.

Oscar shared his rooms on campus with Willie during his second year, an ill-kept apartment where he kept an unfinished landscape in oils permanently displayed sitting on an easel in a prominent place, a practice he would continue in Oxford. The two brothers never entertained in their grimy rooms but should someone drop by Oscar would refer to his unfinished painting. Although Classics was his favourite, Oscar was also a voracious reader of English literature and particularly liked Swinburne's *Poems and Ballads* at this time. Both Oscar and his brother had some poetry published in a new college magazine called *Kottabos* edited by Robert Tyrrell, Trinity's 25-year-old Professor of Latin, who was to be another important influence. In November 1873 Oscar became a member of the College Historical Society, known as the 'Hist' and founded by Edmund Burke. The auditor at the time was Bram Stoker, who became a frequent visitor to Merrion Square where he listened with great interest to Sir William's tales of his early exploits in Egypt. Over thirty years later Stoker followed his successful novel *Dracula* with *The Jewel of Seven Stars*, a story set among the tombs of Egypt. The Wilde brothers did not neglect the social side of student life and were prominent guests at many functions, attending balls and mixing freely in Dublin society.

Oscar also began to develop an interest in the philosophy of aesthetics, which can be defined as the philosophical study of beauty or as a critical reflection on art, culture and nature. This was not a new area – it reached back as far as Plato and Aristotle – but nineteenth-century aesthetics could be said to have developed as a reaction to the materialism and ugliness of the industrial age. This interest led him to the Pre-Raphaelites, a group of reforming painters and poets based in England, and to authors such as Baudelaire and Walt Whitman. The Philosophical Society records show that many other students at the time also had a keen interest in aesthetics and Willie read a paper to the society with the title 'Aesthetic Morality'.

On 17 March 1874 an announcement appeared in the *Oxford University Gazette* stating that Magdalen College was to award two Demyships, or scholarships, in Classics worth £95 per annum, to be held for five years, the recipients to be decided by examination. Five candidates including Oscar Wilde presented themselves for examination that June. G. T. Atkinson, the student who came second to Oscar, remembered years later how the young man from Ireland kept asking the invigilator for more paper. Oscar was by far the worthy winner but this meant that, despite his academic achievements in Dublin, he would now leave Trinity College without graduating. Nevertheless, there was delight all around when he sailed from Kingstown in October 1874 for a new life, as Jane put it in a letter to Lotten von Kraemer, 'at that splendid university where so much talent and genius congregate'. He had just turned twenty years of age.

Oscar did not leave Trinity College empty handed. In 1874, before departing for England, he was awarded the Berkeley Gold Medal for Greek, Trinity's highest award for classical scholarship. The prize, founded by the remarkable prelate and Irish philosopher Bishop George Berkeley[5] (1686–1753), was awarded for his achievements in an examination on the Greek comic poets. He was the second Wilde to gain that distinction as Sir William's Roscommon-born uncle, the Reverend Ralph Wilde, was also awarded the

Berkeley Medal during his student days. Sir William's immediate response to the news of Oscar's achievement in winning the medal was to organise a gathering of friends at Moytura to celebrate. He sent a note to John Gilbert: 'We are asking a few old friends upon Moytura on Thursday, and also to cheer dear old Oscar on having obtained the Berkeley gold medal last week with great honour. You were always a favourite of his, and he hopes you will come.'6 It is poignant to record that after Oscar's death in Paris, a pawn ticket for his Berkeley medal was found among his possessions; his vellum diploma awarded in 1872 went up for auction at Sotheby's in 1911.

With Willie and Oscar now both in England and Sir William spending most of his time in Moytura, there was vague talk of letting out the house on Merrion Square and removing west to Moytura full-time. Sir William's income had been decreasing at a time when his sons had not yet begun to make their own way in the world, but any plans to lease Merrion Square were dropped when Willie was called to the Irish bar in March 1875. It was thought 1 Merrion Square would provide the prestigious Dublin address from where he could launch his career. Unfortunately, a never-ending round of balls, skating rinks and dinners took up most of the new barrister's time and his career at the bar was doomed from the start.

While Oscar and Willie were making their way through university, Sir William was in obvious decline. Asthma had always been a problem for him and he also experienced regular bouts of bronchitis. Jane's letters from this time show a woman deeply concerned about her husband's failing health. To make matters worse, while Sir William was battling with his physical ailments, unknown to the outside world he was also trying to recover from yet another severe emotional blow.

Sir William's two illegitimate daughters, Emily and Mary, were staying with his eldest brother, the Reverend Ralph Wilde, in the Monaghan area during the late autumn of 1871. This was just a month or so after Oscar's entry into Trinity College. The two girls, now aged twenty-four and twenty-two respectively, had been brought up by the Reverend who had accepted them as his wards – hence they bore the Wilde name. Charming girls, they once wrote an epitaph for the most famous greyhound of all time, Master McGrath, three times winner of the Waterloo Cup. It opens with the lines:

> Master McGrath has passed away,
> He breathed his last on Christmas Day.

On 31 October the local bank manager, a Mr Reid, was hosting a ball at Drumaconnor House on the road from Smithboro to Monaghan and the two Wilde sisters were invited to attend. Drumaconnor House is a charming manor house, still standing today and functioning as a guesthouse. The party took place in a medium-sized sitting room and not a grand ballroom as one might imagine. At the end of the evening's entertainment when the other guests had gone, the host took Emily out for a last whirl around the floor. As they waltzed past the open fire Emily's crinoline dress caught fire, an all-too-common occurrence in those days. Her sister rushed to her aid but Mary's dress also became enveloped by flames. The host wrapped his coat about the girls and bundled them outside where they were rolled in the snow but it was too late.

The burns were very severe and after suffering for nine days Mary died. Her sister Emily died more than a week later, on Wednesday 21 November. Only a brief inquiry was held in place of a full official inquest and the name Wylie appears on the report in place of Wilde.[7] Sir William must have used some influence to keep the terrible events as secret as possible. Shocked and grieving, he no doubt wished to be spared the publicity that would surround an inquest, an inquiry being a much more low-key affair. This new information brought to light by Michelle McGoff-McCann in her 2003 study of the old coroner's reports for the area explains the puzzling absence of any reference to the tragedy in the national newspapers, although the *Northern Standard* carried a brief obituary claiming that Mary had died on the 8 November and 'Emma' on 21 November. A large headstone still stands in St Molua's Church of Ireland graveyard, Drumsnat, bearing the following inscription:

> In memory of two loving and loved sisters, Emily Wilde, aged 24, and Mary Wilde, aged 22, who lost their lives by

accident in this parish, November 10th, 1871. They were lovely and pleasant in their lives and in death they were not divided. II Samuel 1 v 23.

Years later, Jack B. Yeats wrote of this sad occurrence in a letter to his famous son, the poet William Butler Yeats:

> There was a dance one evening at the house, to which the Himes went. After Mrs Hime left, one of the girls in her muslin dress and crinoline went too close to the fire and the dress was instantly in flames – after some cries of agony they died. While they were dying, their mother, who had a small black-oak shop in Dublin, came down and stayed with them. After all was over, even to the funeral, Sir Wm. came down and old Mrs Hime told me that his groans could be heard by people outside the house. There is a tragedy all the more intense, because it had to be buried in silence. It is not allowed to give sorrow words. Sir Wm. Wilde's vivacity and stream of talk had its source in this kind of [?] – perhaps like the bubbles that appear on the surface when the water begins to boil. Had Oscar known of them, he would not have been so scornful of his poor father – successful, parsimonious, and bedevilled, yet Oscar benefited by his parsimony.[8]

Old Mrs Hime was the mother of Maurice Hime, headmaster of Foyle College in Derry from 1877 to 1896, and an acquaintance of Yeats. Jack Yeats was quite old when he wrote this chatty letter with its numerous errors. He refers to Ralph as Sir William's father and fails to say that one girl rushed to save the other. Also, there is no evidence to support his belief that Oscar complained of his father's parsimony, if indeed he was ever parsimonious. It is a revealing letter nonetheless.

Once a year for more then twenty years a mysterious woman in black came by train from Dublin to Monaghan where she hired a car to drive to Drumsnat graveyard. She never revealed her identity but once told the sexton that the girls were very dear to her. Did Sir

William share the grief of his dead daughters with his wife and family or did he carry the burden alone? Lady Wilde, ever loyal to her husband, never once mentioned the terrible accident in any of her correspondences, nor did she ever, for that matter, refer to Henry Wilson even though he was a close associate of Sir William's and lived nearby. In the rose garden to the west of Moytura House there is a small square stone delicately carved with laurel leaves and bearing the inscription 'In Memoriam'. Sir William had it placed there, a private memorial to his daughters who were burned to death and probably also to the memory of little Isola. The carved block can still be seen in the garden, serving as a pedestal for a white garden urn.

After the tragedy, Sir William continued to reduce his medical practice even further, with a corresponding loss of income. His once strong financial position deteriorated to the point where he was compelled, in 1872, to take out a mortgage on Merrion Square. He was spending more and more time on antiquarian work and came west to Moytura as often as possible. He completed Part 4 of the catalogue and an index but it remained unpublished, a further bitter disappointment to him. A photograph taken of Sir William around this time and published in the *Dublin University Magazine* shows a man whose whole attitude is brooding and dejected. This photograph unfortunately has come to be the best known image of Oscar Wilde's father and the one most often reproduced.

Sir William continued to write and had enough energy to begin three manuscripts. The first was *A History of Irish Medicine*, the second a proposed collection of *Irish Fairy Lore* for which he gathered large amounts of information on fairy tales and stories, and the third a *Memoir of Gabriel Beranger*, the eighteenth-century artist and antiquarian. William also produced the census return for 1871 but the burden of so doing greatly taxed his ebbing energy. On St Patrick's Day 1873 the Royal Irish Academy awarded Sir William their highest honour, the Cunningham Gold Medal, in recognition of his work on the catalogue. He was greatly cheered and this time accepted the honour, having refused it years before in the belief that it had not been offered with good grace. The Academy had always been an important part of William's life but his relationship with it was often an uncomfortable one and even though he was one of its leading lights he was never fully accepted in certain quarters. William's late friend George Petrie, the artist and antiquarian, had been a previous recipient of the Medal and then went on to be appointed President, an honour Sir William would not attain.

In June of 1874 the Scottish scholar and Professor of Greek at Edinburgh University, John Stuart Blackie, spent four weeks in Ireland. He was introduced to Sir William and the pair went off together on a day trip to visit the archaeological sites around Drogheda. Blackie wrote to his wife saying he found Sir William very easy to get on with and very intelligent, full of knowledge on the Boyne Valley. He described Wilde as being 'a restless, keen-eyed old gentleman, like a Skye terrier, snuffing and poking about'. Blackie went on to describe Lady Wilde, 'a poetess of the very fervid patriotic stamp, and a giantess to boot – the biggest woman I ever saw ... She is a phenomenon and worth considering and with more girth on her little finger then some women have on their whole body.'[9] Her size coupled with a tendency to dress in an increasingly unconventional and extravagant manner made Lady Wilde a formidable sight as she advanced into middle years.

Although Sir William's health was now a constant cause of concern for his wife, he was still involved in various projects. In 1874 he began a campaign to have a monument erected to the sixteenth-century ecclesiastical scholars known as the Four Masters, authors of the *Annals of the Four Masters* that had been recently translated into English by John O'Donovan. The manuscript and the translation were to become very important in the study of early Irish history. To further the cause Sir William contacted his Royal Irish Academy friend Sir John Gilbert, Secretary of the Public Records Office. He was also in correspondence with Dublin Corporation about an appropriate site. Eventually, and after much wrangling, the Four Masters Memorial was erected in Eccles Street opposite the Mater Hospital, the lawn at Leinster House having been refused.

It was at this time that Sir William was cheered to hear about Oscar's achievement in winning the Berkeley Gold Medal at Trinity College and invited his friends to celebrate at Moytura. Then the great news of Oscar's success in the Magdalen College scholarship arrived. As well as relieving some of the financial burden, Sir William was well pleased on another account. Some intellectuals in Dublin at that time had grown fascinated by Catholicism because of the influence of the new Cardinal, John Henry Newman, and Oscar's interest in the Church of Rome had grown to the point where he had begun attending Mass. Sir William hoped that Oxford would be just the place to divert his son's mind away from Rome.

After Oscar's scholarship examination, Jane crossed to London and spent a month there with her two sons. They had a pleasant time meeting with a number of literary figures including Thomas Carlyle before the party continued on to Paris and then to Geneva. Oscar was delighted with his success and he later said that he began work on his poem 'The Sphinx' while staying at the Hotel Voltaire in Paris. He had been reading Edgar Allan Poe's *The Raven* and Swinburne's *Dolores*. Unfortunately, when the happy family group returned to Dublin they found Sir William very unwell and mostly confined to the house.

23

A Weariness of All Things

On 17 October 1874 Oscar went up to Oxford. He had celebrated his twentieth birthday the day before. 'I was the happiest man in the world when I entered Magdalen for the first time,' he said. 'Oxford was paradise to me.' Many of Oscar's fellow students would have been to some of England's top schools such as Eton or Harrow and would have the confidence and expectations associated with their class. There were unwritten conventions he needed to learn and he also decided that his accent would have to change. Years later, on a lecture tour of America, he told an audience in San Francisco that he wished he 'had a good Irish accent to read "The Meeting of the Trials" to you in, but my Irish accent was one of the many things I forgot at Oxford'.[1]

Sir William's health recovered sufficiently for him to join Lady Wilde on a visit to their son in his panelled university rooms where the bowls were brimming for the occasion with gin-and-whisky punch. It is interesting to note that when Oscar's great-grandson Lucian Holland entered Magdalen over a century later he was allocated the room where Oscar had resided. Fellow student David Hunter Blair, heir to a Scottish baronetcy who later renounced all privilege and became the Abbot of a Benedictine monastery, remembered meeting the Wildes on their visit. An 'interesting and delightful family circle' was his verdict.[2] Sir William continued to be concerned about his son's religious inclinations but was somewhat reassured when in February 1875 Oscar, influenced by his good friend J. E. C. Bodley, became a member of the Apollo Lodge of the Freemasons at Oxford University, reaching the level of Master Mason that May. Sir William was himself a leading member of Dublin's Shakespeare Masonic Lodge. Apollo was a very High Church lodge with a great emphasis on ritual and Masonic costume, all of which held a great attraction for the young Oscar.

Fitting into this new world of old Etonians and Wykehamists would present certain challenges for the young Dubliner, even one with Oscar's privileged if bohemian background. He adopted a distinctly English accent that he used to deliver perfectly formed sentences as if, according to W. B. Yeats, they had been written 'overnight with labour'. He was also beginning to make a name for himself for what Yeats called 'the enjoyment of his own spontaneity'.[3] His dress also changed, becoming sportier. It would be a year or two before he developed his more peculiarly distinctive dandyism and his hair, while kept short in first term, was soon allowed to grow longer. His attempts at outdoor pursuits were not always successful. Oscar was dropped from the rowing team for failing to follow instructions but he continued to row occasionally for pleasure. Apart from a little boxing, Oscar for the most part eschewed physical exercise, preferring 'talk to walk'.

The young Irishman and his new friends were involved in the usual rounds of high-spirited student antics. Nevertheless, Oscar did not neglect his studies and continued to read widely in literature and philosophy as well as the required classical texts. He only secured a pass in first term but then settled down to achieve results more in keeping with his ability. When the summer vacation eventually arrived Sir William was happy to see Oscar going off on a trip to Italy with Professor Mahaffy from Trinity College, Dublin, and William Goulding, the young son of a wealthy Dublin businessman, both staunch Protestants. This tour would take him away from his friend, the newly converted Hunter Blair who, since his return from Rome, had been urging Oscar and others to follow his lead and convert to Catholicism. Oscar continued to find the idea of conversion appealing but was justifiably afraid of being cut off by his father if he embraced Rome. The three travellers, Mahaffy, Goulding and Wilde, visited Florence and Bologna and then journeyed on to Venice. From there they went to Padua to see the Giottos spoken of by John Ruskin, the Professor of Fine Art at Oxford. Next stop was Verona. Oscar, however, was by then running out of funds and so returned home.

There are some wonderful letters written by Oscar during that trip to his mother and to Sir William from various parts of Italy. One, dated Tuesday 15 June 1875, was written to Sir William from Florence and describes in great detail the sarcophagi of granite and porphyry he came across in San Lorenzo and how in the Biblioteca Laurenziana he was 'shown wonderfully illuminated missals and unreadable manuscripts and autographs'. When Oscar sets out to detail what he encountered in the Etruscan Museum his prose is an uncanny echo of his father's when Sir William described his own observations on that great adventure with the ailing Mr Meiklam so long ago. 'You first come to a big tomb,' Oscar wrote, 'transplanted from Arezzo; cyclopean stonework, doorway with sloping jams and oblong lintel, roof slightly conical, walls covered with wonderfully beautiful frescoes.' The ageing antiquarian had trained his son well. Not content with words Oscar enclosed a number of detailed sketches of coins and other objects. 'As I was kept there for a long time by an awful thunderstorm,' he explained, 'I copied a few which I send you.' He well knew what his father would appreciate. He signs the letter 'Yours ever truly affectionately Oscar O'F. Wi. Wilde.'[4]

The rest of this summer was spent between Dublin, Moytura and the hunting lodge at remote Illaunroe. If Oscar failed to make it to Rome on this occasion, the Holy City was not far from his thoughts for he wrote a poem called 'Rome Unvisited', much to the delight of Hunter Blair. It was during this summer break that Oscar met the beautiful Florence Balcombe in Dublin. She was seventeen and Oscar was not yet twenty-one. He gave her a gift of a watercolour he had painted of Moytura House and he took to writing love poems. There was also some mild flirting with two other girls before returning to university to commence his second year.

While Oscar was enjoying his first summer vacation as an Oxford man, Sir William was preparing a talk to be delivered in Belfast where the Anthropological Section of the British Association would be gathering in August. His talk would address the question of Irish identity, describing the early settlers arriving 'in a rude, uncultivated state without a knowledge of letters or manufactures'. He would tell his listeners about 'the fair-complexioned Dannans', the dark Firbolgs and about the arrival of the Milesians from Spain, 'brave, chivalrous, skilled in war, good navigators, proud, boastful'. From this race, he would claim, came the O's and the Macs of Ireland. Modern historians, however, would not support these claims. Sir William was on more solid ground when he included recollections from his travels in the Mediterranean and in the Holy Land as a young man.

Sir William's lecture was well received even though he was at his most outspoken, telling his audience that the Irish race was conquered not by Henry II but by the failure of the potato and by the British government altering the price of a grain of corn. He reflected upon his experiences while working on the census, recounting how the native Irish-speaking population had been decimated by the Famine. Sir William praised the results of the intermixture of races, the Saxon and the Celt. There was, he believed, a want of fusion of races in Ireland, of opinions and sentiments. He went on to remind his audience that the Queen of Ireland and Great Britain was descended from the marriage of the Norman knight Strongbow with Eve, daughter of the Irish King Dermot. In this fine lecture, extracts of which Jane would later publish in the back of her two-volume work *Ancient Legends*, Sir William, speaking now as an Irishman himself, was facing up to the difficult and tangled question of Irish identity. The ailing knight had come a long way since his early voyage as Mr Meiklam's young doctor, when he had been more dismissive of his Irishness. This was to be his last public speech.

Sir William's health was now failing badly. He wrote to his friend Gilbert, the historian who had helped him with the catalogue: 'I have been very unwell. You might give me a call, as you know I can always see you in my buff, or get you up to my den. I am not up to dining at the club.' Lady Wilde was now deeply concerned for her husband.

In the autumn of 1875 Lady Wilde had a break from her domestic worries when she visited Paris again. In a letter to her friend Rosalie Olivecrona, Jane maintained she 'would have died altogether' through depression over Sir William's poor health but was now 'quite restored by the fine pure clean air and the great interest and variety Paris offers'. The positive effects Paris had on Jane were not, however, to last for long. 'The sadness is coming on me again,' she wrote to Rosalie, 'a weariness of all things – and now I long for a glimpse of Italy.' But her chances of ever seeing Italy were slim. 'Sir William's health is much broken and I am kept in constant anxiety about him – he is low and languid – scarcely eats and seldom goes out – he complains of gout, but along with this, he seems fading away before our eyes – and has grown so pale and wan and thin and low spirited that I too have fallen like an unstrung instrument and no poet-music can be struck from my heart.'

By now, Jane had taken to sitting by her husband's bedside, writing letters, mostly to Oscar. Willie was at this period trying none too successfully to get his law career off the ground. When Sir William's health allowed, he saw some patients and he was able to travel down to Moytura where he spent the late autumn and early winter of 1875. Jane told Oscar that Sir William did not now mention the possibility of ever returning to Dublin. But Sir William never gave up on his work even in his sick bed and continued compiling the memoir of Gabriel Beranger, working on his notes up to the end.

A second poem from Oscar was published in January 1876 in the *Dublin University Magazine*. Jane told Oscar that his father had carried it off and kept it so she was waiting for her chance to study it closely. The poem was called 'From Spring Days to Winter'.

From Spring Days to Winter
(For Music)

In the glad springtime when leaves were green,
O merrily the throstle sings!
I sought, amid the tangled sheen,
Love whom mine eyes had never seen,
O the glad dove has golden wings!

Between the blossoms red and white,
O merrily the throstle sings!
My love first came into my sight,
O perfect vision of delight,
O the glad dove has golden wings!

The yellow apples glowed like fire,
O merrily the throstle sings!
O Love too great for lip or lyre,
Blown rose of love and of desire,
O the glad dove has golden wings!

But now with snow the tree is grey,
Ah, sadly now the throstle sings!
My love is dead: ah! well-a-day,
See at her silent feet I lay
A dove with broken wings!
Ah, Love! Ah, Love! That thou wert slain –
Fond Dove, fond Dove return again.

On 7 February 1876 Sir William was able to attend a board meeting of the Governors of St Mark's Hospital. His health then took a further turn for the worse and he found himself unable to leave his bed. He was now fading away gently before the eyes of his family. These were to be his final days but he was still making plans as usual for his loved Moytura. At four o'clock in the afternoon on Wednesday 19 April 1876 Sir William Wilde died. According to Jane's account, he passed away 'like one sleeping', without pain or struggle, with his wife holding his hand and his sons about his bedside. William was only sixty-one years of age.

24

A Changed Fortune

On a wet and stormy evening in October 1971, a Portland stone plaque sculpted by Michael Biggs was unveiled at 1 Merrion Square, Dublin. The dignitaries present included the President of the Royal College of Surgeons and the President of the Royal Irish Academy. Sir William would have been very pleased. The plaque, mounted between the two front windows of the imposing Georgian townhouse, which today belongs to the American College, celebrates the great Victorian polymath who once lived there. It reads as follows:

> Aural and ophthalmic surgeon, archaeologist, ethnologist, antiquarian, biographer, statistician, naturalist, topographer, historian and folklorist; lived in this house from 1855–1876

As if to further honour the husband of the rebellious 'Speranza of the *Nation*', a police car arrived to find out what sort of a suspiciously dedicated group would bother congregating in public on such an inclement evening. The escalating 'Troubles' in the Northern Ireland had made the authorities extra nervous at that time.

Sir William Wilde was a truly extraordinary man and he led an amazing life. He was a man full of contradictions. He could be ill-tempered and impatient but also charming and kindly. If he liked to be acknowledged he also gave full praise where it was due. A staunch Protestant and loyal to the Union he married a nationalist poet. He expressed his own love for Ireland through his antiquarian activities and his empathy with the native Irish. His efforts as a folklorist were pioneering as was his work in his chosen field of medicine. His contributions to the Irish census were invaluable. Sir William's charming book on Lough Corrib is still enjoyed today.

Sir William had expressed a desire to be buried at Moytura, if possible, and that his funeral should be small and private. Neither wish came to pass. He died in Dublin and was laid to rest in the family vault at the city's Mount Jerome Cemetery on Saturday 22 April. His funeral cortège was one of the most imposing the city had seen in a very long time. The large attendance included the Lord Mayor, the Lord Chancellor, the Lord Chief Justice, the president of the Royal Irish Academy, several Fellows of Trinity College, eminent physicians, politicians, academics including Mahaffy, thirty-five members of the Royal Irish Academy carrying their mace draped in black crape, artists, members of the professions and many ordinary citizens of Dublin. William's natural son, Dr Henry Wilson, was there but did not take up a prominent position. Lawyer Isaac Butt attended as did Sir William's old adversary, the now aged Arthur Jacob. The official list of mourners numbered 168 people.

Sir William's obituary ran to columns in the Dublin papers and the poet Samuel Ferguson, who had written the famous 'Lament for Thomas Davis' twenty years previously, composed an elegy on the death of his friend Sir William Wilde:

Dear Wilde
An Elegy, 1876

Dear Wilde, the deeps close o'er thee; and no more
Greet we or mingle on the hither shore,
Where other footsteps now must print the sand,
And other waiters by the margin stand.
Gone; and alas! Too late it wrings my breast,
The word unspoken, and the hand unpressed;
Yet will affection follow, and believe

The sentient spirit may the thought receive,
Though neither eye to eye the soul impart,
Nor answering hand confess the unburthened heart.
Gone; and alone rests for me that I strive
In song sincere to keep thy name alive,
Though nothing needing of the aids of rhyme,
While they who knew thee tread the ways of time,
And cherish, ere their race be also run,
Their memories of many a kindness done –
Of the quick look that caught the unspoken need,
And back returned the hand's benignant deed
In help or healing, or with ardour high
Infused the might of patriot-sympathy.
And when we all have followed, and the last
Who loved thee living shall have also passed,
This crumbling castle, from its basement swerved,
Thy pious under-pinning skill preserved;
That carven porch from ruined heaps anew
Dug out and dedicate by thee to view
Of wond'ring modern men who stand amazed
To think their Irish fathers ever raised
Works worthy such a care; this sculptured cross
Thou gatheredst piecemeal, every knop and boss
And dragon-twisted symbol, side by side
Laid, and holy teachings reapplied;
Those noble jewels of the days gone by
With rarest products of progressive man
Since civil life in Erin first began:

These all will speak thee; and, dear Wilde, when these,
In course of time, by swift or slow degrees,
Are also perished from the world, and gone,
The green grass of Roscommon will grow on;
And though our several works of hand and pen,
Our names and memories, be forgotten then,
Oft as the cattle in the dewy day

Of tender morn, by Tulsk or Castlerea,
Crop the sweet herbage, or adown the vale
The ruddy milkmaid bears her evening pail;
Oft as the youth to meet his fair one flies
At labour's close, where sheltering hawthorns rise
By Suck's smooth margin; or the merry round
Of dancers foot it to the planxty's sound,
And some warm heart, matched with a mind serene,
shall drink its full refreshment from the scene,
With thanks to God whose beauty brings to pass
That maids their sweethearts, and that kine their grass,
Fond by His care provided, and there rise
Soft and sweet thoughts for all beneath the skies; –
Then, though unknown, thy spirit shall partake
Refreshment, too, for old communion's sake.

In a letter to Sir Thomas Larcom six days after Sir William's death, Lady Wilde described her husband's end and the sense of loss she was now feeling:

His health was failing in the winter – no actual complaint – except bronchial attack, and we hoped for spring – but spring brought no strength. He faded away gently before our eyes – still trying to work, almost to the last, going down to attend professional duties. Then he became weaker, and for the last six weeks never left his bed. He himself still hoping and planning as usual for his loved Moytura, but still he grew weaker day by day, no pain, thank God, no suffering – the last few days he was almost unconscious, quiet and still and at the last passed away like one sleeping – gently and softly – no struggle – with his hand in mine and his two sons beside him. It was well that his last days were unconscious for he often pined for the strength that would enable him to finish many works left but not yet completed. I think the sentence of death would have been bitter to him. He was spared the knowledge and better so. In any national work he took his part, and his labours were for humanity, for others not for him.

For us the loss is one that plunges our life into darkness. I feel like one shipwrecked. A wife feels the position more fatally then all others – a broken desolate life, a changed fortune, and in the midst of grief the necessity coming for all the exertion that legal affairs demand. It is a sad sorrow for me to leave this house – yet – it must be done. A married man lives on day by day and cannot think of the morrow. Probably at least £3,000 a year goes down in to the grave with him. This forces a sad change in a family. Happily my sons are of age. They will be self-supporting soon, I trust – but while my eyes are blinded with tears, my brain, alas, is filled with many sad bewildering cares and anxieties for the future – and I am very weary after the last eight weeks of exhausting anxiety, during which I never left the house and scarcely for a moment left his side. But I thank God that I was with him to the last hour. The remembrance of your lifelong friendship for him, manifested towards him nobly and affectionately whenever you had the opportunity, will never be effaced from my memory.[1]

T. G. Wilson, Sir William's biographer, describing his death says: 'Speranza was constantly by his side, but it is said that his end was hastened by the heartless conduct of his two sons who came in late and filled the house with their friends. As they tramped noisily up the stairs, their father lay in bed, groaning: "Oh, those boys, those boys!"'[2] But there is another, more irregular, account of Sir William's last days. It is Oscar's own version, as told by Robert Sherard in his biography *The Life of Oscar Wilde*. Talking of his mother, Oscar states:

She was a wonderful woman, and such a feeling as vulgar jealousy could take no hold on her. She was well aware of my father's constant infidelities, but simply ignored them. Before my father died in 1876, he lay ill in bed for many days. And every morning a woman dressed in black and closely veiled used to come to our house in Merrion Square, and unhindered by my mother, or anyone else, used to walk straight up the stairs to Sir William's bedroom and sit down at the head of his bed and so sit there all day, without ever speaking a word or once raising her veil. She took no notice of anybody in the room and nobody paid any attention to her. Not one woman in a thousand would have tolerated her presence, but my mother allowed it, because she knew that my father loved the woman and felt that it may be a joy and comfort to have her there by his dying bed. And I am sure she did right not to grudge that last happiness to a man who was about to die, and I am sure that my father understood her indifference, understood that it was not because she did not love him that she permitted her rival's presence, but because she loved him very much, and died with his heart full of gratitude for her.

Could this be true? If so, who was this mysterious woman in black? Could it have been the same woman who for twenty years visited the churchyard in Drumsnat and, according to Jack B. Yeats, owned a black-oak shop in Dublin? Jane does not mention her presence at the bedside but neither does she mention Henry Wilson who must surely have been called to see his dying father. Jane was always very discreet in these matters. If the account is true, it shows that Sir William's wife had been an extraordinarily tolerant woman. Perhaps she needed to be. At any rate, she never regarded herself or her husband as being entirely conventional people. When Sir William's will was read, among its many surprises was £1,000 borrowed in 1874 for no specified reason. Could it have been borrowed in order to provide for the mother of his two lost daughters whose identity William took with him to the grave?

Sir William's will was destroyed along with many other important public records when Dublin's Four Courts were shelled during the Irish Civil War in 1922. The details, though, can be pieced together from letters. Sir William's practice had been failing, as his health had been, for ten years but a substantial income still needed to be generated.

Even though William had managed to become a wealthy man with property in Dublin, Bray and in the west of Ireland, expenditure had been exceeding income for a number of years and by the time of his death there were no monies left. The situation was actually worse than that, with Sir William having taken out mortgages of £1,000 on both Merrion Square and on the four Bray houses. Sir William's affairs were truly in a very dilapidated condition. His total assets amounted to less than £7,000 with debts running into thousands, including the last £1,000 mysteriously borrowed in 1874. Jane, who was not privy to her husband's affairs and left all business matters in his hands, could not understand where all the money had gone. The future, she wrote to Lotten, was 'all dark and uncertain!' 'When the Head of the House is taken the whole edifice of one's life falls in ruins to the ground.'[3]

Even in the days when money was plentiful, Sir William often managed to get himself into financial tangles. Bills were sometimes left unpaid and the bailiffs knew their way to 1 Merrion Square. A friend of Lady Wilde's once dropped by and found 'two strange men sitting in the hall, and I heard from the weeping servant that they were "men in possession". I felt sorry for poor Lady Wilde and hurried upstairs to the drawing-room where I knew I should find her. Speranza was there indeed, but seemed not in the least troubled by the state of affairs in the house. I found her lying on the sofa reading *Prometheus Vinctus* of Aeschylus, from which she began to disclaim passages to me, with exalted enthusiasm. She would not let me slip in a word of condolence, but seemed very anxious that I should share her entire admiration for the beauties of the Greek tragedian which she was reciting.'[4]

Jane disliked having to deal with the mundane, preferring to share the rarefied atmosphere of Mount Parnassus with the Muses. Until this point in her life she never had to experience real financial difficulties. Jane had her mother's support in Leeson Street and after that her husband looked after the troublesome chore of paying the bills. But now, for the first time in her life, Jane was on her own and in real trouble. Sir William had borrowed a sum of £2,500 from her marriage settlement to purchase Moytura and through some legal muddle she could not now retrieve these monies. The rents from the few Moytura tenants, amounting to £100 or £150 per annum, were to go to Lady Wilde for her lifetime but these were troubled times for landlords in Ireland and the rents were never paid in full nor could they be relied upon. The Land League agitation, which campaigned for tenant rights in Ireland through the 1880s and into the 1890s, and then Gladstone's reforming Land Acts meant that the Wildes would never receive much from Moytura. Willie, as the eldest son, was left 1 Merrion Square, with its mortgage, and Moytura House with its estate of 170 acres and fourteen tenants. Oscar was given the four houses at Esplanade Terrace, Bray, built by Sir William in 1861. But they also came with a mortgage of £1,000. The lodge on Illaunroe was left jointly between Oscar and his half-brother, Henry Wilson.

The financial situation in the Wilde household was grave. Jane, unused to having to handle difficulties of this nature, did not know which way to turn and Willie was of no help at all. He lacked the necessary drive and perseverance to carve out a career as a barrister and instead preferred to spend his time carousing about Dublin. Jane's hopes for Willie now centred on the possibility of him marrying a wealthy lady. In a despairing letter to Oscar she bewailed the situation:

> Oh! It is so miserable . . . And worst of all is when I think of that dreadful debt of £2,000 on you and Willie. How is it to be paid? . . . I think we must give up this house, otherwise how is Willie to live? As a secret, I must tell you, but don't allude to it to Willie, that the whole affair is off between himself and Maude Thomas. The mother won't consent — and she thinks it better to break off entirely and at once. So there is an end to my dreams, and now we must face the inevitable. We could not keep up this house and the female servants, fires, gas, food, rent — there is a mortgage — under £500 a year. Nothing is to be had out of wretched Moytura. I am in a very distracted state of mind. What is to be done?[5]

Jane was never again to experience financial security and Willie would be a constant source of worry for her to the end.

191

Oscar, writing from Oxford, was also complaining about his financial situation but Jane had little sympathy for her spendthrift son who had the rents from his Bray houses and the potential income from their sale whereas she had no income at all and could not 'see from what source I am to look for one'. Oscar, too, believed that marriage was the only way out for him but there was no immediate wealthy candidate presenting herself.

One possible solution to Jane's dire financial predicament would be a civil pension. Sir Thomas Larcom told her to contact an MP as a literary pension was in the gift of the Prime Minister. This was the beginning of a very long campaign. Lady Wilde feared Disraeli would object to her as a nationalist but that her claim for a pension 'on Sir William's general services to the Government and the Country rather than on literary merit' might have a better chance of success.[6] If Jane could secure a pension she might be able to stay on at Merrion Square and this would help Willie in his now feeble efforts to establish himself as a barrister. Her first petition failed in 1876 and she turned for support to T. H. Burke, the Undersecretary at Dublin Castle.[7] Burke tried hard to secure the pension. He had the form of application printed and sought support from persons of influence including the Duke of Leinster. Burke also asked Larcom to write to the Duke of Marlborough who might try to influence Disraeli. Not everybody responded positively to Burke's request for support. Charles Graves, Bishop of Limerick and an associate of Sir William's in the Royal Irish Academy, refused, saying 'I never admired Lady Wilde, and though I did much to help and support Sir William, I never quite liked him either. I tried to: but his intense vanity constantly threw me back.'[8]

Jane wrote directly to the Prime Minister, enclosing an obituary from the *Dublin University Magazine*. All she received was a letter of thanks from his secretary 'for the very interesting memoir'. For all his efforts, T. H. Burke was unsuccessful. He wrote to Larcom: 'If a Liberal Government was in, I think I would get her a pension – somehow or other these are larger-minded.'[9] It was to take almost fifteen years to secure a pension for Lady Wilde. In May 1890 she was eventually awarded a Civil List pension of £70 per annum, not for her own merits as a writer but based on Sir William's services to country, mostly for his work on the census.

Part 6

On the Cusp

'In order to get up to town I have always pretended to
have a younger brother of the name of Ernest, who
lives in the Albany and gets into the most dreadful
scrapes.'

The Importance of Being Earnest

25

The Aesthete

Three months after his father's death, Oscar was awarded a first in Classical Moderations at the end of his second term at Oxford. He came back to Dublin feeling 'an awful dread of going home to our old house, with everything filled with memories'.[1] Oscar planned to complete his father's unfinished memoir on *The Life of Gabriel Beranger*, an eighteenth-century antiquarian who had travelled through Ireland painting and describing the ruins. Instead, he began correcting proofs of Mahaffy's *Rambles and Studies in Greece* while staying with his former professor in his house on the Hill of Howth just north of Dublin. It would eventually fall to Jane to finish her husband's last project.

Oscar at this time was in the process of creating 'Oscar Wilde'. The raw materials included aestheticism, the decadent movement, art and religion, as well as his official Oxford course in *Literae Humaniares* known as the 'Greats'. He was drawn to the ideas of two scholars. The first was John Ruskin, the 55-year-old Slade Professor of Fine Art for whom morality played a part in a more restrained art at the expense of self-indulgent sensuality. Oscar was equally drawn to the arguments of Walter Pater, at thirty-five years old a fellow of Brasenose College, Oxford. Pater believed that one should seize the passing moments with a passion and fill them with as many pulsations as possible and thereby live a fulfilling life. His book *Studies in the History of the Renaissance* was seen in some conservative quarters as an endorsement of hedonism and amorality. Oscar, in *De Profundis*, described it as the 'book which has had such a strange influence over my life'.

Oscar was also involved in an internal struggle with his soul. More specifically he was struggling with the idea of converting to Roman Catholicism and was reading Thomas a Kempis' *Imitations of Christ*. Oscar's close friends at this time at Oxford were William Walsford Ward, known as 'Bouncer', Reginald Richard Harding, whose nickname was 'Kitten', and David Hunter Blair, called 'Dunskie'. 'Bouncer' and 'Kitten' were trying to get Oscar, known as 'Hosky', to see the reasonableness of Protestantism while Hunter Blair was strong in his efforts to persuade him to convert. Oscar took to hanging pictures of the Pope in his rooms. He also liked to host parties in the style of his mother's 'At Homes' but with a more constant flow of wine and gin. Oscar was also developing as a poet and through the intervention of his Catholic friends he began publishing regularly in the *Irish Monthly*, a Catholic journal edited by the Reverend Mathew Russell, SJ. He was also publishing in *Kottabos*, Professor Tyrell's magazine at Trinity College, and in the *Dublin University Magazine*. Oscar always liked to keep his options open.

During that first summer after the death of Sir William, Oscar came west to Moytura House with Frank Miles, a young portrait painter he had met at Oxford. In a letter written by Oscar to his friend Reginald Harding dated 16 August 1876, he says that he and Miles spent some time 'sailing . . . at the top of Lough Corrib . . . situated in the most romantic scenery in Ireland . . . On Friday we go into Connemara to a charming little fishing lodge we have in the mountains where I hope to make him land a salmon and kill a brace of grouse. I expect to have very good sport indeed this season.'[2] Frank Miles, who was two years older than Oscar, enjoyed his time at Illaunroe enough to paint some sunsets and was also moved to paint a fresco on an interior wall of the fishing lodge where it can still be seen today above an entrance archway facing the front door. The fresco shows two naked cherubs angling with high, misty mountains in the background. It bears the inscription 'Tight Lines', the fisherman's good luck cry. Oscar also worked on some paintings that summer, including a watercolour of the view from Moytura House.

Meanwhile, Lady Wilde was trying to come to terms with her new position as widow. In the year following her husband's death, with her eldest son showing more interest in the skating rink than the courtroom and Oscar away at Oxford, Jane once more took up her pen. She started work on Sir William's notes on Beranger and began sending sections of the memoir to the *Kilkenny Archaeological Journal* for publication. Jane eventually completed the project in 1880 and arranged to have the account published in book form. She then wrote an introduction for the book, lavishing praise on her late husband: 'Sir William Wilde was no visionary theorist – nor mere compiler from the labours of other men. His singularly penetrating intellect tested scrupulously everything that came before him, yet with such clear and rapid insight that nothing seemed laborious to his active and vivid intellect. His convictions were the product of calm rational investigation, and facts, not theories, always formed the basis of his teaching.' Jane also began to contribute poetry and articles to the *Dublin University Magazine* but the publication was going through a bad financial patch and could not afford to pay its contributors.

In Oxford Oscar had by now made something of a name for himself both inside and outside the university. His remark, probably inspired by two blue china Sèvres vases he had purchased with Hunter Blair, that he was finding it 'harder and harder every day to live up to my blue china' had already made him famous. A sermon was preached in Oxford against the 'form of heathenism' then gaining ground in the college. The magazine *Punch* would later pick up on it. 'Oscar Wilde the aesthete' was taking shape as he listened to Ruskin and read Pater. Oscar was also enjoying being a Freemason, having proceeded into the Apollo Rose-Croix Chapter. He loved the order's elaborate regalia and accessories such as the sword and scabbard as well as the accompanying ceremony. Hunter Blair had been a Mason but had to give it up when he converted to Catholicism. Oscar knew he too would have to resign if he converted and this was another good reason for remaining Protestant.

Hunter Blair decided to try once again to lure his Dublin friend away from Protestantism by inviting Oscar to join himself and William Walsford Ward in Rome for the spring vacation of 1877. He provided Oscar with £60 for the journey, supposedly won at Monte Carlo when a £2 bet was placed on Oscar's behalf. A divine sign if ever there was one. But Oscar typically decided to experience both 'Popery and Paganism'. He would visit Greece with Professor Mahaffy and his friends William Goulding and George Macmillan, the son of Alexander Macmillan, founder of the famous publishing house, before meeting up with Hunter Blair and 'Bouncer' Ward in Rome. Oscar and his companions travelled down through Italy and then across to Greece to explore the glories of the ancient world. They visited, among other places, Olympia, Athens and Mycenae, before Oscar left his Dublin group and sailed through a terrible storm to reach port at Naples. He then travelled on to join his Oxford friends in Rome. One is reminded of his father's heroic travels in this area a generation before.

Mahaffy was confident that he had saved his former student from the clutches of the Catholic Church. The remarkably persistent Hunter Blair, however, managed to arrange a private audience for himself and Oscar with Pope Pius IX. Oscar, left speechless for once in his life, locked himself in his room after the meeting and wrote a sonnet. But even this stirring experience failed to convert Oscar who shortly after took himself off to the Protestant cemetery and prostrated himself on the grass before the grave of Keats. The soul of Oscar Wilde would not be so easily won. When he returned to Oxford a month late for term after his travels in Italy and Greece, Oscar was shocked to be fined £47 and sent down (suspended) for the rest of term. A trip to Greece was not deemed to be sufficient reason, even for a student of the Classics, to be late for term. He was greatly annoyed and described the dean as an old woman in petticoats. His mother was likewise disgusted with Oxford's attitude to her son. But Oscar was to have some satisfaction the following year. On being awarded a First Class in the 'Honours Finals', it was agreed that his fine should be returned.

His expedition to the ancient world also contributed to his great success the following year when he won the prestigious Newdigate Prize with a poem called 'Ravenna', the first victory for Magdalen College since 1825. He had visited the Italian town on his journey to Greece and was able to turn the experience to his advantage on the page. Oscar was saluted all around and Jane wrote to congratulate her brilliant son, 'the Olympic Victor'.

> Oh, Gloria, Gloria! Thank you a million times for the telegram. It is the first pleasant throb of joy I have had this year. How I long to read the poem. Well, after all, we have Genius – that is something attorneys can't take away.
>
> Oh, I do hope you will have some joy in your heart. You have got honour and recognition – and this at only twenty-two is a grand thing. I am proud of you – and am happier than I can tell – This gives you a certainty of success in the future – You can now trust your own intellect, and know what it can do. I should so like to see the smile on your face now. Ever and ever with joy and pride, Your loving Mother.[3]

Returning to events at the time of his late return from Greece, the dejected student decided that if he was to be sent down for the term he might as well cheer himself up by visiting Frank Miles in London. Oscar decided to make an impression by ordering a spectacular coat cut in the shape of a cello. He wore this eccentric garment to the opening of the Grosvenor Gallery by Sir Coutts Lindsay where he rubbed shoulders with the Prince of Wales as well as Gladstone, Ruskin, Henry James and others. Oscar delighted in all the attention he received and was well able to match his outlandish appearance with lively conversation. He decided there and then to 'take up the critic's life'. An article on the opening of the gallery, his first published prose piece, appeared in the *Dublin University Magazine*.

This article made reference to a number of paintings including Guido Reni's St Sebastian, a favourite with homosexuals, to an 'open-mouthed St John' as well as works featuring 'Greek island boys'. All of these, he said, were examples of 'adolescent beauty'. Oscar sent a copy of the piece to Walter Pater in Oxford whose curiosity was obviously aroused as he wrote back immediately to thank the young man for sending such an 'excellent article' and inviting him to visit as soon as he returned to Oxford. Oscar had not yet met with the scholar who advocated an aesthetic philosophy where the cultivation of beauty and moments of sensation in life as well as in art was extolled. Pater was not free of controversy. A student called William Money Hardinge, who had attracted unfavourable attention as a result of outspoken homosexuality, had recently left Oxford to avoid further scandal involving an exchange of letters with Pater, some of which were signed 'Yours lovingly'. A friendship now developed between Oscar and Walter Pater, who was almost forty at this stage and whose written works tended to focus on male beauty, friendship and love. Pater was to exert an influence over the young Irishman who was at this stage working hard on developing a recognisable persona of his own.

After his week in London, Oscar came home to Merrion Square to reflect on his situation but was in for an unpleasant shock. On Saturday 9 June Oscar attended a dinner party given by his half-brother, Henry Wilson, now the senior surgeon at St Mark's Hospital. Henry had been out riding that afternoon and appeared to be in perfect health but later in the evening he began to feel unwell. By the following day his condition had deteriorated to the point where his life was in danger. To the great astonishment of his friends and despite the best efforts of his colleagues Henry died three days later on the evening of Wednesday 13 June 1877. The *Freeman's Journal* said he had been suddenly seized with rigour and inflammation of the lungs that then developed and spread rapidly to the heart. He had only just reached his fortieth year and was unmarried. His obituary in the *Irish Medical Journal* is revealing:

> As Dr Jacob and Sir William Wilde, who at that time, divided the ophthalmic and aural practice of Dublin were both growing old, the one by right of years, the other prematurely, and Mr Wilson had returned to Dublin with a knowledge of the ophthalmoscope, then but recently introduced, he very soon obtained some private practice, and might have secured more had he not been scrupulous to avoid any interference with Sir William Wilde's patients; and over and over again it happened that patients who had

left Sir William, were allowed by Henry Wilson to go to London for operations, when he might easily have retained them in his own hands, if he had not been so careful to avoid becoming Sir William's competitor.

The writer was obviously well informed and knew that Sir William had been losing patients for some time.

Henry Wilson's funeral, only a year after his father's, was attended by many of Dublin's leading citizens including the Lord Mayor. Willie and Oscar were the chief mourners and expected to be the main heirs. But the brothers were to be disappointed once again by a will. Henry left most of his money, £8,000, to St Mark's Ophthalmic Hospital. The bequest, according to an obituary in the *British Medical Journal*, was subject to a life interest intended for two unnamed female relatives. Was one of them his mother? Willie received £2,000 and Oscar was not forgotten. He got £100 and Wilson's half-share in the lodge at Illaunroe but only on condition that he would not become a Catholic within five years. Oscar wrote to his Oxford friend Reginald Harding complaining that 'My brother and I were always supposed to be heirs but his will was an unpleasant surprise, like most wills ... He was, poor fellow, bigotedly intolerant of the Catholics and seeing me "on the brink" struck me out of his will. It is a terrible disappointment to me; you see I suffer a good deal from my Romish leanings, in pocket and mind ... Fancy a good man going before "God and the Eternal Silences" with his wretched Protestant prejudices and bigotry clinging still to him.'[4]

Oscar needed money to finance his increasingly extravagant lifestyle and the few pounds of rent from Bray would not suffice. He continued to write poems and have them published in various journals but this could not form the basis of a career with an income. But he also continued to be concerned about religious matters once back at Oxford. Troubled, he went to London to see the Reverend Sebastian Bowden, well known for his numerous conversions among the English upper classes. The priest spoke to Oscar of 'escape from your present unhappy self' by converting to Rome and warned him against 'bad influences mental and moral' and against becoming corrupt through 'positive sin'.[5] Positive sin is a euphemism for sexual activity. It was decided. Oscar was to be received into the Catholic Church. But when the appointed day arrived he failed to appear. Instead, a package arrived and when opened it was found to contain a bunch of lilies.

Oscar Wilde was now constantly constructing and reinventing himself at Oxford. His ingredients were much the same as before and included religion, aestheticism, Greece and Rome, Freemasonry and conduct. A fluctuating sexuality would also be added to the fitful mix. This did not impede his studies and in June 1878 he achieved a rare double first in his final examinations. Oscar now had only to pass his divinity examination to take his degree. No fellowship was offered, however, so his career path was still unclear.

Oscar needed money and decided to sell the four houses at Esplanade Terrace, Bray, but the sale was complicated when two different selling agents found clients for the properties. One of the purchasers sued and the case was heard in July 1878. By the time legal fees and the mortgages were paid there was little left. To add to his woes he was greatly upset to hear that his old flame in Dublin, Florence Balcombe, had become engaged to Bram Stoker who had accepted a position as business manager of the Lyceum Theatre, only recently taken over by Henry Irving. Florence had an ambition to act and eventually took to the boards at the Lyceum two years later.

Oscar passed his divinity examination and was conferred with his Bachelor of Arts Degree on 22 November 1878. He was unhappy having to leave his beloved Oxford behind and would continue to return as often as possible. Facing an uncertain future, he set out for London where he used the monies from the Bray sales to set up in bachelor quarters with Frank Miles. Oscar named his new three-story rambling abode at 13 Salisbury Street 'Thames House' for its view of the river. Here, just off the Strand, he would begin the task of creating 'Oscar Wilde' the Oxford graduate. Personal qualities he had inherited, such as his mother's grandiosity and his father's charm and his ability to make important friends, would now stand him in good stead but Oscar knew he would need more than a handful of published poems and a fresh buttonhole if he were to make it in the Empire's capital.

The house at 13 Salisbury Street soon attracted some interesting guests. Lillie Langtry appeared on the scene and her beauty had the men swooning. Edward, Prince of Wales announced he would not attend a party unless 'The Jersey Lily' was a guest. Soon, with help from Oscar and his friends, Lillie Langtry would be reborn and accepted as an actress despite having to withdraw for a period to have a baby daughter she discreetly left behind in Jersey. The circle expanded to include actress friends such as Ellen Terry and then Sarah Bernhardt. Now Oscar knew what he wanted to do. How wonderful it would be to hear a great actress deliver lines he had written from the stage. In September 1880 Oscar presented Ellen Terry with a red leather-bound volume bearing her own name in gold letters. It was a copy of his first play *Vera; or, The Nihilists*. Set in Moscow, the plot involved the killing of the cruel and despotic Czar. Oscar, adding politics to his list of concerns, declared himself to be a socialist.

He now had an answer for those who wondered if Oscar Wilde could actually do something other than speak wittily and be seen about town. Ellen Terry thanked him politely for the beautiful book, but the play did not live up to the quality of its binding. Henry Irving who received his own copy also sent his thanks but neither actress nor manager made any concrete offers. Hermann Vezin, an American-born actor working in England, also received a copy. Vezin was one of W. S. Gilbert's favourite actors and was also a teacher of elocution. He did not make an offer for the new play but would later coach Oscar before he set out on his lecture tour of America some years later. Nothing definite came of this first attempt to get a play noticed. But it was still early days for Oscar Wilde.

26

Leaving Dublin

Willie was living with his mother at 1 Merrion Square and struggling to make his way as a barrister. His main plan now was to find and marry a wealthy woman and then live the easy life. Although Willie could be charming and had many liaisons, he was finding it difficult to locate a woman of wealth who would agree to marry and support a man whose real love was for the good life. Willie was also writing. Several of his poems appeared in the Trinity College magazine *Kottabos* and he had begun contributing pieces to the *World*, a London society journal. In a letter to Margaret Campbell, one of his many lady friends, he spoke of the 'strong poems' he would like to send her and told her that 'I want you to know me as a poet'.[1] Even at this early stage the elder brother was sensing the presence of his younger sibling's shadow. Jane, too, took up the pen around this time to write a pamphlet called *The American Irish* in which she saw a future generation of Irish Americans playing a role in challenging 'the degraded position Ireland holds in Europe'. It was to be her final tirade as Speranza.

With the £2,000 he had received from Henry Wilson's estate dwindling rapidly and his legal career in the doldrums, Willie began to tire of Dublin and perhaps Dublin was also beginning to tire of Willie. Jane wrote to Oscar saying that his brother had decided if no briefs came in he would 'throw it all up . . . and he and I will try London'. This would be a drastic step and an unthinkable one if Sir

William was still alive. Jane would undoubtedly find it hard at her age to leave her fine Dublin mansion for an uncertain future in rented accommodation in a city where she was virtually unknown. But Sir William was not alive and circumstances had radically altered. Jane now began to convince herself that Dublin was really a backwater and that her two fine sons needed 'the focus of light, progress and intellect'[2] offered by London. Anyway, financially there was little choice. Willie's idea of finding a rich wife or one who at least could bring in briefs was nothing more than wishful thinking in a city as insular as Dublin.

Willie encountered a pretty seventeen-year-old as they were crossing to England and such was his charm that by the time they reached London the pair were engaged to be married. The girl was puzzled by his request to keep the engagement a secret for the moment although he did present her with a ring. The engagement lasted all of three weeks and Willie, assuming the role of munificent Irish gentleman, allowed her to keep the ring. The short-lived courtship is even more extraordinary because the girl in question was Ethel Smyth, who went on to become the first important female composer in Britain. She claimed she was charmed by his penchant for making up entirely new endings for Chopin preludes.[3] The brief relationship was to be Miss Smythe's first and last engagement. She had a preference for women and would later have affairs with the Princess de Polignac, formerly Winnaretta Singer, the American musical patron and heir to the Singer sewing machine fortune, and also with Emmeline Pankhurst, the British suffragette. Ethel herself also became an active suffragette and served some time in prison for the cause. She came to further prominence when in her seventies she very publically sexually pursued Virginia Woolf.

Eventually, in the spring of 1879, the decision to leave Dublin once and for all was taken. 'We have done with Dublin,' Jane wrote to Oscar. 'This is what is now in my head. What profit or respect has a man here? Times is hard.'[4] The house on Merrion Square was bought by a Dr O'Leary, an acquaintance of the old family friend Professor Mahaffy, for £3,500. Willie went on ahead to search for appropriate lodgings and Jane wrote to Oscar telling of the situation:

Willie in London, looking after rooms and lodgings, but all are so dear! I think a house would be quite beyond us involving two servants. Perhaps we could get the upper part of a house over a ware room, and we could furnish. But it is certain we quit Dublin even if we go into furnished lodgings in London, which can be had at any moment, and let off everything here. Willie has got good openings with the press. The editor of the *Athanaeum* wants him ... He says he wants young men, that everyone is tired of the old stagers. Willie has dined with Yeats and he has had a meeting with the editor of the *Morning Advertiser* ... says Willie could make £1,200 a year in London by press work. I think after all, Willie is more suited for it than anything else.[5]

Jane painted a prettier picture in a letter to her Swedish friend Mrs Olivecrona: 'We have arranged to leave Ireland, and this is my last note from the old family mansion in Merrion Square. Both my sons prefer residing in London ... and we have taken a house there, and disposed of this on very good terms. It belongs to my son and he gets £3,500 for it. I may hope to see you in London which is a much more attractive place than Dublin to foreigners.'[6] However, time passed and there still was no definite word from Willie in London. An alarmed Jane wrote to Oscar signing herself 'La Madre Desolata' and complaining that Willie 'writes seldom – we have only eight weeks more in this house and not an idea where to lay our heads'. Yet even in the midst of her distress she could quickly change tone and pass on to mention some trivial items of gossip or news of acquaintances.

Willie eventually wrote with news of lodgings in Ovington Square, Chelsea – not then a fashionable address. He also mentioned the possibility of marriage, which left Jane in a tizzy of indecision. In the end Willie's marriage plans once again came to nothing and in May 1879 Jane left Dublin, the city where her carriage was once cheered in the streets, for a new address and a new life at 1 Ovington Square. She would live there with Willie and a female Irish servant. The brave Lady Wilde was fifty-eight years of age.

27

Literary London

By the time Lady Wilde moved to London her son Oscar was a minor celebrity and in a position to introduce his mother into the capital's literary and artistic circles. After a year in London she felt confident enough to begin hosting a Saturday afternoon salon along the lines of her Merrion Square 'At Homes'. Oscar made a point of telling his acquaintants to visit as they were sure to meet some interesting company. Jane's 'At Homes' were to last for fifteen years and attracted many famous people, including W. B. Yeats, George Moore and George Bernard Shaw. Many other young Irish writers trying to find their feet in London appreciated the opportunity to mingle with some of the city's leading lights. Visiting Americans such as Henry Ward Beecher, the famous opponent of slavery, and Oliver Wendell Holmes also found there way to the salon, as did Eleanor Marx, daughter of Karl. Numerous accounts exist of Jane and her salon and some of them are most unkind. But many of those descriptions appeared in biographies in the early twentieth century when anything associated with the Wilde name was treated with hostility, hence the derogatory tone sometimes found in the reports.

Lady Wilde's 'At Homes' were conducted, as before, by candle-light with the drapes closed. This was in part to create atmosphere but also to conceal the dingy rooms and furnishings and the fact that the large hostess skilfully making her rounds was no longer young. Lady Wilde's style of dress also attracted comment. What was accepted in Dublin as eccentricity was often sneered at in London. As the years passed Jane continued to dress in gowns she had once worn to Castle functions in the long-gone glory days of the 1860s. Perhaps she wore her old clothes for sentimental reasons, but even if she had the desire to update her wardrobe she did not now posess the means. One account describes how 'She seemed to wear two dresses. They were covered over with flounces in an entirely departed style, huge bodices with vast trimmings, draperies, caps, ribbons on her head – and her favourite colour seemed to me mauve.'[1] Another guest describes Jane in 'a low-cut lavender-coloured silk dress over a crinoline, with a piece of crimson velvet about a foot deep round the skirt and a miniature, some six inches by four, pinned on her breast . . . Her hair was dressed in ringlets, surmounted by a high head-dress of lace and hanging loosely round her waist was a Roman scarf which was bright green, with stripes of scarlet, blue and yellow.'[2]

In the winter of 1881 Jane and Willie moved to the more upmarket 116 Park Street in the West End. The house was tiny and just one door away from a corner pub but it was more accessible for her salon guests. Oscar and Frank Miles had also moved from Salisbury Street and were living close by in Tite Street. The 1881 census lists Miles as head of the household and describes Oscar as a 'boarder'. It was Oscar, however, who renamed the building 'Keats House'. Among the many society guests visiting 'Keats House' was the Prince of Wales, probably because his then mistress Lillie Langtry was a regular guest. The Prince had made a point of meeting the young man from Ireland who was rapidly becoming a sensation in fashionable London circles. He was quoted in *Harper's Bazaar* as having said 'I do not know Mr Wilde, and not to know Mr Wilde is not to be known.'[3] Oscar's other friends at this point included Rennell Rodd, whom he knew from Oxford, and the famous painter James McNeill Whistler. Oscar and Rodd took trips together to Belgium in 1879 and the Loire Valley in 1881. Oscar was for a time made welcome at Whistler's studio and the witty pair enjoyed the rivalry of each other's clever conversation. But Whistler, who could be vain, egotistical and sharp, did not make lifelong friendships.

While Oscar was rubbing shoulders with the great and the good of London society his mother was experiencing real poverty for the first time in her life. Jane's major problem was that she had no regular source of income. Trouble in Ireland meant that the meagre rents from Moytura went unpaid so Lady Wilde began to look at the possibility of earning some income from her pen. After she had completed the memoir of Gabriel Beranger she began to write regular articles for the *Burlington Magazine*. A two-part article in the summer of 1881 was actually called 'The Laws of Dress', this from a woman who had scant regard for the rules herself. Jane also wrote for the *Pall Mall Gazette* and the weekly magazine *Queen* but the scattered earnings from occasional pieces were insufficient and Willie was not contributing in any way to the paltry family coffers.

An American widow, Anne, Comtesse de Brémont, provides an interesting account of Jane and her circumstances at this time. She describes arriving in London with a letter of introduction to Lady Wilde and making her way to Park Lane where she was surprised to find her living in so simple an abode. She raised the rusty knocker and the door was immediately opened by an Irish servant with 'a delicious brogue'. She was led through a long dark hall to a 'large low-ceiled panelled room dimly illuminated by red-shaded candles' and into the presence of Lady Wilde waiting in the shadowy interior. The Comtesse describes 'the old-fashioned gown, the towering head-dress of velvet, the long gold ear-rings . . . the yellow lace fichu crossed on her breast and fastened with innumerable enormous brooches – the huge bracelets of turquoise and gold, the rings on every finger! Her faded splendour was more striking than the most fashionable attire for she wore that ancient finery with a grace and dignity that robbed it of its grotesqueness.' Jane appeared quite unconscious of 'the dowdy maid, the poorly furnished room, the badly served tea, the dust and dinginess, the flickering candles'.[4]

Willie, meanwhile, had by now put any thoughts of making a success of it in the legal profession well behind him. But there were plenty of opportunities in London for good journalists and Willie had more than a little talent in this area. Writing came effortlessly to him but he was easy-going, lacked any sense of responsibility and did not have his father's drive. He lived with his mother but was absent for much of the time and even though it was obvious that Jane could do with some financial support from a son who was now approaching thirty years of age, Willie would never become a provider.

Willie Wilde did eventually break into journalism and for a time during those early years in London his prospects looked reasonably good. He produced excellent work for the *World* and this led to further offers. He became drama critic for *Punch*, *Gentlewoman* and *Vanity Fair* and his short stories, a popular and relatively lucrative genre in those days, appeared with Oscar's in *Blackwood's* and *Lippincott's Monthly Magazine*. When the *Daily Telegraph* offered Willie the job of chief correspondent and leader writer his mother was delighted. Perhaps now there would be a steady income to ease her worries.

Willie's life, however, revolved around the Café Royal, the Spoofs Club and other drinking clubs and all-night venues. With his black moustache and pointed beard he was a charmer and a ladies' man but could become devious if short of money. He was not above borrowing from friends or filling his pockets with free cigars at receptions. Instead of demanding money for his keep Jane indulged him as one would a spoilt child. Willie had talent – some believed he was every bit as clever as Oscar – but talent without effort is of little use. 'He established himself among the kind of company which made a point of honour not to go to bed on the same day they got up'.[5] At the Owls Club, Willie was once asked to come up with a couplet as a motto for the club. Instantly, he wrote:

> We fly by night, and this resolve we make,
> If the dawn must break, let the damned thing break.

Willie's approach to his work at the *Daily Telegraph* was casual in the extreme. He never appeared in the office before noon when the editor would ask if he had an idea. With his idea accepted he would be off again. According to his own – no doubt embellished – description:

> I may then eat a few oysters and drink half a bottle of Chablis at Sweeting's, or, alternatively, partake in a light lunch at this admirable club . . . I then stroll towards the Park. I bow to the fashionables. I am seen along incomparable Piccadilly. It is grand . . . I repair to my club. I order out my ink and paper. I go to my room. I am undisturbed for an hour. My pen moves. Ideas flow . . . Three great, meaty solid paragraphs, each one-third of a column – that is the consummation to be wished . . . Suddenly someone knocks at the door . . . it is an old friend. We are to eat a little dinner at the Café Royal and drop into the Alhambra for the new ballet.

With his copy sent off to the paper by messenger Willie and his friends make off to partake in 'that paradise of cigar-ashes, bottles, corks, ballet, and those countless circumstances of gaiety and relaxation, known only to those who are indwellers in the magic circles of London's literary Bohemia'.[6]

At this stage the two brothers were still good friends. They would eventually quarrel when Oscar learned that his older brother had been taking money from his mother, money Oscar had given her. The two brothers moved in different circles but, at this time, were glad to see each other when their paths crossed. Jane was anxious they remain on good terms and when their disagreements eventually came to a head she constantly pleaded with Oscar to make it up with his elder brother.

Willie could be charming and was a brilliant conversationalist. But he was not always liked as a person. The famous essayist Max Beerbohm certainly had little time for the man. 'Quel monster!' he wrote. 'Dark, oily, suspect yet awfully like Oscar: he has Oscar's coy, carnal smile and fatuous giggle and not a little of Oscar's esprit. But he is awful – a veritable tragedy of family likeness!'[7] Otho Lloyd, brother of Constance, Oscar's future wife, also felt something unpleasant and artificial in his personality. Willie managed to stumble along for a number of years but by the spring of 1883 an exasperated Jane was writing to Oscar in Paris how 'as to Willie I give him up – his debts are now about £2,000 ... I am very stupid and sick and dull and weary.'[8]

28

The First Collection

Even though her life was plagued by financial worry Lady Wilde still managed to enjoy certain London delights such the magnificent Grosvenor Gallery, built to resemble a Venetian palace, the place where Oscar had made his London debut after being sent down from Oxford. The traditional Royal Academy had dominated painting up to this time but now the Grosvenor offered an exciting alternative. People could appreciate new schools of painting and Lady Wilde greatly enjoyed the Pre-Raphaelites, especially Rossetti. The circulating libraries were also popular at this time and a regular visit to Maudie's in New Oxford Street was a must for fashionable society. Jane had many books of her own, having brought a large quantity with her from Merrion Square. Sadly, Sir William's own library had been auctioned off before she left Dublin.

Jane took great pleasure in observing Oscar's entry into London's fashionable society. By 1880 he had established himself as an attraction with his witty epigrams and his shocking opinions. He also knew how to get noticed, dressing outrageously and making ostentatious gestures. He deliberately mixed in the proper circles and made a point of being seen at first nights. Characters closely resembling Oscar and his companions Whistler and Frank Miles began to appear in humorous sketches and burlesques. A number of plays were staged, all featuring aesthetes with Oscar's obvious mannerisms. Oscar was not always charmed by the depictions but understood that all publicity was good publicity. His fame, or notoriety, further increased when *Punch* began regularly poking fun at him and his aesthetic stance through a series of caricatures. But it was time to show the world that there was more to Oscar Wilde than a pose with a bunch of lilies or a sunflower.

In April 1881 Oscar's friend from Oxford, Rennell Rodd, published a collection of poems with David Bogue, a minor publishing house. This prompted Oscar to send a letter to the same publishers that May:

> I am anxious to publish a volume of poems immediately, and should like to enter into a treaty with your house about it. I can forward you the manuscript on hearing that you will begin negotiations. Possibly my name requires no introduction.
>
> Yours truly,
> Oscar Wilde[1]

Oscar's first book, *Poems*, appeared soon after in the summer of 1881.

The collection was an attempt to explore a nature divided. Oscar was all too aware of his own conflicting desires and impulses, such as his constant oscillating between Catholicism and aestheticism, between Ancient Greece and the Rome of Pius IX. It is also unclear how far Oscar had as yet progressed in exploring the conflicts he must have been experiencing between his homosexuality and his attempts to live a heterosexual life. He appears to have been genuinely wounded by the collapse of his relationship with Florence Balcombe in Dublin and more recent friendships included an interest in Violet Hunt, daughter of painter Alfred Hunt and novelist Margaret Hunt. There were some positive reviews of the collection but it was also controversial and received harsh criticism. Oscar was accused of plagiarism, of insincerity, even of indecency. One poem, 'Charmides', has a young man sexually caressing, possibly even attempting to ravish, the polished marble statue of a naked Athena. Conservative English readers would have found this shocking.

Canon Robert Miles, the Canon at Bingham in Nottinghamshire and father of Oscar's housemate Frank, wrote to Oscar telling him the book was 'licentious and may do a great harm to any soul that reads it'.[2] The Canon's wife had also found one poem, presumably 'Charmides', 'painful and dangerous'. Oscar, the Canon continued, had departed from 'Revealed Truth' and his verse was anti-Christian. As a father he had to think of his own son's good name and was advising a separation for a time. Frank Miles told Oscar he had no choice but to obey as he was financially dependent upon his father. Oscar was incensed. He was being judged morally unworthy by a man whose son had brought the police to the door just a short time before because of his predilection for very young girls. Oscar saved Miles that time by telling the police that he was away on the Continent when he was in reality escaping over the rooftops. Miles' fondness for underage girls was a strange counterpoint to his friendship with Lord Ronald Gower, well known among the homosexual community, who regularly had him to stay at his Windsor house. Oscar flew into a rage and told Miles he would never speak to him again. He then hurriedly packed a trunk with some clothes and tipped it over the banister smashing a valuable antique table below. He called a cab and left the house never to return. Their friendship ended that night.

Frank Miles' subsequent life was short and unhappy. He was committed to Brislington Asylum near Bristol in 1887 and died there four years later from what was diagnosed as 'general paralysis of the insane'.

Oscar was now in desperate need of money. His poetry may have stirred the emotions and caused trouble but it was not profitable. The new author had to mortgage his hunting lodge at Illaunroe and try to hang on until a forthcoming production of his play *Vera* entered rehearsal stage. He rented two rooms on the third floor of 9 Charles Street – present-day Carlos Place – off Grosvenor Square and started work on what would become *The Duchess of Padua*. He had been living with his mother since leaving Tite Street in a huff. Then, out of the blue, a cablegram arrived at Jane's house. It was for Oscar and had come from New York. Good news at last. The cablegram was from an agent enquiring if Oscar Wilde would consider an offer to give fifty readings in the United States beginning in November. Oscar replied the following day: 'Yes, if the offer is good.'

Oscar's expenses would be covered and he would receive an equal share of the profits of the readings. Other details were discussed and some more time was needed to prepare for the tour. Eventually, all was settled to everyone's satisfaction. The proposed production of *Vera*, meanwhile, was cancelled, probably for political reasons as it dealt with issues such as anarchism and the murder of a head of state.

On Christmas Eve 1881 Oscar departed for the America on board the SS *Arizona*, arriving in New York harbour on the evening of 2 January. The waiting reporters were wild with excitement and Oscar did not disappoint them. He appeared wearing a long green coat and a round cap of seal or otter skin. Disembarking the following day he told the reporters who were hanging on his every word that he had come 'to diffuse beauty'. He declined, however, to give a definition of aestheticism, the philosophy he was there to expound.

It was when passing through customs that Oscar is supposed to have uttered one of his most famous remarks. Replying to the question 'Have you anything to declare?' his immediate retort was 'I have nothing to declare except my genius.' The remark went unrecorded at the time so there is no solid proof that it was ever actually said. Nevertheless, it sounds very much like Oscar and is exactly the kind of quip he would have at the ready for such an occasion. So began what would turn out to be a full year of lecturing, touring and entertaining across the United States. He would be both praised and pilloried in the press on both sides of the Atlantic but at the end of the year the name of Oscar Wilde was known all over the world.

The initial plan was to bring Oscar over to promote *Patience*, the new comic opera by Gilbert and Sullivan that was to run at the Standard Theatre, New York. The operetta, which satirises the aesthetic movement, had been a great success in London but it was felt that American audiences might not be so familiar with the movement or its disciples. The main character in the opera is Bunthorne, a 'Fleshly Poet', who people mistakenly believed was a parody on Oscar Wilde but was actually an amalgamation of well known aesthetes such as Rossetti and Swinburne with Wilde and his friend Whistler also evident. Impresario Richard D'Oyly Carte thought it would be a good idea to have Oscar come over to deliver a series of lectures as a spokesperson for aestheticism. With his flamboyant ways he would surely build up the box office for *Patience*. This concept quickly grew into a series of nationwide engagements that brought Oscar all over the United States and into Canada.

Oscar delivered his first lecture on 'The English Renaissance' at the Chickering Hall, New York, on 9 January 1882. He immediately realised that adjustments would be required in both content and delivery. Editing resulted in two separate lectures, 'The Decorative Arts' and 'The House Beautiful', both later adjusted to have an even broader appeal. As with any long tour there were occasional difficulties and the press soon discovered that ridicule made better copy than praise. Of course it was easy to ridicule a man given to wearing knee breeches and silk stockings at the lectern.

Oscar was surprised to discover that being the son of Speranza gave him an advantage among the Irish-American constituency. He did not like to overemphasise the difference between being born in Ireland or in England and had made a conscious effort to lose his Irish accent. Nevertheless, he remained enough of an Irishman to believe in the country's right to her independence and quickly learned when to play the Irish card. Among the personal highlights of his tour was a meeting with an ageing Walt Whitman where the pair drank home-made elderberry wine, discussed poetry and became friends. They would meet once more before Oscar returned home. He had a less successful meeting with Henry James, who found his style of dress and mannerisms distasteful. Perhaps James detected Oscar's homosexual tendencies and found that alarming. Henry James always kept his own homosexuality well out of sight.

As Oscar criss-crossed America, Jane revelled in all the newspaper publicity her son was receiving at home in England and was pleased to hear that people both in London and Dublin were discussing the vast amount of money they assumed he was earning. She wrote to Oscar every week. Whatever about her son's supposed earnings, the reality was that Jane was still very short of money. Oscar was eventually able to send back £80, enough to pay his overdue accounts and still have some left over for his impoverished mother. Jane was delighted with any crumbs and sent him a long list of paid bills. She told him that such a 'large overplus' would allow her to stay on in Park Street at least for the winter 'and then see what fate brings'. 'It is dreadful taking your money,' she wrote. 'Destiny does such very ill-natured things, whenever one member of a family works hard and gets any money immediately all the relations fling themselves on his shoulders.' Willie had not been home for several days, Jane complained, and she did not know where he was. She would, however, give him the money Oscar had sent him. The contrast between Oscar's life in America with his black manservant and fancy hotels and that of his mother and brother back in London can be seen in Jane's delight at being able to pay Willie's laundry bill with Oscar's money. This, she said in her letter, was 'a great matter to have off our minds'.[3]

After finishing his last engagement Oscar decided to stay on in New York for a couple of months to attend to some unfinished business. He wanted to get his play *Vera* staged and to explore possibilities for his new work *The Duchess of Padua*. He was also ill for a time with malaria but perhaps the principal reason for his delayed return was the impending arrival in town of Lillie Langtry. When her ship docked in late October, Oscar was there to theatrically present the famous actress with an armful of lilies. He also organised the American publication of his friend Rennell Rodd's collection of poems. In doing so, however, he overstepped the mark by writing a preface to the collection and including a dedication that read: 'To Oscar Wilde, "Heart's Brother" – These few songs and many songs to come.' It made Rodd look like a 'disciple' of the sexually ambivalent Wilde. The preface also mentioned their visits to the Continent together, not good for Rodd's fledgling career with the Foreign Office. Another friendship was over.

By the end of December Oscar, now an established celebrity, was back in London sporting a red suit and with tall tales of his American adventures. But Oscar could not settle in London after the excitement of his year on the other side of the 'disappointing' Atlantic. He needed further stimulation and knew just where to go to find it. Before January 1883 was out he was ensconced in a suite on the second floor of the Hotel Voltaire looking out on the River Seine from the Left Bank. Decadent Paris would welcome him in ways the less complicated America could not.

29

A Proposal

Oscar was not long in Paris when he met a young man by the name of Robert Sherard. He was a great-grandson of Wordsworth and trying to succeed as a writer and journalist. His father was the Reverend Bennet Sherard Calcraft Kennedy, the illegitimate son of the 6th Earl of Harborough and Jane Stanley Wordsworth, granddaughter of the poet. He had fallen out with his father after being sent down from Oxford in 1880 and had stopped using his last names. Oscar found him an interesting fellow, his blond hair and his youth being potent assets, and after an initial coolness the pair became firm friends. They went about the city together, dining in the Café de Paris and visiting Les Folies-Bergère. Gradually the young writer found himself succumbing to Oscar's charming spells.

Robert Sherard published his first novel, *A Bartered Honour*, in 1883. This was followed a year later by a collection of poems, *Whispers*, which he dedicated to Oscar. Their friendship was particularly intense at this time but Sherard was heterosexual and appears to have never fully understood or come to terms with Oscar's homosexual leanings. Sherard would prove a loyal friend to Oscar during his trial and imprisonment but their friendship eventually faltered due to Wilde's homosexual activities following his release from prison. At this early stage, however, Oscar appears to have been still 'undecided' – as Henry Adams' wife had remarked in America – about his sexual preferences. He spent a night with a well-known

Parisian prostitute he met at the Eden Music Hall but was rather more disgusted than charmed with the event, reflecting that people were 'as beasts'. Later, at a reception in the home of Victor Hugo, he ignored the advances of a Polish princess, preferring instead to discuss literature. It was around this time he wrote 'The Harlot's House', a fantastical poem peopled with frightening, shadowy characters dancing in a house of lust until the 'dawn, with silver-sandalled feet' comes creeping 'down the long and silent street . . . like a frightened girl'.

Oscar's stay in Paris was fruitful. He spoke with many of the great writers including Zola, Hugo, Paul Verlaine and painters such as Degas and Pissarro. He worked on 'The Sphinx' but most importantly he managed to complete *The Duchess of Padua*,[1] a play exploring the idea of forgiveness for the helpless casualty of a passion that is immoral but cannot be ignored. Unfortunately, plans he had made while in America to have the play staged came to naught at this time. However, rehearsals for a production of *Vera* were to commence in the autumn. On returning to London and once more low in funds, Oscar had to move in for a time with his mother at Park Street. Even more aware now of the limitations of the aesthete, Oscar knew he needed to assemble a new guise. Marriage was one possibility.

Oscar found men sexually attractive, particularly young men, but it is difficult to say with certainty if he had allowed himself to experience sexual relations with a man up to this point. He had certainly been moving in the right circles had he wished to do so. On the other hand, it is known that he occasionally slept with women. And there was his serious courtship of Florence Balcombe back in Dublin. He also proposed to two other women in 1880 or 1881: Violet Hunt, who later lived with Ford Madox Ford and went on to be a novelist herself, and Charlotte Montefiore. Both ladies refused. Maybe they suspected his motives given his uncertain financial circumstances? Or perhaps they detected something about his sexuality in his manner – Oscar the flamboyant dandy, Oscar the effeminate aesthete?

Surely his homosexuality was obvious to anyone who cared to look, but this after all was Victorian England. Alan Sinfield puts forward a plausible explanation as to why even a number of his close friends did not believe the charges that eventually brought him to ruin. People, he argues, 'did not recognise Wilde as a homosexual because they didn't know what that unnamed creature looked like. They didn't know, as we do, that he looked like Oscar Wilde'.[2] But some quarters did know or at least suspect. *Punch* called him a 'Mary-Ann' while Courtenay Bodley wrote in the *New York Times* how Wilde had lost out on a chance for a fellowship at Oxford because he assumed 'a guise which sturdier minds still look upon as epicene'.

Shortly after returning from Paris, Oscar decided to make contact with a lady friend he had first met two years before when he went with his mother to visit a family they had once known in Dublin. He had taken note of this pretty young woman at that time and Jane invited her to attend one of her Saturday 'At Homes'. Oscar was subsequently invited to tea at her home and the pair struck up a regular friendship, something that was encouraged by other family members. She liked Oscar as did her brother who remembered him from his own Oxford days. Back now in London from his famous travels Oscar once again made contact, inviting her to come to his mother's house. The girl's name was Constance Lloyd.

Constance lived with her grandfather, John Horatio Lloyd, QC, and her aunt, Emily Lloyd, in a large house at 100 Lancaster Gate. Her father had died in 1874 and her mother remarried. Her relationship with her mother had been strained since childhood so she chose instead to live with her ageing grandfather. She was tall, slim and good looking with long dark, wavy hair. She was intelligent, shy but not reticent, liked music and the arts and had a practical mind. Constance was kind and loving by nature and Jane, from the start, saw her as the perfect daughter-in-law. During the spring and into the summer of 1883 Oscar and Constance met regularly, usually with her brother Otho or Lady Wilde present as chaperone. It was becoming clear that an attachment was forming but Oscar's finances were in a dilapidated state. He had even borrowed £1,200 from a moneylender to keep going. Something needed to be done.

Oscar contacted his lecture manager from the United States, a Colonel Morse who happened to be in London on business at the time. They arranged a lecture tour of the British Isles. He would speak on 'The House Beautiful' and 'Personal Impressions of America'. Oscar had earned almost £6,000 (over £490,000/€550,000 today) after expenses from his American adventure but that, of course, was all gone. His English series, paying between ten and twenty-five guineas per talk, would not match that sum. Nevertheless, pleased to have any income at all, he began a series of lectures up and down the country.

In the meantime, his play *Vera* finally opened in New York on 20 August 1883. Oscar was present, having crossed over on the SS *Britannic*. The reviews, however, were not complimentary, and Oscar himself had reservations about Marie Prescott in the title role. Attendances dropped and the play was withdrawn on 28 August, much to Oscar's disappointment. *Punch*, ever ready with the jibe, ran a drawing of a tearful Oscar with his head resting on his brother's large shoulder for comfort. With *Vera* failing, Oscar had no choice but to return home and commence once more delivering lectures in any venue that would have him. At least he could continue his relationship with Constance, to whom he was drawing ever closer.

Oscar was booked to give two lectures in Dublin, on 22 and 24 November. Constance was also in Dublin at the time visiting with her grandmother who lived in Ely Place. Constance attended both lectures and Oscar came to tea. On Sunday 25 November the couple found themselves sitting together in the drawing room at 1 Ely Place enjoying a rare moment alone. Constance knew that this was the same room where, a generation before, her father had proposed to her mother. It must have been a place favoured by Cupid for, to her great delight, Constance received her proposal from Oscar that very afternoon. 'Prepare yourself for an astonishing piece of news!' she wrote to her brother Otho. 'I am engaged to Oscar Wilde and perfectly and insanely happy.'[3]

Part 7

Conquests

"'Culture and corruption," echoed Dorian, "I have known something of both.'"

The Picture of Dorian Gray

30

The House Beautiful

Lady Jane Wilde was delighted at Oscar's engagement to Constance Lloyd. A rich wife for one or both of her sons had always been her simple solution to their financial problems and Constance's grandfather John Lloyd was certainly wealthy. She wrote to congratulate Oscar on 27 November:

> I am intensely pleased at your note of this morning – You have both been true and constant and a blessing will come on all true feeling. But one feels very anxious . . . it always seems so hard for two lovers to get married. But I have hope all will end well. Willie is greatly pleased, but says he feels so old and venerable – quite shelved by 'the young people'. What endless vistas of speculation open out? What will you do in life? Where live? Meantime you must go on with your work. I enclose another offer for lectures. I would like you to have a small house in London and live the literary life and teach Constance to correct proofs and eventually go into parliament. May the Divine Intelligence that rules the world give you happiness and peace and joy in your beloved. La Madre.[1]

Jane's letter touched upon some very pertinent issues. Oscar had no choice other than to continue earning a living by travelling the country delivering lectures. The two lovers snatched a little time together whenever he returned to London but Constance wept at his every departure. She loved him truly as can be seen from her surviving letters. She calls him 'my hero and my god' and tells him that he must read her heart 'and not my outward semblance if you wish to know how passionately I worship and love you'.[2] Oscar was also in love, as can be seen from a letter postmarked 16 December 1884, some months after their marriage, and written from Edinburgh: 'Dear and Beloved, Here I am, and you at the Antipodes. O execrable facts, that keep our lips from kissing, though our souls are one . . . I feel your fingers in my hair, and your cheek brushing mine . . . my soul and body seem no longer mine, but mingled in some exquisite ecstasy with yours. I feel incomplete without you. Ever and ever yours.'[3] It is the only letter from Oscar to his wife to have survived and shows how very close they were, at least in the early years of their marriage.

The ageing John Horatio Lloyd liked Oscar but was concerned about his uncertain financial circumstances. Oscar was honest with the old gentleman who advised them to wait a few months so that his granddaughter's future husband could pay off some of his debts through his lecturing. Constance had an income of £250 per annum. This would increase to £900 when her grandfather died, a sizeable sum. He generously advanced £5,000 against her eventual inheritance so that the young couple could secure the lease on a nice home at 16 Tite Street, Chelsea. They commissioned the architect Edward Godwin to oversee the renovation work and the redecoration. Oscar would now learn that creating a 'house beautiful' takes an awful lot of money.

Money also continued to be a serious issue for Lady Wilde. She was in dire financial difficulties with nothing coming in from Moytura and Willie spending his meagre income on himself. He was now with *The Word* but often had to go into hiding, even occasionally fleeing to Illaunroe, in order to escape the debt collectors. After a long break Jane began to correspond once again with her Swedish friends and she could now boast to Rosalie Olivecrona of Oscar's engagement. But she also admitted that her life had 'many troubles and anxieties', telling her friend that London was 'too ponderous and expensive' and that she had received no rents from Ireland where 'all the gentry are ruined and the shops are bankrupt'.[4]

Jane also wrote to her friend Lotten von Kraemer looking for more up-to-date information on Sweden as she planned to publish a series of articles on her travels there. In a further letter she admitted 'Life grows sad as years go on – and my life was rent and broken when Sir William died.' Lotten and Rosalie sent some information and Jane began to work her notes into a book called *Driftwood from Scandinavia*. It was eventually published by Richard Bentley in 1884, who paid fifty guineas for the first printing of 1,000 copies with the promise of a further fifty guineas for a second edition. The book on Scandinavia is interesting in that it reveals Jane's sense of humour. The reader can also enjoy her obvious fascination with the legends and antiquities of Scandinavia and the way she finds links with Ireland. Jane wrote to Lotten saying 'The book has had a good success here and the publishers are very content with the sale.'

Oscar Wilde and Constance Lloyd were married on 29 May 1884 at St James Church, Sussex Gardens, Paddington. Surprisingly, the wedding was kept small and somewhat secret, perhaps because Constance's grandfather had fallen seriously ill. One is reminded of Sir William's wedding to Jane in Westland Row and their own desire for privacy. The *New York Times* of 22 June carried a description of the bride's dress. Designed by Oscar, it was

> of rich creamy satin ... a delicate cowslip tint; the bodice, cut square and somewhat low in front, was finished with a Medici collar; the ample sleeves were puffed; the skirt, made plain, was gathered by a silver girdle of beautiful workmanship ... the veil of saffron-coloured Indian gauze was embroidered with pearls and worn in Marie Stuart fashion; a thick wreath of myrtle leaves, through which gleamed a few white blossoms, crowned her fair frizzed hair; the dress was ornamented with clusters of myrtle leaves; the large bouquet had as much green in it as white

Jane stood near Oscar, wearing 'a handsome costume of silver-grey brocaded silk and satin; on the bodice was fastened a large spray of roses and pink carnations; grey and pink feathers trimmed her hat'.[5] Oscar sported a rose buttonhole and a touch of pink in his tie. Willie was best man.

The couple honeymooned in Paris at the Hotel Wagram near the Tuileries Gardens but Oscar soon made a point of meeting his young friend Robert Sherard and they took off for a walk together. Matrimony and its associated respectability might be all very well but Oscar enjoyed being in the company of men. The honeymooners attended the theatre where Oscar's friend and probable one-time lover, Sarah Bernhardt, was playing Lady Macbeth. They also visited galleries and dined with friends. Oscar managed to find time to read Stendhal's *Le Rouge et le Noir* and he got hold of a copy of Huysmans' new work *À Rebours* or *Against the Grain*, a novel that greatly influenced him. The principal character in Huysmans' novel, which is also known in English as *Against Nature*, is Jean Des Esseintes, a man who becomes disgusted with human society after leading an extremely decadent life in Paris, an existence that includes both heterosexual and homosexual activity. He flees the city and starts a new life in a country house where, among other strange activities, he creates a garden of poisonous flowers. Oscar, well aware of his own internal oscillations, was fascinated.

Constance was delighting in her new role as the wife of Oscar Wilde. Life in her grandfather's house had not been easy as her aunt, Emily Lloyd, tended to treat her as a guest. Oscar was her saviour and she worshipped him. The couple spent a further week in Dieppe in northern France and then returned to London where their first task was to find a place to live while 16 Tite Street was being expensively refurbished. They moved for a short time into Constance's home at Lancaster Gate but when her grandfather died on 18 July, freeing up some finances for the spendthrift husband and his compliant new wife, they took up temporary lodgings at Oscar's old abode in 9 Charles Street.

Oscar had still to earn a living so he set out once more on the lecture circuit and spent the winter of 1884 and spring of 1885 touring. In January 1885 Oscar and Constance were thrilled to be able to move into their splendidly decorated four-storeyed house in

Chelsea. Here at last was the 'house beautiful'. Constance had her own bedroom with pink walls and apple-green ceiling. It also contained a large bath and Oscar, who had his own bedroom and study, always knocked before entering. The dining room was painted white and off-white with white curtains embroidered with yellow silk and there was a Moorish-style library on the ground floor. A white staircase with gold and yellow matting led to the second-floor drawing rooms. The front drawing room had a ceiling of Japanese leather with pink walls and a lemon-gold cornice while the drawing room to the rear had dark green walls and a pale green ceiling with gold dragons painted by Whistler in two corners. One wall contained Oscar's portrait by Harper Pennington, and a bust of Augustus Caesar, his Newdigate Prize, was placed in a corner. The bedrooms were on the third floor with servants' quarters on the fourth.

Jane was overjoyed with developments. She grew very fond of her new daughter-in-law and they became companions with Constance calling regularly to take Lady Wilde shopping or occasionally to a reception. Constance was expected to entertain and Jane was often present when Oscar and his new wife hosted their many friends and well-known personalities. Guests at Tite Street included Sarah Bernhardt, Lillie Langtry and Ellen Terry, friends who remembered the previous residence on Tite Street that Oscar shared with Frank Miles. Other visitors would include Algernon Swinburne, Henry Irving, Robert Browning, Herbert Beerbohm and a visiting Mark Twain. The Pre-Raphaelite painters were also regular visitors. Jane must surely have been reminded of the many wonderful gatherings at 1 Merrion Square so many years ago with Sir William dominating the table with his wit and their children sitting quietly, watching all. Then, on 5 June 1885, Oscar's own son Cyril was born, to the delight of all.

Jane continued to host her own 'At Homes' every Saturday from four o'clock to seven o'clock. They were usually well attended as, since Oscar's tour of America, many people came in the hope of meeting her famous son. But this was still a far cry from the celebrated afternoons in her Dublin mansion. Jane continued to employ her old strategy of keeping daylight at bay by making sure the heavy curtains were always drawn so the guests had to peer at each other in candlelight. Lady Wilde presented herself in outrageous costumes. Bedecked with large pieces of jewellery, she dominated proceedings in low-cut dresses that she may have worn to Castle balls in her glory days over twenty years before. She also liked to wear her hair in ringlets beneath an outrageously tall headdress of velvet or lace. She mingled, keeping the conversations going, introducing guests to each other and often grossly exaggerating their achievements in the process. Jane was a skilled hostess, surveying the gathering regally and oblivious to the dowdy surroundings.

Willie was doing reasonable amounts of journalistic work, for a time he held the post of dramatic critic for *Vanity Fair*, but was of no real help in sorting out the regular household bills. A letter to Oscar in 1885 shows how difficult Jane's position was: 'I am obliged . . . to ask you to lend me £2 which I shall return as soon as Willie sends me anything – perhaps you would call today with it. I had to borrow from Teresa and had to pay her back. Would you buy a dressing table and glass – I'll sell it for £2.10 – it cost £5.'[6] But Oscar himself had no regular income, his only earnings coming from scraps of journalism, writing reviews and a few essays. In the summer of 1885 he applied for a post as a school inspector but was unsuccessful. Illaunroe had been sold the previous year when bookings for his lecturing began to dwindle.

Jane was forced to begin selling her library of books through the book-dealer Walter Spencer, who later wrote about his visit to Park Street in his memoirs *Forty Years in my Bookshop*:

> In 1886 Lady Wilde ordered some books on Irish antiquities from one of my catalogues and when acknowledging their receipt she invited me to see her library. I called at the house and was shown into a room whose walls were crowded with books from floor to ceiling, and in many places along the floor. Lady Wilde received me in state: that is, she welcomed me from a dais at the far end of the room, like a queen on a throne. 'Look round, Mr Spencer,' she said regally, 'and tell me what you

would wish to buy.' I picked out a few volumes, including Browning's *Bells and Pomegranates*. I said, 'What will you take for these, your Ladyship?' She answered with splendid indifference, 'Whatever you offer, Mr Spencer, whatever you offer.' So I suggested £10. She seemed pleased and accepted it readily, saying that I might visit her once a fortnight at eleven in the morning as long as I felt there was a parcel worth giving £10 for. Thus it came about that I saw a good deal of the pathetic, faded old lady.

Constance became pregnant with their second child in 1886 and often had to pass on the many invitations to dinner parties and social engagements that continued to arrive. Oscar, who thrived on such occasions, continued to attend. They continued to host their own dinners in Tite Street where Constance was known to ruffle Oscar occasionally by interrupting his telling of a story or finishing an anecdote while her husband was still in full flight. Although his affection for Constance was real, he was privately struggling with his own sexual conflicts. To make matters worse, it would appear that Oscar was finding his wife's altered body unattractive due to her pregnancy, at least according to his friend Frank Harris. In November 1886 Constance gave birth to their second son, Vyvyan. They had hoped for a girl but both parents were thrilled with their new arrival. Oscar continued to lavish tenderness on his two sons as the years passed and was an excellent father whenever he was at home. They were to have no more children.

During late 1885 and into 1886 Oscar began corresponding with a youth called Harry Marillier, a student at Cambridge, and he even travelled north to attend a college play. He was drawn to young men's company and the tone of his letters reveals a mind stretched between opposites. Nevertheless, there is no evidence that he was sexually intimate with Marillier or indeed anybody else other than his wife up to 1886. He was playing the role of loving father and husband, while all the time he could hear Huysmans' *À Rebours* decadently whispering in his ear. Meanwhile, the law in England was taking a position on such whisperings, with Queen Victoria signing the

Sir William Wilde aged around sixty, from *Dublin University Magazine*, 1875.

Reproduced with permission of the William Andrews Clark Memorial Library,
University of California, Los Angeles.

Oscar Wilde in New York, 1882.

A portrait drawing of Oscar Wilde from 1885.

National Library of Ireland

Constance and Cyril Wilde, November 1889, with an inscription
to author Edgar Saltus.

Oscar Wilde and Lord Alfred Douglas (Bosie), probably in the summer of 1893.

Oscar Wilde in Rome sometime after his release from
Reading Gaol, probably 1900.

Oscar Wilde two hours after his death in Paris, 30 November 1900.
Taken by Maurice Gilbert at the request of Robert Ross.

Reproduced with permission of the William Andrews Clark Memorial Library,
University of California, Los Angeles.

Plaque in honour of Sir William Wilde at
1 Merrion Square, Dublin.

Statue of Oscar Wilde in Merrion Square, Dublin, sculpted by
Danny Osborne and unveiled in 1997.

Criminal Law Amendment Act in 1885 prohibiting gross indecency between consenting adults of the same sex. From the moment this Act was signed into law anybody involved in overt homosexual behaviour ran the risk of being charged with gross indecency and, if found guilty, could face two years with hard labour.

31

Robbie Ross

In 1886 Oscar met Robert 'Robbie' Baldwin Ross, a seventeen-year-old youth who was visiting at Oxford. This was a meeting that would change his life forever. Ross's Irish-born father had risen to become Canada's Attorney-General in 1853 before dying at the age of fifty-three in 1871. His mother was the daughter of the Canadian Deputy Premier, Robert Baldwin. The family moved to London after his father's death and Robbie at the time of his meeting with Oscar was preparing for admission to King's College, Cambridge. He was small with the face of a young boy and was openly homosexual. If Oscar had managed to avoid consummating any of his same-sex attachments up to this point, he could not resist this youth's confident sexual advances, revealing much later to his journalist friend Reggie Turner that it was 'Little Robbie' who first seduced him.[1]

Robbie went up to Cambridge in 1888 where he adopted an aesthetic manner, made no secret of his sexual inclination and wrote outspoken articles in the university press. He experienced some harassment around college and managed to antagonise a number of students. Meanwhile, he and Oscar continued their affair whenever they could meet. Robbie's university career came to an abrupt end when he was thrown into the fountain by a group of students with, he claimed, the full support of a don. Outraged, he managed to extract a public apology from the students but failed to have the don removed from his post. Robbie left Cambridge soon after.

When he revealed his homosexuality to his mother and sister they reacted negatively, telling the young man that he was no longer welcome in the family home. Robbie took off for Edinburgh where he worked on the *Scots Observer*. He would later work, often without pay, for a friend who owned an art gallery. He would also write occasional art criticism for little money. Luckily he had an allowance and later an inheritance from his wealthy family. He and Oscar remained lifelong friends. After Oscar's death, Robbie accepted the onerous task of becoming his literary executor, a task he carried out bravely and with great integrity, eventually rescuing Oscar's estate from bankruptcy. Robbie also felt responsible for the well-being of Oscar's two sons because he had been the first to seduce their father. Today, an urn containing Robbie's ashes sits in a special compartment in Oscar's famous Epstein tomb in Paris.

Oscar was now actively homosexual. Having succumbed to young Robbie's advances he now felt free to enjoy a series of relationships with other young men. The new excitement and the liberation he was experiencing from having acknowledged his secret urge appears to have provided a new impetus for his writing. He turned out a series of superbly written articles and reviews, mostly for the *Pall Mall Gazette*, and also wrote some fairy stories and short stories. He began to stay in hotels for increasing periods, claiming he needed seclusion to write. Constance, even if she was unhappy with the arrangements, had to acquiesce.

Jane, meanwhile, was in constant need of money. She decided on another book based on Sir William's notes, the ones he had gathered many years before for his *Irish Popular Superstitions*. They had been preserved in a shoebox. From these scraps Jane put together *Ancient Legends, Mystic Charms and Superstitions of Ireland, with sketches of the Irish past*. It was published early in 1887 and brought in a little badly needed cash. W. B. Yeats praised it highly in *Women's World* in February 1889. Jane later reworked extracts from *Ancient Legends* for use in various magazines and thereby was able to eke out some further payments from the work.

Jane always had an eye out for possible outlets for her writings and was delighted both for her son and for herself when Oscar was appointed editor of *The Lady's World*, a magazine of fashion and society, in April 1887. This was his first salaried job, one that he was offered partly for his profile as an aesthete with an interest in fashion and beauty but more so because the quality of his recent reviews had caught the attention of Thomas Wemyss Reid, general manager of Cassell & Co., the publishers who had started up *The Lady's World: A Magazine of Fashion and Society* the year before.

Oscar began work in the summer of 1887 with great enthusiasm, soliciting articles from his many celebrity and aristocratic acquaintances and attending at the offices twice a week, on Tuesdays and Thursdays. He changed its name to *The Woman's Weekly* and managed to revamp its style and content successfully. After his bright start he gradually lost interest. He remained in charge, however, until October 1889 and was paid £6 per week.

Jane was now spending a good deal of her time alone in her rented house on Park Street. Nonetheless, she continued to venture out to occasional receptions. Elizabeth Robins in her book *Both Sides of the Curtain* has a description of Jane at a reception given by Lady Seton at Durham House. She was 'tall, dark-eyed, with a big nose and heavily rouged under a double white gauze veil drawn close like a mask over the features'.[2] Lady Wilde was a brave woman but the constant struggle for daily bread was taking its toll on the ageing authoress.

Lady Wilde also enjoyed attending the debates in Parliament, probably because they were free entertainment and also because it was a dizzy time in Irish politics. Charles Stewart Parnell was the leader of the Irish party in the House of Commons and to the fore of both the Land War and the struggle for Home Rule. For many in Ireland he was a hero but he had made some powerful enemies. In April 1887 a copy of a letter allegedly written by Parnell appeared in *The Times*. If authentic, it showed that he had secretly approved of the savage murders in Dublin in 1882 of Lord Frederick Cavendish, Chief Secretary for Ireland, and of his Permanent Undersecretary Thomas Burke. The two most senior officials in Ireland were walking towards the Viceregal Lodge in the Phoenix Park when there were set upon by members of a Republican organisation called the 'Irish

National Invincibles' and stabbed to death. The atrocity became known as the 'Phoenix Park Murders'. As other letters surfaced Parnell loudly proclaimed his innocence. In response to the furore the government set up a commission of three judges to investigate.

Lady Wilde was a supporter of Parnell and both her sons attended the commission's hearings. Willie reported on the meetings for the *Daily Telegraph* and the articles he wrote at this time are regarded as his best work. Parnell was completely exonerated when the letters were found to have been forged by an Irish journalist called Richard Pigott. Parnell won damages from *The Times* and with his reputation restored resumed his place in Parliament to a standing ovation. Unfortunately for Parnell, his career was wrecked shortly afterwards when his affair with a married woman called Katharine O'Shea, the wife of another Irish MP, came to light.

Lady Wilde remained interested in the politics of Ireland after her move to London but refrained from writing on the topic, wisely perhaps as she was still seeking a government pension. With money continuing to be scarce the house at Park Street proved too expensive and in October 1888 Jane and Willie moved to 146 Oakley Street, Chelsea, a pleasing thoroughfare leading from the Albert Bridge to the King's Road. Here, in surroundings even less salubrious than Park Street, Jane continued to hold her Saturday afternoon salons. Even though Jane was pleased to be closer to Chelsea's Tite Street, the move had been a further financial burden. She wrote to Constance saying 'we have arrived here yesterday and I have no end of work and expense to get it in order and I have no money except this cheque which will you kindly cash for me as soon as possible, all in gold. But now can you lend me one sovereign for present expenses – that makes three I have borrowed from you, which please deduct from the £10 cheque. If possible send me the pound now by Mrs Faithful, as I have nothing in hand.'[3]

Back at her writing desk Jane turned out a companion to *Ancient Legends* called *Ancient Cures, Charms and Usages of Ireland: Contributions to Irish Lore*. Once more she had raided Sir William's old notes and put together amusing descriptions of cures and charms involving incantations and unpleasant concoctions to be taken at certain times of the day. *Lady's Pictorial* said it was a 'curious and interesting book'. But Jane had padded out the volume by including her old essay on 'The American Irish', written in her best nationalistic Speranza style. The *Athenaeum* was critical, saying 'It was sad to think that all the years that Lady Wilde has dwelt in London have taught her nothing but hatred.'[4] In 1888, through Oscar's efforts, Jane received a grant of £100 from the Royal Literary Fund. Much more importantly, on 24 May 1890, fourteen years after the death of Sir William, she at last received a Civil List pension of £70 per annum. It was awarded by the Prime Minister, Robert Gascoyne-Cecil, 3rd Marquess of Salisbury, 'in recognition of the services rendered by her late husband Sir William Wilde, MD, to statistical science and literature'. Jane's early revolutionary writings went unmentioned.

The following summer Jane was pleased to hear that she had won 78 per cent of the votes in a competition run by the Dublin magazine *Lady of the House* to find the greatest living Irishwoman. Speranza had not been forgotten and in July 1891 she published an impressive collection of essays and reviews in a book called *Notes on Men, Women and Books* published by Ward and Downey. These articles reflected the fact that Jane had always read widely and held strong personal views on literature, philosophy and history as well as views on the role and position of women in society and on politics in general.

Oscar had also been productive, writing several fine short stories including 'The Canterville Ghost', 'The Devoted Friend' and 'The Nightingale and the Rose'. He then wrote his excellent exploration of vanity, 'The Remarkable Rocket'. On something of a roll now, Oscar wrote 'Lord Arthur Saville's Crime' and in July 1889 published 'The Portrait of Mr W. H.' against the advice of some of his friends, including politicians Arthur Balfour and Herbert Henry Asquith, both future Prime Ministers. This was a complex short story based on the well-known theory that Shakespeare was attracted to boys. The tale involves intrigue and secret lives, fact mixed with fiction. The author was by this time leading his own multilayered life.

The *Athenaeum* compared Oscar to Hans Christian Andersen when in May 1888 he published *The Happy Prince and Other Tales*. He then went on to publish a series of fine essays including his great dialogue 'The Decay of Lying' in the *Nineteenth Century* magazine. Oscar's friend Frank Harris was at this time editor of the *Fortnightly Review* and he published a discursive prose piece called 'Pen, Pencil and Poison'. He would later prove to be one of Oscar's most faithful allies.

When a young W. B. Yeats came to 16 Tite Street for Christmas dinner in 1888, proofs of 'The Decay of Lying' were produced and discussed in detail. Yeats was impressed and would be influenced by what he heard that day. Oscar was at this time skilfully formulating new theories on art or, more correctly, he was reassembling his aesthetic ideas in the context of the subversive and the decadent in order to create a post-aestheticism. He had found some kind of inner freedom when he accepted his homosexuality. He was seeing a number of young men including John Grey, whom he would flatter by using a variant of his name in his short novel *The Picture of Dorian Gray*. The ink and creativity were now flowing. Perhaps it was the thrill of being a secret outlaw and at the same time associating with the highest law-makers in the land or the idea of being a husband and father while consorting with young men. Whatever the spur, Oscar was now on the cusp of great achievements in literature.

32

Bosie

*T*he *Picture of Dorian Gray* was first published in *Lippincott's Monthly Magazine* on 20 June 1890. Oscar had managed to bring homosexuality on to the pages of an English novel. 'The love that dares not speak its name' was never directly mentioned but the reader is left in no doubt. Like Oscar, Dorian loves both women and men. Lord Henry Wotton is married but the marriage is anaemic and his wife leaves him. He takes Dorian off to Algiers, a recognised destination for English homosexuals at the time. Oscar had managed to free himself from his repressed nature and now had Lord Henry Wotton state: 'To realise one's nature to perfection – that is what we are here for.' Oscar then has him elaborate even further: 'Every impulse that we strive to strangle broods in the mind, and poisons us . . . The only way to get rid of temptation was to yield to it. Resist it, and your soul grows sick.' Richard Ellmann, Wilde's greatest biographer, declares *Dorian Gray* to be 'the aesthetic novel par excellence, not in espousing the doctrine, but in exhibiting its dangers'.

The reaction was strong. Oscar was accused in reviews of writing a novel that was offensive and immoral but he stoutly defended himself in long letters of reply. Asked by Samuel Henry James, the critic with *St James's Gazette*, if he really meant what he had written, Oscar replied 'I meant every word I have said and everything at which I have hinted in *Dorian Gray*'. James' reply was prophetic: 'Then all I can say is that if you do mean them you are likely to find yourself at Bow Street one of these days.'[1] By Bow Street he meant the courts of law. Constance is reported to have said that 'Since Oscar wrote *Dorian Gray*, no one will speak to us.' Jane, however, was delighted with the novel.

When *Dorian Gray* finally appeared in book form in April 1891 W. H. Smith refused to sell it, saying it was 'filthy'. But there were others who thought it excellent. The young men who gathered around Oscar could not praise it highly enough. One young man in particular, at this time a student at Magdalen, Oxford, read the book at least nine times. He was a cousin of Lionel Johnson, the poet and essayist who was a friend of Oscar's. This young man availed of an opportunity to meet with the author of *Dorian Gray* by accompanying his cousin on a visit to 16 Tite Street in the summer of 1891. Oscar took note of this pale-faced, blond youth, offering to help him with his study of the Classics. This young guest who obviously delighted Oscar so much was Lord Alfred Douglas, known as Bosie to his friends, the youngest son of the Marquess of Queensberry.

Oscar's future may already have been written in the stars but for now there was much work to be done. He wrote two fine essays 'The Critic as Artist' and then 'The Soul of Man Under Socialism'. Frank Harris from the *Fortnightly Review* was greatly impressed. Oscar was proving himself to be a fine scholar and a far cry from the young man with a sunflower parading about Piccadilly. Oscar was then surprised to be asked by an American actor, Lawrence Barrett, if he could him stage *The Duchess of Padua* in New York. They decided to change the play's name to *Guido Ferranti* and to keep Oscar's name off the billboard. *Vera's* failure might still be remembered. Everything agreed, the play opened in the Broadway Theatre on 27 January 1891 and was a success. The play was soon recognised as Oscar's but this did not damage the reviews. The author's name was then attached to the production and it ran for three successful weeks. It could have had a longer run had Barrett not fallen ill. He died two months later. However, Oscar's career as a playwright had been resuscitated.

Towards the end of 1890 George Alexander took over the St James's Theatre in London and asked Oscar for a play. He refused *The Duchess of Padua* but gave Oscar £50 in advance for a new play to be delivered by January. The time was too tight and Oscar failed to deliver but the shrewd manager refused to accept his money back and gave the playwright more time. Oscar took himself off to the Lake District during the summer of 1891 and returned with a substantial part of what would become *Lady Windermere's Fan*. At this point it had the working title of *A Good Woman*. Jane wrote to her son complaining about the name: 'I do not like it, *A Good Woman*, it is mawkish. No one cares for a good woman. *A Noble Woman* would be better.' She also told him to attend the opening night, saying 'if you go away, it will look cowardly, as if you feared the result'.[2] That last piece of advice would be tendered again a few years later in far more calamitous circumstances.

Alexander was so impressed with the finished product that he offered the author £1,000 for the play. But Oscar, out of generosity or shrewdness or perhaps both, refused the kind offer insisting instead on a percentage. They could sink or swim together. In the event, Oscar was to make £7,000 (£570,000/€640,000 today) from the play in its first year.

While Oscar was off working on his satire on marriage and gazing upon Lake Windermere, his brother, Willie, was also about the business of matrimony. Florence Miriam Frank Leslie, a wealthy American widow and newspaper publisher, was visiting London where she attended a number of Lady Wilde's salons and also visited Constance at Tite Street. She had known the Wildes since the early 1880s when she first attended one of Jane's salons on a previous visit to London. Willie, of course, made it his business to meet this well-to-do lady who had been married on three previous occasions and who, at fifty-five, was sixteen years his senior.

There was a certain air of mystery and rumour surrounding Mrs Frank Leslie, a former actress. It was whispered that she was the illegitimate daughter of a black slave and that her mother once ran a New York brothel. Mrs Frank Leslie was born Miriam Florence Folline in New Orleans in June 1836 of a French Huguenot family but was brought up in New York where she received a sound education, particularly in languages. Mrs Leslie's third husband, the publisher Frank Leslie, died in 1880 leaving debts of $300,000, but his formidable widow took the business in hand and managed to restore the publishing house to profit. During the process of rescuing the business she had her name legally changed to Frank Leslie in 1881. Willie, who had managed to get himself declared bankrupt in August 1888, wasted no time in proposing to the tough American who by now was the owner of seven newspapers. Attempts were made to arrange some lectures in America. These plans came to nothing and Mrs Frank Leslie left for home in early August, leaving Willie behind without giving him any definite commitment. They kept in touch, however, and in September Willie set sail for New York where the unlikely pair married on 4 October 1891 in the aptly named Church of the Strangers. The bankrupt journalist had at last fulfilled his ambition to secure a wealthy bride.

Oscar advised his indolent brother to have this affluent and worldly-wise woman agree a prenuptial settlement but Willie did not heed the good counsel. 'When she has glutted her lust on him and used him up, she'll pitch him his hat and coat and by means of an American divorce get rid of him legally and let him starve to death for all she'll care' was Oscar's prophetic comment.[3] But Jane, ever optimistic, was only too pleased to have her wayward son settled at last and, better still, with a woman of wealth. She wrote to Oscar: 'I think it is altogether a fine and good thing for Willie. Her influence may work great good in him and give him the strength he wants.'[4] Such had been her hope ever since Willie's career as a barrister in Ireland had come to naught.

In October Oscar took off for Paris to expand his ideas for a new play based on the much-used story of Salome who danced for King Herod and then demanded the head of John the Baptist as her reward. There he met with many of the great French writers of the day. Oscar generally delighted his listeners with his witty conversations and enjoyed convivial evenings in the company of the Parisian literary set, becoming particularly friendly with two young authors Pierre Louÿs and André Gide.[5] Later, in letters to friends, Gide, who was soon to discover his own homosexual nature, revealed the powerful effect Oscar had upon him at that time. Back at home, Jane and Constance were feeling lonely. The two women kept each other company but Jane was upset at the way Oscar left his wife alone so often. She wrote asking him to return but Oscar was now living in his clandestine world of homosexual lovers, a place that would eventually lead to his downfall. In November 1891 he did at least dedicate his new collection of short stories, *A House of Pomegranates*, to Constance.

Lady Windermere's Fan opened on 20 February 1892 at the St James's Theatre and was an immediate success. Oscar took Constance to the first night as Jane had advised. At the end of the performance the audience called loudly for the author and Oscar spoke a few words from the stage holding a cigarette in his mauve-gloved hand and sporting a green carnation in his buttonhole, as were a number of young men in the audience. Lord Alfred Douglas, the youth who had been so taken by *Dorian Gray*, was there, as was Oscar's lover Robbie Ross. Pierre Louÿs, his friend from Paris, who was not homosexual but was accepted in such company perhaps because his libertine themes often included lesbianism, had come to London for the occasion. He was seated beside another young man by the name of Edward Shelley, a clerk in a publishing house and one of twelve boys Oscar would later be accused of soliciting to commit sodomy. The date in Shelley's case was one week after the triumph of the opening of *Lady Windermere's Fan*.

Jane was not at the opening night, in fact she never did see any of her son's plays on the stage as she was in such frail health at this time, but Oscar presented her with an inscribed copy of the play when it was published. A delighted Jane wrote to her son after the triumph of the opening night: 'You have a splendid success and I am very happy and proud of you. I warmly give you my congratulations. You are the great success of the day.' She then went on to ask him for tickets for all her friends and to come to her next Saturday 'At Home'. Oscar had been good to his mother, paying her bills and giving her some money. Now, with this great success, perhaps the scrimping would end for the Wildes.

But Oscar's lifestyle altered with his circumstances. He had never been careful with money and now there was travel, expensive hotels and late suppers at the Café Royal. His new friend Alfred Douglas was also proving to be extremely expensive and expected Oscar to pay for all his extravagances. Bosie liked to gamble, usually without much luck, and would then turn to Oscar for money to cover his losses. He also liked to frequent the murky world of rent boys and Oscar found himself drawn into this dark underworld of young male prostitutes with all the inherent risks, including blackmail. Infatuated by Bosie's youthful beauty, the now famous playwright was helpless to resist his increasingly outrageous demands. The two lovers were also being indiscreet in public. Indeed, Oscar flaunted his relationships with Douglas and other young men on the basis that he would not be hypocritical. The more success he gained the more he abandoned discretion.

Over in America, Mrs Frank Leslie's strong work ethic was showing up Willie. 'She rose early, enjoyed or endured a cold bath, did physical exercises, turned up at the office at nine a.m. arrayed in black silk.'[6] She expected her new spouse to work as a journalist and as the husband of the owner of a newspaper empire there would have been many great opportunities. But Willie could not understand why both partners in the marriage should labour. He liked to stay in bed until midday. He would then call around and collect his wife at the office and take her for a drive in her own carriage. There would be drinks and dinner before he left to spend the night at one of his favourite clubs. Willie liked to explain to his acquaintances that in his view what 'New York lacked was a leisured class'. Willie Wilde was determined to introduce such a class.[7]

By January 1892 the marriage was showing signs of strain. Willie was being insulting and Mrs Frank Leslie told an interviewer that she would not take the name of Wilde until Willie had proven himself in the world of American journalism, ending with the barbed remark that 'I really think I should have married Oscar.'[8] Willie, finding that his allowance had been reduced, reluctantly began writing a series of articles for the *New York Recorder*, but when his new wife saw that he was refusing to exert himself and was sinking more and more into alcohol she arranged a visit to England in the spring. 'I'm taking Willie over, but I'll not bring Willie back,' she told friends.[9] After arriving in England she engaged private detectives to have her husband followed with a view to gathering evidence that could be used in divorce proceedings.

Willie managed to change his wife's mind and the couple returned to New York but his behaviour continued to deteriorate. With his allowance cut off he began sponging drinks in the Lotus Club where he liked to try to ingratiate himself with other members by poking fun at his famous brother and mimicking Oscar's speech. When Willie's attempts at lampooning his famous brother were later revealed in the *New York Times*, together with news of his expulsion from the Club, Oscar was outraged at what he saw as betrayal.

Mrs Frank Leslie was now determined on divorce and she had the ammunition. The private detective had gathered sufficient evidence on the grounds of drunkenness and adultery. Willie, it was claimed, had been consorting with women of disreputable character and frequenting places of low resort. Mrs Frank Leslie's domestic staff corroborated allegations of Willie's intemperance and cruel conduct towards his wife. The couple were formally divorced on 10 June 1893. Mrs Frank Leslie called the marriage 'a blunder' and declared that Willie 'was of no use to me by day or by night'.[10] Willie failed to benefit from Mrs Frank Leslie's wealth but others did and at the end of her life she bequeathed her entire fortune to the suffragette movement.

Jane was greatly upset by the turn of events but still managed to find the newspaper reports of the divorce amusing. She laughed at the headlines 'Tired of Willie' or 'Willie Won't Get Up and Won't Work'. However, it was less amusing when he returned from America to live once more with his hard-pressed mother. His allowance was gone and he was offered only occasional work as a journalist. Robert Sherard in his biography *The Real Oscar Wilde* said that Willie 'went out to America a fine, brilliant, clever man, quite one of the ablest writers of the press' but returned 'a nervous wreck, with an exhausted brain and a debilitated frame . . . it soon became apparent that his power for sustained effort was gone'. He had left for America a drinker and returned a drunkard. Willie and Oscar were still on good terms at this point, as reports of Willie's behaviour at the Lotus Club had not yet reached London. Oscar asked him if his marriage had really broken down. Willie said 'No, it has broken up.' 'What is the difference?' asked Oscar. 'She is up, I am down,' came the caustic reply.[11]

33

A Brilliant Success

Actress Sarah Bernhardt, in need of a London success, approached her old friend Oscar for a play. He suggested *Salome* and the play went into rehearsals in June 1892. A problem arose when the Censor refused to grant the drama a licence on the grounds that it breached the law forbidding the depiction on the stage of Biblical characters. The play had been written in French and a furious Oscar publicly declared his intention of becoming a citizen of France to show his disgust at England. Anyway, he was an Irishman, he thundered, and not English, 'which is quite another thing'.

In the event, Oscar did not change nationality. Instead, he published *Salomé* as a book in France in February 1893. Later that year it was published in England with illustrations by Aubrey Beardsley. But the play remained cancelled and so Oscar took Bosie off to Bad Homburg, a spa resort near Frankfurt that also boasted a casino. He had been advised by his doctors to 'take the waters' for health reasons. In Bad Homburg he was put on a diet, made to drink the mineral waters and told not to smoke cigarettes. High living had been taking its toll.

Back in London, and possibly feeling refreshed from his spell in Germany, Oscar made contact with his friend Herbert Beerbohm, principal actor and manager at the Haymarket Theatre, to whom he had promised a play. Oscar's new work would eventually be called *A Woman of No Importance*. In order to write the play Oscar rented a farmhouse near Cromer in Norfolk for August and September while Constance and the children holidayed in Torquay. Bosie soon joined Oscar in Norfolk. He fell ill but Oscar managed to nurse his young lover back to health and at the same time find the peace to write. The result was a play containing perhaps his harshest epigrams and involving a character with a dreadful secret. By October 1892 the play was ready to be delivered to Beerbohm. It went into rehearsal the following March.

Jane had also been working hard at her desk in spite of being distracted by bills and demands. She wrote a collection of essays and two translated short stories that were published in the spring of 1893 with the title *Social Studies*. But this did not relieve her financial difficulties, compounded now by having to move temporarily to new accommodation while repair work was carried out at her house.

A Woman of No Importance opened on 19 April 1893 at the Haymarket Theatre and was very well received although the author heard a few boos and hisses when called to the curtain, possibly because of a harsh line or two with decidedly unpatriotic sentiments that were later dropped. Balfour and Chamberlain were there and the Prince of Wales attended the second performance. He and Oscar chatted together after the play. 'You had a brilliant success!' Jane wrote, 'and I am so happy. I receive many notices of congratulations . . . I had a crowd here on Saturday and many had seen the play and nothing else was talked of . . . You are now the great sensation of London and I am very proud of you.' She ended with a plea for Oscar to 'Take care of yourself and your health and keep clear of suppers and late hours and champagne. Your health and calm of mind is most important.'[1]

But Oscar had not been taking care of himself. He was drinking too much, had put on a lot of weight and that was not all. He was now living mostly in hotels and avoiding his home. He was sleeping with a string of youths who accepted his money and his gifts and often sought ways to exploit his generosity further, sometimes through the threat of blackmail. One seventeen-year-old youth, Alfred Wood, who was sleeping with both Douglas and Oscar, came upon private and sensitive letters written by Oscar to Bosie in the pockets of cast-off clothes he had received from Douglas. Wood attempted to get £60 from the famous playwright in return for the letters. Oscar refused to pay £60 but did pay £30 (over £2,400/€2,700 today) to the young blackmailer. However, he failed to secure the return of all the letters including a particularly personal one to Bosie, which would later become known as the Hyacinth Letter. This sensitive document would eventually find its way into the hands of Oscar's enemy, the Marquess of Queensberry, and be used against him at his trial. Wood used the money he received from Oscar to leave for America but he later returned. There were other such scrapes as Oscar and Bosie continued their reckless pursuit of young lovers. Oscar had other regular and constant companions such as Robbie Ross and John Grey but Bosie knew he was Oscar's favourite and liked to lord it over his male rivals.

Lord Alfred Douglas and Oscar certainly had a strong romantic attachment to each other but they were also being extremely promiscuous. It was Alfred Douglas who, towards the end of 1892, had familiarised Oscar with the dubious excitements of the male prostitute underworld. Douglas introduced Oscar to a young man called Maurice Schwabe, a nephew of the Solicitor General, who in turn introduced Oscar to an ex-member of the Royal Fusiliers called Alfred Taylor who was running a sort of male brothel in his flat at 13 Little Cottage Street. Through Alfred Taylor, Oscar found a group of youths, mostly in their late teens or early twenties, who were willing to indulge in sexual activities for a few pounds or the price of a meal. This dark gangland excited Oscar and he called it 'feasting with panthers'. He was always kind and generous with the boys and often gave them gifts and extra money. These were the mostly working-class youths, Wood, Allen, the Parker brothers Charles and William, who tried to blackmail their famous client and who would eventually be called upon to give evidence against Oscar at his trial. Alfred Taylor, the man who inducted many of these hard-up young men into the murky world of prostitution, was the son of a wealthy cocoa manufacturer who once attended Marlborough public school and later joined the army. In 1883 he inherited the princely sum of £45,000 but squandered the lot and was eventually declared bankrupt. His interests in cross-dressing and homosexual activities led him to get involved in supplying young men to wealthy clients and he became known to police. He is the man who would later share the Old Bailey dock with Oscar Wilde. To his credit he refused to testify against Oscar.

On 16 August Oscar attended the last night of his play in the company of Aubrey Beardsley, Robbie Ross and, of course, Lord Alfred Douglas. But he was failing under the pressure of a hectic year and the intensity of his relationship with Bosie. Bloated by success and surrounded by his troupe of loyal followers Oscar waved his cigarette about and acted in a presumptuous manner. His band of young men all sat around with vine leaves entwined in their hair and people took notice of the pompous author and his devotees. Victorian society did not like its standards to be so publically derided and certainly not by a haughty Irishman. Had not Charles Laver noted something of the same pomposity in Sir William and his friends when the aristocracy of Europe began calling to see their museum so long ago?

With the run over, Oscar left for Dinard in France alone. He was later to write of this time in *De Profundis*: 'I required rest and freedom from the terrible strain of your [Bosie's] companionship.' Frank Harris, in his biography *Oscar Wilde*, claimed Oscar told him that young Bosie frightened him as much as he attracted him and that 'I held away from him. But he wouldn't have it; he sought me out again and again and I couldn't resist him.' One is reminded of Sir William and his infatuation with Moll Travers and his inability to extricate himself from the dangerous entanglement.

Meanwhile, Jane had a problem of her own on her hands. In August she received a summons from the agent of her rented house for damages to the property. Outraged, Jane fired back a twelve-page letter outlining the dilapidated state in which she had found the house. It makes for grim reading. The house had not been cleaned down for Jane's arrival, having been unoccupied for the eight months prior to their taking up residence. The kitchen was in a state of rust and neglect, the carpets were shabby, the muslin curtains were very soiled, and the articles named 'missing' on the summons were most certainly not taken away by Lady Wilde or her servant, she claimed. Distressed, Jane wrote to Oscar twice on the matter telling him he was not to pay. But Oscar did pay, and Jane was very grateful 'to find it all settled! This was truly something though I must regret all the money I have cost you and which you have paid so freely and so generously. Again and again I thank you dear Oscar – you have always been my best and truest help in everything.' She then went on to mention Willie, saying he had met a new woman. 'He seems bent on Lily Lees – and who can say how all will end.'[2] Sophie Lees, known as Lily, was the youngest daughter of a William Armit Lees from Dublin. Willie had only recently met her. She was to become Willie's second wife.

If Oscar was feeling the strain of his own clandestine world he was also growing weary of his older brother's lifestyle. Willie was drinking heavily and his indolence and above all his dependency upon his ageing mother for free board and lodgings were seriously irking his younger brother. Willie's standing about town was sinking fast. He was borrowing from his friends and had become careless of his appearance. 'He sponges on everyone but himself,' was Oscar's opinion.[3] When the *New York Times* of 18 September 1893 carried the scathing article about Willie and his habit of amusing his friends by mimicking his brother, the situation came to a head. The paper had found a club member who said that Willie 'owed most of his celebrity to his . . . excellent imitations of his brother, the Aesthete. These latter were simply killing. You know, Oscar had a fat, potato-choked sort of voice and to hear Willie counterfeit that voice and recite parodies of his brother's poetry while he struck appropriate and aesthetic attitudes was a rare treat.'[4] Why did Willie resort to making fun of his brother? Probably for free drinks, but it was also, perhaps, his way of dealing with the fact that Oscar was leaving him far behind. The paper found its way to London and when Oscar saw it he felt deeply betrayed. Willie could not understand why Oscar was so hurt by what he considered to be harmless fun and put it down to his famous brother's inflated ego. A rift developed between the pair and there was worse to follow.

That same month, September 1893, Constance Wilde received a letter from a Miss Mynous, a friend of Lady Wilde's, telling her of a shocking state of affairs she had heard from her friend Mrs Faithful concerning Willie and Miss Lees. Mrs Faithful was Lady Wilde's loyal servant and housekeeper. 'Lady Wilde will utterly break down and die if something is not done to prevent the tormenting worry. It seems that Miss Lees has confessed that she and Mr W. Wilde have been living together as man and wife at Malvern and Broadstairs and the wretched woman has actually asked Mrs — to give her a powder to prevent the birth of a baby! And she says he has treated her with great brutality.' The letter went on to claim that Willie 'is always asking his mother for money and stamps his foot and swears at her if she hesitates'. The writer called to visit Jane but 'I was sorry to find her in bed and suffering . . . you and Mr Oscar are so good to her, but she conceals the state of affairs . . . the house is not safe and wholesome, Lady Wilde is always being asked for money and worried to death.' Miss Mynous finished by asking Constance to 'please destroy this letter'.[5]

Constance did not destroy the letter. She showed it to Oscar and it was to be the final nail in the coffin for his relationship with his brother. In his anger, Oscar wrote to Willie and also to his mother. Willie apologised to Oscar by letter. Jane, distressed at the hostility that had developed between her sons, wrote to Oscar pleading with him to make up with Willie. 'Try and do Willie good – be a friend to him, speak truly and wisely, but kindly . . . He feels your coldness most bitterly . . . he is reckless and extravagant, preach to him, but do it kindly. Willie has some good points . . . I am miserable at the present position of my sons.' Jane then turned to the fact that she gave him money. 'I pity Willie in that he does not get a sixpence from Moytura and so I am content to give him what I can. At my death he will at least have something – but till then I try and help him a little . . . He has never injured you. Why should you hate him? If he has taken help from me in money, why that does not injure you and I don't want you to hate Willie on my account . . . You will both have to meet by my coffin and I want you to meet before that in friendly feeling . . . I shall hope to see you soon – if not I'll die of grief.'[6]

Jane's efforts were in vain. Oscar's attitude towards his brother did not soften but he continued to support his mother in his own way. He paid the urgent bills, checking the pile in a rack above the mantelpiece for the most pressing ones when he dropped by and writing a cheque there and then. Jane's urgent appeals by letter make for distressing reading: 'Dare I ask you for a little help? I know it is very dreadful to ask you to give or lend money – but I am helpless . . . I am poorly and have not left my room.' Another letter reads: 'I am in much trouble, overwhelmed with threatening letters for rent . . . I therefore reluctantly ask you for the sum of £10 to help me over the difficulties and I shall be ever grateful.'[7] Oscar answered these pathetic cries but he could have made Jane much more comfortable in her old age. He lavished a fortune on a wealthy aristocrat's spoilt son while his mother existed in uncertain penury and even his own family's bills often went unpaid.

Near Christmas 1893 a writ was served on Willie for an unpaid debt. Oscar did not have sufficient funds and Jane was in dread of the bailiff calling. There was nothing for it but to ask Mrs Frank Leslie for help. She came to the rescue but the price was an angry letter sent to Jane telling her that she had received 'two of the rudest and most under-bred letters' from Willie who then 'put you forward to ask a service from me and then proceeded to pelt me with abuse'. She also withdrew an invitation to holiday on the Continent saying it had not been seriously meant: 'I should as soon think of hoping to move the Obelisk from its Embankment home as to tempt you from yours when you will not go out for even a drive once a year.'[8]

Jane, it was true, rarely ventured out now but she continued to host her Saturday 'At Homes'. Henriette Corkran, one of Jane's regular visitors, brought an American novelist, Gertrude Atherton, to call on the aged Lady Wilde. Atherton wrote about the visit in her memoirs, *The Adventures of a Novelist*. She recalled asking her companion Henriette why she was carrying a large plum cake. 'Lady Wilde is frightfully poor,' came the reply, 'her sons do little or nothing for her. Her friends don't dare offer her money or real food, for she's very proud, so we always take her a cake, which we beg her to "try as we have made it ourselves". I only hope the gas isn't turned off, and you will be able to see her.'[9]

Atherton is something of a hostile witness. She told her readers that Jane lived in 'an obscure street', which was untrue, and said her drawing room 'into which the miserable slavery conducted us' was 8 square feet when in fact it was much larger. She then went on to describe the meeting:

> But the strange figure that rose as we entered received us with the grand air. She might have been a queen graciously giving a private audience. In her day she must have been a beautiful and stately woman; she was still stately, Heaven knew, but her old face was gaunt and grey, and seamed with a million criss-cross lines, etched by care, sorrow, and (no doubt) hunger. Her dress was a relic of the 'sixties', grey satin trimmed with ragged black fringe over a large hoop-skirt. As her hair was black, it was presumably a wig, and it was dressed very high, held in place by a Spanish comb from which descended a black lace mantilla. She pressed her withered lips to Henriette's red cheek, and extended me a claw-like hand. I wondered if I were expected to kiss it, but gave myself the benefit of the doubt. She received the cake graciously, but put it aside without a glance. Poor thing, no doubt she devoured it whole as soon as we left; but her manner was lofty and detached, almost complacent. She always remains in my mind as a leaning tower of courage.

This account was written forty years after the visit by a woman who had herself grown old. It was also written in a time when the name of Oscar Wilde was still odious to many. Nevertheless, it has a certain ring of truth.

Mrs Atherton continued:

> The room was close and stuffy, the furniture as antiquated as herself; the springs could not have been mended for forty years. She talked to Henriette in a weak quavering voice, mainly of the triumphs of her exalted son, although she drifted back to the past when she had been one of the lights of Dublin with her literary and political salon, the

words of wisdom that flowed from her facile brain to an admiring world over her nom de guerre. But to her present circumstances she made no allusion, and the walls seemed to expand until the dingy parlour became a great salon crowded with courtiers, and the rotting fabric of her rag-bag covering turned by a fairy's wand into cloth of gold shimmering in the light of a thousand wax candles. But the dream faded – Once more she was a laboriously built-up terribly old woman who subsisted mainly on indigestible cake contributed by the few friends who remembered her existence.[10]

But Lady Wilde had not been forgotten by all. In December 1893 publishers William Morris bought the rights to *Sidonia the Sorceress*, the first book she had ever translated, for £25 and produced a beautiful, well-illustrated edition complete with vellum cover. However, the new year was about to bring further distress for the ageing Lady.

34

Swept Away

On 11 January 1894 Willie married Sophie 'Lily' Lees in a registry office, a very quiet affair as Lily's stepmother did not approve of Willie. Sophie, or Lily as she was known, was Irish, born at 31 Upper Pembroke Street, Dublin, in 1859. Her father had been appointed to a number of municipal positions in Dublin. He moved to London with his second wife and two daughters, Georgina and Sophie, in 1882 and they settled in the Bayswater district. He died in 1885, his will providing generously for his two daughters but subject to the 'life estate' of his second wife. Perhaps Lily's inheritance was withheld by her stepmother because of her disapproval of her choice of husband.

Jane was alarmed at the news of the marriage and wrote to Oscar who was away in Brighton working on *An Ideal Husband*:

> Willie is married to Miss Lees – though not yet publicly announced as her stepmother objects . . . and they look forward to come to live here in March next with me, but as they will have no income, I am alarmed at the prospect – and I feel so bewildered and utterly done up that I would be glad to have a talk with you all about it. I am also dreadfully hard up as to income . . . I have ever so many bills to meet and unless I can get at least £30 to meet them I shall be utterly crushed – what is to be done? Willie

is utterly useless — and now, just when my income has fallen so low, he announces the marriage and the whole burden of the household to fall upon me . . . Miss Lees has but £50 a year and this just dresses her . . . she can give nothing to the house and Willie is always in a state of utter poverty. So all is left upon me. I sometimes think of taking apartments for myself and leaving the house and furniture for I have an immense dislike to sharing the house with Miss Lees, with whom I have nothing in common . . . The idea of having her here is quite distasteful to me . . . La Madre Dolorosa.[1]

With her finances in ruins and saddened by the rift between her two sons, the spring of 1894 was a difficult time for Lady Wilde. She had to ask Oscar for financial help in February and again in March: 'I am in dreadful financial difficulties and have literally not a shilling in the world . . . could you advance me £20.' For a time she believed the house on Oakley Street would have to be given up but with Oscar's help she managed to hold on. Lily Lees, however, proved to be less of a burden on Jane than expected. In fact she soon got used to having Willie's kind-hearted wife in the house and wrote to Oscar saying that 'Willie and his wife get on very well here. Mrs Willie is sensible and assists me in arranging the house and is very good tempered.'

Jane was now seventy-three years of age and the strain of her troubled life was telling. She rarely ventured out of doors and even wrote to W. B. Yeats resigning her membership of the Irish Literary Society, of which she and her two sons were original members. The committee would not hear of her resigning and immediately elected her among the first honorary members. She acknowledged the compliment on 13 April 1894: 'Lady Wilde's compliments, and writes to request that Mr Rolleston will kindly express to the Committee of the Irish Literary Society her sincere thanks for being placed on the list of honorary members. But Lady Wilde much regrets that her very uncertain health will prevent her having the pleasure of attending the Lectures and Receptions illustrated by so many distinguished representatives of Irish genius.'[2]

While his ageing mother was struggling with debt her celebrity son was living on the precipice of disaster, consorting with a gang of male prostitutes and blackmailers, many of them petty criminals, some known to the police. Wilde's biographer Richard Ellmann, writing of this period, states: 'If Queensberry had not brought Wilde down, someone else might well have done so . . . Wilde had to pick his way among blackmailing boys and furious fathers . . . Only self-assurance, and the thoughtless flurry of his activities, made him trust to his luck.'[3]

In the spring of 1893 Oscar and Bosie took rooms at the Savoy Hotel after spending time away in Devon where they had quarrelled. Bosie threw regular tantrums, an aspect of his nature that greatly distressed Oscar though he was quite unable to leave his troublesome lover. Pierre Louÿs dropped by the hotel one morning and observed that there was only one double bed in the suite. Constance came around with letters while Pierre was there and he later reported how she tearfully begged her husband to come home but Oscar dismissed her sad plea with a flippant remark about being away so long that he had forgotten the number of his house. Louÿs was upset for poor Constance and soon ended his friendship with Oscar. Meanwhile, Bosie refused to be discreet at the Savoy, preferring to flaunt his relationship with Oscar by entering and leaving through the front door in full view of all.

Oscar had spent much of that spring and summer of 1893 with Bosie, first at Oxford, where the young aristocrat failed to turn up for his Greats examination and therefore did not graduate, and then in a rented house at Goring-on-Thames. Oscar's family came down for a short visit at this lovely country cottage with its lawns running down to the river but Alfred Douglas was the main guest. It was here that Oscar began work on his next play, *An Ideal Husband*. Bosie, at one point, had another of his regular temper fits at Goring and stormed off. Oscar, exasperated by his lover's outrageous behaviour, tried to end their relationship but the young aristocrat pleaded for forgiveness. This was a regular pattern and Oscar always relented. That summer Oscar managed to get through the colossal sum of £1,340 (around £109,000/€123,000 today).

Oscar tried to encourage Bosie by inviting him to write the English translation of *Salomé* but the young man was not able for the task. When Oscar pointed out the flaws in his weak translation Bosie once more exploded in rage. Bosie's father, John Sholto Douglas, 9th Marquess of Queensberry, was another man with a quarrelsome nature. As a young man he had managed to introduce order into the sport of boxing, which was, along with hunting, one of his favourite pastimes. He also wrote a number of poems, including 'The Spirit of the Matterhorn', his brother having died while attempting to climb the peak. His first wife divorced him in 1887 claiming adultery but the Marquess continued to take an active interest in his children's welfare.

The year 1893 was not a good one for Queensberry. He was incensed by his youngest son's reckless lifestyle and blamed Oscar for Bosie's failure to finish his degree at Oxford. He was also worried about his eldest son, Francis, Viscount Drumlanrig, who was private secretary to Archibald Primrose, Lord Rosebery, Gladstone's Foreign Secretary and a future Prime Minister. Rosebery was a suspected homosexual and Queensberry feared his son, Drumlanrig, was being tempted in that direction. He went so far as to follow the Foreign Secretary to the spa at Bad Homburg where he threatened to assault him with a whip. It took the police and the intervention of the Prince of Wales, who was also present, to have him sent away. It has been strongly suggested that Rosebery and Viscount Drumlanrig were lovers. If so, their relationship would have major consequences for Oscar when he was placed on trial. It provides a good explanation for the vigour with which the state was to prosecute Oscar Wilde. Queensberry, it would appear, threatened to reveal the new Prime Minister's own homosexuality if Oscar's case was dropped.[4] The Marquess had to be pacified.

Queensberry was driven to further anger when his second son, Lord Percy Douglas, also defied him and married the daughter of a clergyman against his father's express wishes. But worse was to come. Queensberry married a young woman, Ethel Weedon, on 1 November 1893 but she immediately filed for divorce, claiming that her new husband's genitals were malformed and that he was frigid and impotent. A humiliated Marquess hired solicitor George Lewis to fight the case. Lewis understood delicate matters, indeed he was often used in cases where homosexuals were being blackmailed. It was unfortunate for Oscar that he had been engaged to work for Queensberry because he would have been Oscar's obvious choice when it came to his own case.

There were many homosexuals in London – the police knew of at least 20,000 – but discretion was expected and Oscar was not being discreet. Instead, since his major theatrical successes, he had thrown all caution to the wind and now appeared to be flaunting his sexual leanings. London society was buzzing with rumours about Lord Alfred and Oscar Wilde. Queensberry was determined to put an end to their relationship.

Oscar wrote to the first Lady Queensberry advising her to find some way of getting Alfred away from England because he believed the young man was not in good health, mentally or physically. He suggested a visit to the Cromers, the family of the British Consul in Egypt, who were based in Cairo, and Bosie agreed to go. It was a good time to be absent because another potentially dangerous situation was brewing following the revelation that he and Robbie Ross had slept with the sixteen-year-old son of an army colonel. Oscar had also slept with the youth but his name was not mentioned. Ross had to leave the country and went as far as Davos in Switzerland, ostensibly for health reasons. It would appear that Richard Ellmann was correct and that any one of a number of incidents could eventually have brought down Oscar, such was the extent of his circle's recklessness.

Bosie left for Cairo in December 1893. Oscar could now get down to serious work and managed to complete *An Ideal Husband*. He also started writing *A Florentine Tragedy*, which was never finished, and wrote the short play *La Sainte Courtisane*. Later that year Oscar began work on what would be his finest play, *The Importance of Being Earnest*, but by then Bosie had come back to England and with his return came all the pressures of Queensberry's relentless harrying of the pair. If *Earnest* would be Oscar's finest play, it would also be his last.

Oscar would have been content to let the relationship end with Bosie away in Egypt. He even advised Lady Queensberry to keep her son out of the country by securing some position for him. Plans to have him made honorary attaché to Lord Currie, British Ambassador at Istanbul, came to nothing. Bosie bombarded Oscar with letters from Egypt but he refused to reply. The spurned lover even wrote to Constance begging her to have her husband write to him. Oscar continued to refuse to correspond and instead sent a telegram in March 1894 saying he would not write and he would not see him. Bosie travelled to Paris and threatened suicide. Oscar relented and crossed to Paris where he once again fell under Bosie's spell. They dined together and made up. There is an essay in Lady Wilde's last book, *Social Studies*, called 'Venus Victrix'. It contains the lines 'Reason can do little against the force of beauty; the first impulse, the irresistible instinct of a man's nature is the homage to physical beauty. It has a mystic power that sweeps down all before it, the strongest and wisest.' All indeed would now be swept away.

Back in London Queensberry came upon Oscar and Bosie as they lunched together at the Café Royal on April Fools' Day 1894. They invited him to join them at their table. He accepted the invitation and was temporarily impressed by Oscar. However, on returning home he changed his mind and wrote immediately to his son:

> Alfred, – It is extremely painful for me to have to write to you in the strain I must, but please understand that I decline to receive any answers from you in writing by return. After your recent impertinent ones I refuse to be annoyed with such, and I decline to read any more letters. If you have anything to say do come here and say it in person. Firstly, am I to understand that, having left Oxford as you did, with discredit to yourself, the reasons of which were fully explained to me by your tutor, you now intend to loaf and loll about and do nothing? All the time you were wasting at Oxford I was put off with an assurance that you were eventually to go into the Civil Service or to

the Foreign Office, and then I was put off with an assurance that you were going to the bar. It appears to me that you intend to do nothing. I utterly decline, however, to just supply you with sufficient funds to enable you to loaf about. You are preparing a wretched future for yourself, and it would be most cruel and wrong of me to encourage you in this. Secondly, I come to the most painful part of this letter – your intimacy with this man Wilde. It must either cease or I will disown you and stop all money supplies. I am not going to try and analyse this intimacy, and I make no charge: but to my mind to pose as a thing is as bad as to be it. With my own eyes I saw you both in the most loathsome and disgusting relationship as expressed by your manner and expression. Never in my experience have I ever seen such a sight as that in your horrible features. No wonder people are talking as they are. Also I now hear on good authority, but this may be false, that his wife is petitioning to divorce him for sodomy and other crimes. Is this true, or do you know of it? If I thought the actual thing was true, and it became public property, I should be quite justified in shooting him on sight. These Christian English cowards and men, as they call themselves, want waking up.

Your disgusted so-called father,
QUEENSBERRY.

To Oscar's dismay Bosie, who loved a good quarrel, replied by telegram: 'WHAT A FUNNY LITTLE MAN YOU ARE.' Queensberry was enraged and Oscar realised he was being drawn into the middle of a feud that was essentially between father and son. Oscar and Bosie thought it best to be away for a spell and took off for Paris and then travelled on to Florence.

When Oscar returned on 30 June a bellicose Queensberry arrived unannounced at Tite Street. A confrontation ensued, with Queensberry in a fury and Oscar denying all charges. Following this unpleasantness, Oscar went for legal advice to a solicitor, C. O. Humphreys, who was recommended by Robbie Ross, George Lewis being unavailable. Humphreys was not an ideal choice, having no experience in dealing with the delicate matter of homosexuality. Action was not taken immediately but Oscar later asked him to write to Queensberry threatening litigation if he did not retract his accusations. The reply was that he only wanted the friendship between his son and Oscar to end.

Oscar carried on with his work, publishing *The Sphinx* in a limited edition. In August he took his family to Worthing in West Sussex to begin writing *The Importance of Being Earnest*. This was actually remembered as a happy family time. Vyvyan could later recall his father being in good spirits at the seaside, boating with Cyril and fishing and building sandcastles with his youngest son. Oscar had always been a kind father to his two beloved children.

It was at this time that the novel *The Green Carnation* by Robert Smythe Hichens appeared. The main character, the dominant Mr Amarinth, was a slightly disguised portrait of Oscar, and his follower, Lord Reggie, was obviously Bosie, with Willie appearing as 'Teddy'. Jane found it a clever and amusing book, not understanding just how damaging it was by adding further fuel to the rumours of Oscar's homosexuality. Queensberry also read it and was further incensed.

Bosie managed to coax Oscar to the Grand Hotel in Brighton where the young Lord had to take to his bed with the flu. Oscar nursed his lover back to strength but then fell ill himself. Bosie refused to help his ailing companion who was even too weak to get out of bed for a drink. Instead he flew into a rage so violent that Oscar felt in danger. Bosie then stormed off leaving his ailing friend to fend for himself. Oscar recovered and prepared to return to London on Friday 19 October. Deeply hurt by Bosie's cruelty, he determined to finish with his tempestuous friend once and for all. But when he read the morning paper he was in for a shock. Viscount Drumlanrig, Queensberry's eldest son, was dead. He had been killed the day before in what was described as a hunting accident but suicide was the more probable cause. Had Oscar been able to foresee the veiled significance this tragedy was to have on his own life he might have acted differently. However, such foresight is not often available. His anger vanished and he telegraphed Bosie with his sympathies. They were friends again.

Queensberry received a second blow the following day when his new marriage was annulled. Deeply wounded, he thrashed about looking for people he could hold responsible for his son's death. In a ferocious letter to his first wife's father, dated 1 November, he lambasted his wife and her family, the Montgomerys, and 'Queers like Roseberry & certainly Christian hypocrite Gladstone the whole lot of you'. He blamed them for setting his son against him and hints at a concealed scandal saying 'I have already heard something that quite accounts for it all.'[5] The Marquess came to believe that his son and heir died because he was involved in a homosexual affair with powerful Lord Rosebery. He would now do all in his power to make sure his youngest son did not also fall victim to a similar scandal with the famous author.

An Ideal Husband opened on 3 January 1895. Rehearsals had been intense, with Oscar insisting the cast meet even on Christmas Day but the result was an outstanding success in front of an audience that once again included the Prince of Wales, Balfour, Chamberlain and many government ministers. *The Importance of Being Earnest* was also ready. Oscar wanted to stay and help out with the production but Bosie would not hear of it as they had planned a trip to Algeria. Oscar and Bosie stayed first in Algiers then moved 30 miles north to Blidah, a town much frequented by Englishmen on the lookout for boys. There they met with André Gide who recalled in his autobiography *Si le Grain ne Meurt* (*If I Die*) that Oscar and Bosie quarrelled fiercely and that Bosie took a boy off to Baskra for some weeks. He records Oscar complaining that Queensberry was tormenting him and Gide saw danger. 'But if you go back, what will happen?' he asked. 'Do you realise the risk?' 'That one can never know,' Oscar replied. 'My friends advise me to be prudent. Prudent! How could I be that? It would mean going backward. I must go as far as possible. I cannot go any further. Something must happen.' Oscar was now set on being accepted on his own terms. But a hypocritical society would not accept his terms and the consequences would be terrible.

While Oscar was off in Algeria, Constance tripped on loose carpet at the top of the stairs in Tite Street and tumbled all the way to the bottom. She injured her spine and her right hand and was left unable to walk for some time. She did not know her husband's exact whereabouts and had to write to Robbie Ross in the hope that he could pass on a message. Even in her distress Constance was concerned for the welfare of her mother-in-law, leaving directions to ensure Lady Wilde had 'everything she needs'.[6]

Oscar left Bosie behind somewhere in Algiers and returned to London in time to see the last of the rehearsals for *Earnest*. Queensberry was now going about London issuing threats and vowing vengeance against the playwright. By a stroke of luck a friend told Oscar that Queensberry was planning a demonstration on the first night of the new play. The producer, George Alexander, took evasive action by cancelling Queensberry's ticket and ensuring he would not gain entry. On St Valentine's Day 1895 *The Importance of Being Earnest* opened at St James's Theatre. It was a freezing cold night and Oscar arrived in a coat with a black velvet collar and wearing a green carnation. Queensberry failed to get in but made a statement by having a bouquet of carrots and turnips sent to the stage door. The play was a magnificent success. Max Beerbohm proclaimed it a masterpiece and the next day the *New York Times* announced that 'Oscar Wilde may be said to have at last, and by a single stroke, put his enemies under his feet'.

Oscar now had two successful plays running simultaneously in the West End. As a dramatist he had no rivals. Fortune was sure to follow. But the hugely successful playwright was troubled and could not savour his success. On the one hand he was being harassed and bullied by Queensberry while on the other he was being pressurised by Bosie, back now from Algeria. Bosie wanted his lover to take up the fight against his father. Oscar and Bosie moved into the Avondale Hotel but they quarrelled and the young Lord once again departed in a temper. He then fired off a series of letters to Oscar urging him to take legal action against his father and accusing him of being a coward. Oscar was growing increasingly anxious but, caught between father and son, could not decide on a definite course of action. Meanwhile, Queensberry was threatening destruction on Oscar Wilde.

Jane, cut off as she was from any real contact with the outside world, knew nothing of her son's dilemma. She wrote to say 'You have been a splendid success and I am so glad. Someone said you were now the foremost man of the day and I am so proud of you.'[7] Ground down by poverty, Oscar's mother had by now closed the door on a harsh world. She had given up her salons and also stopped writing; even her letters to Oscar were getting scarce. She rarely left the house and discouraged visitors. Vyvyan, Oscar's son, remembered his grandmother in Oakley Street and called her 'a terrifying and very severe old lady seated bolt upright in semi-darkness' dressed 'like a tragedy queen, her bodice covered with brooches and cameos'. He did not like having to visit but was forced to call occasionally out of duty to the old Lady despite his protests. He recalled the drawing room 'lit by guttering candles arranged in the corners of the room, as far away from my grandmother as possible, so that the heavy make-up with which she tried to conceal her age could not be detected'.[8] Jane's final sole pleasure was in reading reviews of her famous son's plays. Soon, even this satisfaction would be denied her.

Part 8

Calamity

'So they pulled down the statue of the Happy Prince.
"As he is no longer beautiful he is no longer useful."'

The Happy Prince

35

Arrest

On the morning of 28 February 1895 Oscar left the Avondale Hotel where he was staying and travelled the short distance to his club, the Albemarle. He was somewhat distressed, having just that morning received an unpleasant letter from Bosie. The hall porter at the Albemarle, Sidney Wright, handed him a card left by the Marquess of Queensberry ten days before. It was difficult to make out the words but Oscar understood it to read 'To Oscar Wilde, ponce and Somdomite', the misspelling possibly showing a degree of agitation in the writer. What was actually written was 'To Oscar Wilde posing Somdomite'. In court Queensberry maintained he wrote 'To Oscar Wilde, posing as a Somdomite'.

Oscar was upset and angry. Persecuted by both father and son he could not now even rely on his private club for sanctuary. His first instinct was to leave for Paris but the hotel demanded payment of the bill before it would release his luggage and Oscar did not have the money. Even though he was on the cusp of making an absolute fortune with two successful West End plays, the monies had not yet begun to come through.

He consulted his friend Robert Ross who wisely advised Oscar to do nothing about the card. Oscar persisted, however, and the following day went with Bosie to see C. O. Humphreys, his solicitor. Bosie pressed for action and Humphreys chose to believe the pair's protestations of innocence. He advised that a prosecution of

266

Queensberry was bound to succeed. When Oscar claimed that he did not have sufficient funds to press a charge Bosie announced that his brother and Lady Queensberry would be delighted to pay the costs. Humphreys and Bosie escorted Oscar, a white flower in his buttonhole, to a carriage that brought them to Marlborough Street police station. There, on 1 March, Oscar swore out a warrant for the arrest of John Sholto Douglas, the 9th Marquess of Queensberry, on a charge 'that he did unlawfully and maliciously publish a certain defamatory libel of and concerning one Oscar Wilde'. By this act Oscar killed the thing he loved, his own celebrity.

At the preliminary hearing it was stated that the Marquess would plead justification and the case was set for hearing on 9 March. George Lewis stepped aside, allowing Edward Carson, a Dubliner who knew Oscar from his time at university, to take the case. 'No doubt he will perform his task with the added bitterness of an old friend,' was Oscar's pointed response to this piece of news. The case was sent forward for trial but instead of getting down to work to prepare for what would obviously be a difficult suit, Bosie persuaded Oscar to take him off to Monte Carlo as they had originally planned. The pair left on 13 March for a week but the trip did not raise Oscar's spirits. Instead he sat on his own looking forlorn and anxious while Bosie gambled at the tables.

Meanwhile, back in London, Queensberry and his team were about the business of destroying Oscar. A private detective found his way to the flat in Little College Street that was rented to Alfred Taylor. The tip-off came from a female prostitute disgruntled because she believed she was losing clients to male youths operating from that address. Here the detective found a list of boys who, when confronted, all confessed to consorting with Oscar Wilde. This new evidence, together with incriminating letters written by Oscar to Douglas that had fallen into the hands of Queensberry, would prove damning.

When Humphreys called Oscar and Douglas in to look over Queensberry's Plea of Justification they were horrified to see before them a list of boys – ten of them named – and fifteen separate counts accusing Oscar of soliciting to commit sodomy. The list was as follows:

1. Edward Shelly, between February and May 1892.
2. Sidney Mavor, in October 1892.
3. Freddie Atkins, on 20 November 1892 in Paris.
4. Maurice Schwabe, on 22 November 1892.
5. Certain (unnamed) young men, between 25 January and 5 February 1892 in Paris.
6. Alfred Wood, in January 1893.
7. A certain young man, on or about 7 March 1893 in the Savoy Hotel.
8. Another young man, on or about 20 March 1893 in the Savoy Hotel.
9. Charles Parker, in March and April 1893.
10. Ernest Scarfe, between October 1893 and April 1894.
11. Herbert Tankard, in March 1893 at the Savoy Hotel.
12. Walter Grainger, in June 1893 in Oxford and in June, July and August at Goring.
13. Alfonso Harold Conway, in August and September 1894 at Worthing and about 27 September in Brighton.

Accusations of immorality concerning *The Picture of Dorian Gray* and maxims published in the *Chameleon* in December 1894 made up the remaining two counts.

Friends urged Oscar to drop the case but Bosie pressed him to continue. Oscar asked Frank Harris to give evidence in support of the morality of *Dorian Gray*, which prompted the shrewd Harris to explore the facts of the case. When he heard that Queensberry had managed to get hold of some letters from Oscar to Bosie he advised his friend to give up the lawsuit as it was sure to go against him. Harris decided to make even further enquiries. He spoke with a person in the office of the Director of Public Prosecutions and realised that Oscar had no chance of winning. He told Oscar this the following day in the Café Royal, advising him to leave at once for Paris and to take his family with him. From there he could plead his case through the press. Unfortunately, just as Oscar appeared to be taking heed of this good counsel, Bosie arrived and upon hearing the advice immediately accused Frank Harris of being no friend to Oscar. Deaf to any further pleading from the rational Harris, Oscar sided with Bosie and the pair left the café.

The trial proper began at a packed Old Bailey on 3 April 1895. Oscar put on a show, arriving in style with a carriage and a pair of liveried attendants. But in reality he was troubled. Sir Edward Clarke, an eminent barrister in his mid-fifties who had previously held the position of Solicitor General, opened for Oscar and the prosecution. Oscar's letters to Douglas were defended and the question of paying blackmail money was explained. The letters, according to Oscar, were works of art or drafts of prose poems. Indeed one already had been published in France. He also explained that the money he had paid for their safe return was to compensate the young chap Wood for having to hire a detective to locate them after they had been stolen from him by a youth called Allen. Wood had found them in an old suit he had been given by Lord Alfred Douglas. Now Wood claimed he was being threatened by Allen and his associates and needed to leave London for his own safety. Oscar's defence was that he had agreed to cover the young man's expenses and had given him money in response to his strong appeal. Oscar went on to say that shortly after this meeting he received a visit from another young man who returned a rather grubby copy of another letter. This would be a copy of the original Hyacinth Letter which was now in the possession of Queensberry's team.

Then Sir Edward Carson, who had been admitted to the English bar only one year before, rose to cross-examine. He immediately forced Oscar to admit that he was not thirty-eight years old as stated by his lawyer or thirty-nine as he himself had claimed but actually forty: a clever move as Oscar was shown to be unreliable even on trivial matters. Carson was efficient and there were several clashes with Oscar. The wealth of evidence the defence had at their disposal ensured it would be only a matter of time before they won the day. Oscar at one point had to remind the court that he was actually the prosecutor in this case. One cannot help but recall the Travers case when a newspaper had to remind its readers that Sir William Wilde was not the person on trial.

Queensberry's team had done its work well. When it came to the list of homeless and shiftless boys, as Carson called them, with whom Oscar had associated, all was lost. The youths were willing to say anything to remain free. Their names had been found on the list in Alfred Taylor's flat and Queensberry's defence had intimidated them into believing that they could receive stiff sentences for their homosexual activities. Carson continued by explaining his client's actions to the jury in terms they could understand. Queensberry 'had one hope alone – that of saving his son', whereas Wilde had been consorting with 'some of the most immoral characters in London', including Alfred Taylor, 'a most notorious character – as the police will tell the court'. Carson carried on relentlessly. He asked about certain love letters, questioned whether Oscar had kissed a boy called Walter Grainger, a servant in a house in Oxford, raised issues about paying blackmail and then read the list of boys with whom Oscar had consorted.

Clarke attempted to regain ground by reading letters written by Queensberry to his son. He had hoped to show that the Marquess was not in fact a caring father at all but an irrational bully. The letters unfortunately made reference to both the Prime Minister Lord Rosebery and to Gladstone. This was a fatal error as the names of the two politicians appeared in the Continental press linking them, albeit extremely loosely, to the case. This almost certainly ensured that Oscar would be charged with indecency to avoid any allegations of a conspiracy.

On 5 April Oscar's counsel requested on behalf of his client to withdraw from the prosecution to save 'going through day after day, it might be, matters of the most appalling character'. It was clear that Oscar's prosecution would now fail and that he was in danger of himself being charged. Clarke offered to keep the trial going to give his client a chance of fleeing to France but Oscar declared that he would stay. Carson had the upper hand and in discussions with Clarke insisted that the whole Plea and not just part of the Plea of Justification be allowed. Oscar's barrister had no choice but to agree.

This was disastrous as it meant that Queensberry was found to have been fully justified in calling Wilde a sodomite in the public interest. Mr Justice Collins instructed the jury to so rule. Frank Harris, who was in court for the verdict, noted that the judge made no attempt to subdue the cheering that broke out in the chamber. In fact, he sent a note of congratulations to Carson.

Within hours of the verdict a warrant was issued for Oscar's arrest. Robbie Ross was sent to tell Constance the terrible news. She wept and said she hoped her husband would go abroad. Oscar was torn between staying or fleeing to France and his bag was half-packed. His friends, congregating at the Cadogan Hotel where Bosie had been staying, advised flight but the idea of wandering the Continent as a fugitive did not appeal to Oscar. He would prefer to stay and be martyred by a hypocritical society and its unjust laws. He drank some wine – he had been drinking heavily all afternoon – and waited for the knock on the door.

At ten minutes past six it came. A waiter arrived, followed by two detectives. 'We have a warrant here, Mr Wilde, for your arrest on a charge of committing indecent acts.' He was taken to Bow Street police station and put in a cell. Bosie came to the station but was refused permission to see the prisoner. He had received a message from Oscar telling him to get his brother Percy and George Alexander and Lewis Waller from the theatres where his plays were running to come in the morning with bail money. Only Percy agreed. Oscar, feeling wretched, ate a little chicken, drank some coffee and was not allowed to smoke. 'With what a crash this fell! Why did the Sibyl say fair things? I thought but to defend him from his father,' he wrote to his friend Ada Leverson two days later from Bow Street.[1] Robbie Ross hurried to Tite Street and gathered some clothes for Oscar but was not allowed to leave them or to see his friend. Fearing that Oscar's papers would be ransacked by police or private detectives acting for Queensberry, Ross dashed back to Tite Street and with the help of a servant – Constance had locked the rooms and left – broke into the library and saved some of Oscar's letters and manuscripts.

The reaction to Oscar's arrest was immediate. It was reported that 600 gentlemen crossed from Dover to Calais that very night, ten times the normal number of passengers. Oscar's name, large outside the theatres in the West End, was covered over and his books were removed from shops. His friends began destroying even harmless letters. Oscar was formally charged at Bow Street Police Court the following morning, 6 April, and bail was refused. This was unusual in that the crime was a misdemeanour. The hearings dragged on and, instead of bail, Oscar was transferred on remand to Holloway Prison to await trial. Robbie Ross, named in the papers as being with Oscar at the time of his arrest, was forced to resign from some of his clubs and his mother offered him £500 towards Oscar's defence if he would leave England. He crossed to Calais and later travelled to Rouen. Many of Oscar's friends had already left but Bosie was determined to stay and help, most likely because it would antagonise his father.

Oscar's plays were soon taken off entirely both in London and New York. And Willie did not help matters. Oscar complained in a letter to Ada Leverson that his brother 'has been writing me the most monstrous letters. I have had to beg him to stop . . . I don't know what to do. My life seems to have gone from me. I feel caught in a terrible net. I don't know where to turn.'[2]

The hearings were drawn-out affairs. On the last hearing, on 23 April, a trial date was set for 26 April. Oscar was charged with indecency and sodomy, charges the magistrate believed so grave as to rule out bail. Meanwhile, Queensberry forced a bankruptcy sale of Oscar's effects. The beautiful house at Tite Street was effectively ransacked. A Mr Bullock was appointed to conduct a public auction of Oscar's private possessions on Wednesday 24 April with a public viewing the previous day. Even the children's toys were included in the sale as were Oscar's beautiful books, bundled and disposed of for a pittance. Many of these books had been presented to him by literary colleagues such as Hugo and Whitman. There were also first editions of Sir William's books. Included in the lots were drawings by Whistler and Thomas Carlyle's writing desk, beautiful china, letters and manuscripts. All were scattered. It was legal pillage and heartbreaking for Constance and for Oscar. Some items were purchased and saved by loyal friends and Jane's letters, written to

Oscar over the years and which he had faithfully retained, were among the belongings to survive. It would be many years before the faithful Robbie Ross could eventually rescue the Wilde estate from receivership.

Bosie continued to visit Oscar in prison on almost a daily basis. Eventually, Sir Edward Clarke, who together with young Travers Humphreys, C. O. Humphreys' son, was still representing Oscar, convinced him to leave England as his presence was more of a hindrance than a help to the case.

36

Prosecution

The first trial of Oscar Wilde opened in the Old Bailey on 26 April 1895. There was a desire on the side of the prosecutor, Charles Gill, to have a speedy trial, which meant the cases against Alfred Taylor and Oscar were joined even though Sir Edward Clarke protested. The case involved twenty-five counts of gross indecency and conspiracy to commit gross indecency. The accusation was that Wilde and Taylor had conspired together to commit sodomy, but sodomy was an extremely difficult crime to prove. Alfred Taylor was linked to Oscar, having been the one who had procured the young men whose names were found on the list at Taylor's flat. Clarke continued to protest but Mr Justice Sir Arthur Charles agreed with the state prosecutor. The conspiracy charges were soon dropped but the two cases remained joined, much to Oscar's disadvantage.

There was an amount of activity going on behind the scenes. Prosecutor Gill reached an agreement with Charles Russell, solicitor for Queensberry, to keep Lord Alfred Douglas' name out of the proceedings as far as was possible. It is also very strange that George Wyndham MP, a cousin of Bosie's and friendly with Oscar, could not find one person of influence willing to help Oscar. The theory is that Queensberry had threatened Lord Rosebery, who was now Prime Minister, with a scandal if Oscar Wilde was not prosecuted with the utmost vigour. This would certainly explain the government's extraordinarily aggressive position throughout the entire case.

The trial went ahead along the same lines as the libel case. A list of witnesses was produced, all willing to testify against Oscar, who was now looking thin and anxious. Oscar answered the questions evenly but rose to the occasion when asked by Gill to explain the phrase 'The love that dare not speak its name'. His reply drew applause from the gallery, and a few hisses. It has become a celebrated speech from the dock and reads as follows:

> The love that dare not speak its name in this century is such a great affection of an elder for a younger man as there was between David and Jonathan, such as Plato made the very basis of his philosophy, and such as you find in the sonnets of Michelangelo and Shakespeare. It is that deep, spiritual affection that is as pure as it is perfect. It dictates and pervades great works of art like those of Shakespeare and Michelangelo, and those two letters of mine, such as they are. It is in this century misunderstood, so much misunderstood that it may be described as the 'Love that dare not speak its name', and on account of it, I am placed where I am now. It is beautiful, it is fine, it is the noblest form of affection. There is nothing unnatural about it. It is intellectual, and it repeatedly exists between an elder and a younger man, when the elder has intellect, and the younger man has all the joy, hope, and glamour of life before him. That it should be so, the world does not understand. The world mocks at it and sometimes puts one in the pillory for it.

The jury and those in the gallery may have been impressed by Oscar's extemporaneous eloquence but he was in fact using parts of a speech he had delivered in 1891 on the night he was elected a member of Wilfrid Blunt's Crabbet Club, a group of forty-five men who met annually at Blunt's family estate in Crabbet Park. He was also quoting from his own creation *Dorian Gray*.

The jury in the trial was out from just after half past one to a quarter past five but they failed to reach a verdict. Oscar could have been acquitted at this point. T. M. Healy, barrister and politician, asked

Sir Frank Lockwood, the Solicitor General, not to put Oscar on trial again. Lockwood replied: 'I would not but for the abominable rumours against Rosebery.'[1] Edward Clarke sought a postponement, presumably to let sentiment abate, but Gill, the prosecutor, pressed for a retrial to be heard at the next session and the judge agreed. The establishment obviously wanted Oscar's ruin. A new trial was fixed for 20 May and once again bail was refused. Two days later a different judge set bail at £5,000, half to be allowed on Wilde's own recognisance. It took seven days to organise the funds. Bosie's brother, Percy, Lord Douglas of Hawick, put up half. Ernest Leverson, the wealthy diamond-broker husband of Oscar's friend Ada, was behind the raising of the remaining sum. He managed to get an acquaintance of his, the Reverend Stewart Headlam, a man who had met Oscar Wilde on only two previous occasions, to put up the bail monies. Headlam was a controversial priest of the Church of England and a pioneer of Christian Socialism who felt that Oscar deserved his freedom at least until he was convicted of a crime. Oscar was released from Bow Street on 7 May but he emerged into a very altered and hostile world. Thus would be his life for his remaining days.

Two rooms had been booked for Oscar at the Midland Hotel at St Pancras, well away from the places he would have normally frequented, but as he sat down to dinner the manager asked him to leave. Queensberry and a gang of roughs had been following him and arrived at the hotel where they threatened the manager for receiving the disgraced author. He drove to another hotel but the same thing happened. He then drove around aimlessly trying to find shelter, all the time pursued by Queensberry's thugs. Eventually, around midnight, he had no alternative but to knock on the door of 146 Oakley Street where Willie and his wife were now living with Jane. 'Willie, give me shelter or I shall die in the streets,' cried Oscar as he staggered into the narrow hall.[2] Willie later described his brother's arrival: 'He came tapping with his beak against the window-pane, and fell down on the threshold like a wounded stag.'[3] The pair had not spoken in eighteen months.

Willie gave his worn-out brother a small camp-bed between the fireplace and the wall in the corner of a poorly furnished room. Oscar remained there for some days, physically ill and distressed. Robert Sherard came from France to see his friend and found his face 'flushed and swollen'. 'Oh, why have you brought me no poison from Paris?' Oscar asked in a broken voice. Willie had written cruel letters to Oscar in his prison cell; now he was claiming the high moral ground. 'At least my vices were decent,' W. B. Yeats heard him declare. Yeats also claims in his *Autobiographies* that Willie was secretly pleased that his 'successful brother who had scorned him for a drunken ne'er-do-well was now at his mercy'. Vanity, according to Willie, was the cause of Oscar's anger over the reports of him being mimicked in the Lotus Club in New York and now it was his vanity that had 'brought all this disgrace upon him'.[4]

'Willie makes such merit of giving me shelter,' Oscar told his good friend Frank Harris, who called at Oakley Street and insisted on bringing him out to lunch against Willie's wishes. Harris put forward plans for the defence but Oscar interrupted saying: 'You talk with passion and conviction, as if I were innocent.' 'But you are innocent,' Harris replied, 'aren't you?' 'No,' said Oscar, 'I thought you knew all along.' Harris then pleaded with Oscar to flee. Oscar would not agree to go. Frank Harris claimed that Oscar believed his brother would inform the police if he did not return to Oakley Street. Harris further claimed Oscar told him that 'Willie . . . has made my solicitors buy letters of mine; he has black-mailed me.'[5] Robert Sherard checked this story years later by asking Humphreys if it was true but the solicitor could not recall. Sherard believed that Willie stood by Oscar most loyally at this time. Willie told Oscar that he was defending him all over London and Oscar commented to a friend: 'My poor, dear brother, he would compromise a steam engine.'[6]

Oscar's biographers all agree that Willie was determined to see his brother stay and stand trial: 'Oscar is an Irish gentleman and he will face the music.'[7] Jane also believed he should not flee: 'If you stay, even if you go to prison, you will always be my son. It will make no difference to my affection. But if you go, I will never speak to you again.'[8] Yeats called to see Oscar at Oakley Street but instead encountered Willie who asked him his business. Yeats had letters of encouragement from Ireland and Willie wondered if the letters were urging Oscar to run away: 'Every friend he has is urging him to, but we have made up our minds that he must stay and take his chance.' Yeats replied: 'No, I certainly would not advise him to run away.' Yeats later wrote 'I never doubted, even for an instant, that he made the right decision, and, that he owes to that decision half of his renown.'[9]

And what of the other Wilde living at Oakley Street? Jane's life had been blessed at times but it had also been tragic. She had experienced fame as Speranza and mingled with royalty and aristocrats. She had been mistress of one of Dublin's finest mansions, honoured in castles, had magical times visiting European cities and holidaying in their west of Ireland lodges. But she had also lost her beloved Isola to fever and then her husband, too, plunging her into poverty at a relatively young age. She had lived through the stressful experience of the Travers case and had tolerated Sir William's complicated relationships. Now her only source of joy, her beloved son who had supported her and brought so much glory to a tattered family, was being destroyed.

Jane had been tough and brave but now she had enough. The door in Oakley Street was closed and the old Lady retreated to her bedroom, far from prying eyes. The Comtesse de Brémont wrote of the 'mournful train of friends that went silently to the closed door of the house in Oakley Street to drop a word of tender enquiry or reassurance into the letter-box'.[10] Robert Sherard recorded the awful events: 'during all those dreadful days in May, 1895, when I was a constant visitor to my friend, who had been released on bail, she was confined to her room, indeed to her bed'.[11]

Ada Leverson, Oscar's great friend and supporter, whom he liked to call Sphinx, invited him to dinner and saw how unhappy he was staying with Willie at Oakley Street. She and her husband offered him a room in their own home. There was space because their son was in the country and so it came to pass that the man once proclaimed the new Hans Christian Andersen left his mother's house to spend his last days of freedom hidden away in a nursery surrounded by children's toys.

Most of Oscar's friends were now imploring him to escape. Even Percy Douglas, who stood to lose his bail money, urged him to get away to France. Constance called at the Leversons and she too begged him to leave. She spent two hours with her husband but left in tears when he refused to go away. Ada Leverson was so moved that she sent up a note to Oscar asking him to do what his wife had asked of him. When he later came down to dinner his only remark was to say 'That is not like you, Sphinx.' She saw 'a look of immovable obstinacy' on his face. Oscar believed that if he was to retain any dignity he must not run. He was not prepared to live the life of a fugitive, skulking in shadows. The beautiful thing to do was the courageous thing. He would stay.

The night before his trial Oscar spent 'a long hour with his mother, deeply loved and deeply honoured, whom he would never see again'.[12] He asked Ada Leverson to leave out a sleeping draught for him. He would not take it but its presence would have a magical effect. He left a little gift for each of his friends as a souvenir and asked Ada to write to him if the worst came to the worst. In the morning More Adey, another literary friend of Oscar's, came by to accompany him to court.

On 22 May 1895 the second and final trial of Oscar Wilde opened in the Old Bailey. Sir Edward Clarke requested separate trials, one for Alfred Taylor and another for Oscar. Lockwood, the Solicitor General, opposed the motion but Mr Justice Sir Alfred Wills agreed to Clarke's request. Unfortunately, he then proceeded to hear Taylor's case first. This was a blow to Oscar as Taylor, who was well known to police, was certain to be convicted. There would undoubtedly be an overlap in evidence and the same jury could hardly be expected to acquit Oscar if they found Taylor guilty. The charge was reduced from sodomy, which would be difficult to prove, to indecency and Taylor was promptly found guilty on two counts. Sentencing was deferred.

Oscar's retrial lasted six days. The press were for the most part on Queensberry's side, praising him for bringing down the 'High Priest of the Decadents', as the *National Observer* labelled Oscar. One notable exception was *Reynold's News* and Oscar's biographer Richard Ellmann makes the interesting comment that this newspaper 'had private information about the extraordinary zeal with which Wilde was being prosecuted'. Meanwhile, the state witnesses were being very well looked after by the Crown. The Parker brothers, Charles and William, were living at the prosecution's expense in a residence at

Chiswick with Charles Parker, a very important witness because he was willing to testify that he was sodomised by Oscar, being supplied with a new suit. It has even been suggested that all state witnesses had been receiving £5 per week since the first prosecution by Oscar against Queensberry.

Sir Edward Clarke achieved some early successes. He got the judge to rule that Edward Shelley was an unreliable witness for the Crown and, in an interesting aside, it was revealed that the person who introduced Taylor to Oscar in the first place happened to be Sir Frank Lockwood's nephew by marriage, one Maurice Schwabe, one of the many who had recently crossed to France. As the case dragged on the Comtesse de Brémont attempted to visit Jane at Oakley Street but could not gain access. She happened upon Willie and enquired about her friend. 'Mother is bearing up bravely – she hopes for the best,' he replied. 'It was so good of you to call, but she cannot see any one, no matter how dear a friend.' Willie must have thought his brother still had a chance for he told the Comtesse that 'Oscar will need me when the verdict is given. I must take care of my poor brother – for, one way or another, he will be a wreck after this terrible business!'[13] As for Jane, one of her strongest traits had always been loyalty. She never lost faith in her husband during the Travers case and she continued to believe in Willie's ability even when his own brother had given up on him. Now she was locked away in her room, still loyal to her brilliant son and hoping for the best, even though all of London's press condemned him.

At half past three on the afternoon of Saturday 25 May 1895, the jury in the second criminal trial of Oscar Wilde retired to consider its verdict. This time they were ready to convict. Oscar Wilde was found guilty of committing indecent acts.

Mr Justice Wills in his summing up called it the worst case he had ever tried and the sentence of the court was the harshest he could impose, imprisonment and hard labour for two years. The prisoners, Taylor and Wilde, were taken immediately from court to Newgate Prison and from there to Holloway. A few weeks later Oscar was moved to Pentonville before being transferred on 4 July to Wandsworth. Finally, Oscar was moved to Reading Gaol on 21 November 1895 to complete his full sentence without any remission.

37

Incarceration

Robert Sherard says that Jane, when told of the verdict, 'only turned over on her side in bed and said, "May it help him!"' Whatever her immediate response, and Sherard's account of her reaction may not be exact, she must have been totally crushed. Many years before, following the birth of her second child, Jane had written a letter to her friend in Scotland in which she chided herself for not being as happy as a mother ought to be. Instead, she was filled with apprehension for the future because life held endless potential for woe[1] and how right she was.

Constance had engaged a French governess to take her two boys to Switzerland to escape the turmoil of London and now she also left England to join them. Their lives had been thrown into chaos by events of which they knew little or nothing. Plucked from their schools in Kent and Sussex they were hauled back to London, then hurriedly shipped abroad. Vyvyan was to later say that he knew nothing about the nature of his father's offences until he was eighteen. Cyril said that he learned the truth when he read about the terrible events in a newspaper while staying with relations in Dublin before being sent to Switzerland. He must have been bewildered and devastated by what he read, having been particularly close to his father.

Constance booked herself and her sons into a hotel near Lake Geneva but the manager, on finding out that he was hosting the family of Oscar Wilde, asked them to leave. They went to friends near Genoa in Italy and later joined her brother, Otho, back in Switzerland. On returning to England for a short visit, Constance changed the family name by deed poll to Holland, an old family name on Constance's side. Oscar's two sons, Cyril and Vyvyan, assumed the name Holland for the rest of their lives. His grandson Merlin, born in 1945, and his great-grandson Lucian, born in 1979, continue to be known by the name of Holland.

Bosie, always one for the grand gesture, petitioned Queen Victoria from Rouen for clemency but without success. As for Willie, he was sinking more and more into alcoholism. A few weeks after the trial, Lily Wilde, Willie's wife who was now heavily pregnant, wrote to the governor of Pentonville Prison asking him to pass on her 'fondest love' to her 'unhappy brother-in-law' and to let him know 'what will give him the most pleasure, that his mother is wonderfully well'.[2] This was untrue as Jane was seriously ill but it was thought best to keep this news from Oscar. She had problems with her breathing and had lost the will to live.

Behind bars, Oscar was suffering greatly. The prison diet was poor and insufficient, consisting of thin soup or bacon and beans, potatoes, weak gruel, suet and water, with a little cocoa and bread for breakfast. Oscar was a big man and not accustomed to starvation rations. The prisoners were locked up for the night at five o'clock and spent their first month sleeping on a bare plank raised a few inches from the ground. Sleep was virtually impossible. If deemed fit enough, they would spend six hours on the treadmill, twenty minutes on and five off, and one hour in the exercise yard walking around in strict silence. The treadmill was a great wheel that was turned by the prisoners who had to 'climb' or step on to the timber steps as they came down to meet them where they stood in narrow individual booths. The continuous 'climbing' was monotonous and physically gruelling.

After the first month the prisoner was assigned work detail such as picking oakum, a torturous procedure whereby loose fibres are disentangled from lengths of old tarred rope. It was very severe on the fingers and nails and a prisoner was expected to produce a certain quota every day. Oscar always struggled to achieve his quota, much to the annoyance of the prison authorities, and he suffered great pain in the process. To add to Oscar's misery he fell ill with diarrhoea in Pentonville, which persisted despite doses of medicine. There was no plumbing in his cell, only a tin container, which he quickly filled. The sight awaiting the warders who opened his cell door in the mornings was 'indescribable'. On at least three occasions the warders fell to vomiting.

Oscar's first visitor was R. B. Haldane, a member of a Home Office prison committee, who had known the famous playwright before his fall. He found a man who was in deep depression. Haldane tried to comfort the prisoner by telling him that he had not used his great literary gifts to their full potential up to that point because of his lifestyle and that this period of misfortune might prove a blessing by providing a great subject. Oscar burst into tears but then agreed that he had fallen to temptation and would take heed of what Haldane had said. They drew up a list of books and Haldane made arrangements for Oscar to receive them. Pen and ink, however, were still forbidden. Haldane received an anonymous package through the post some years later. It contained a copy of *The Ballad of Reading Gaol*.

Meanwhile, as life continued on the outside, Bosie fell into his old ways, causing a scandal with youths on a hired boat in Le Havre before leaving there for Italy. Lily Wilde had her baby girl, Dorothy Irene Wilde, on 11 July 1895. Willie had no money at all so Oscar gave the couple £50 pounds towards the child's expenses. He had been given £1,000 by a friend called Adela Schuster while out on bail and had passed this on to Ernest Leverson to hold with instructions that his mother was to be looked after. The rent on Oakley Street was paid out of this money and Jane also received about £280 for expenses. Willie and his wife continued to stay on at Oakley Street with their new baby. Jane now needed someone to look after her but could no longer afford a servant.

Oscar was allowed to send and receive one letter every three months from Wandsworth Prison. Jane was counting the weeks in the hope that she would soon hear from her beloved son. In the event, Oscar sent his first letter through to Constance in Switzerland. She had been persuaded by Robert Sherard to try to reconcile with her husband instead of proceeding with her initial plans to look for a divorce. Constance wrote to Oscar promising forgiveness and sent a letter to the prison governor seeking permission to visit her husband in prison. A disappointed Jane wrote to Ernest Leverson on 29 August: 'Accept my grateful thanks for your kind attention in bringing me news of dear Oscar, as I am very poorly and unable to see friends or to leave my room . . . I thought that Oscar might perhaps write to me after three months, but I have not had a line from him, and I have not written to him as I dread my letters being returned.'[3]

Jane spent the autumn and winter of 1895 alone in her room, never venturing out and refusing any visitors. The suffering of this once proud woman can barely be imagined as she sat in her chair or lay on her bed, crushed by poverty and surrounded by the ruins of her dreams, one son firmly in the grip of alcoholism and the other disgraced and imprisoned. If there was one comfort perhaps it was Lily Lees, a kindly woman, who tended to her baby and looked after her deteriorating mother-in-law while her husband sank beyond the point of rescue. Willie took to selling Oscar's belongings to fund his drinking and Lily had to ask her own family for help. In a letter from Lily to More Adey, in which she misspells her husband's name, she writes: 'Kindly understand that I take no responsibility as regards Wily and that any money from the sale of [Oscar's] clothes I had nothing to do with. Also, Wily has not earned one farthing for the last ten months and I and my family have had to keep my home over my head.'[4]

In September Constance came over from Switzerland after receiving permission to see Oscar. They met in a vaulted room behind many locked doors where prisoner and visitor sat divided by rows of iron bars, watched over by a warder. It was more awful than she had imagined. Oscar told her that he had been mad the last three years and that he would kill Douglas if he saw him. By renouncing Bosie, Oscar removed a major obstacle preventing his possible return to his family upon release and Constance, always kind, now believed that he had been misguided and weak rather that evil. Constance was deeply moved by her visit and reported that her husband was 'very altered in every way'.

Oscar was indeed in a bad state physically and mentally. Hunger and dysentery had weakened him and he believed he would soon be dead. Though weak, he was compelled to follow the prison routine and pick his measure of oakum. One day while attending chapel he fainted and collapsed, causing injury to his right ear; he had already been experiencing some deafness in that ear. This fall and his general weakness led to Oscar spending two months in the prison infirmary. Haldane came to see him again and realised that the situation was not satisfactory. He arranged for the prisoner to be transferred to Reading but the transfer process occasioned an incident that was to haunt Oscar for a long time. On the afternoon of the transfer, 21 November 1895, Oscar was left standing for half an hour, handcuffed and in his prison clothes, in full view on the platform at Clapham Junction. He was soon recognised and a jeering crowd gathered. One man stepped forward and spat at him. Oscar wrote later in *De Profundis*: 'For a year after this was done to me, I wept every day at the same hour and for the same space of time.'

In Reading, Oscar was given cell C.3.3, cell three on landing three in C wing, and set to work in the garden and in the library. These tasks would have been regarded as lighter labour and a relief from picking oakum. But Oscar continued to struggle and clashed regularly with the governor, Lieutenant Colonel J. Isaacson, a strict disciplinarian. These confrontations often led to Oscar being repri-manded; he would find himself on even shorter rations or confined to the punishment cells. On 19 February 1896 Constance came to Reading to see her husband. It was an unscheduled visit. Even though her own health was poor she had travelled all the way from Italy to bring further devastating news. Jane had fallen seriously ill with bronchitis in January. As she grew weaker she asked if Oscar could be brought from prison to see her but the request was denied. Her condition deteriorated further and on Monday 3 February Lady Wilde died. The official cause of death on her death certificate was sub-acute bronchitis. But the months spent alone in a drab room, grieving and pining for her beloved son, must also have taken their toll.

In one of her many romantic flights, Speranza had expressed a hope that her body would be thrown into the sea or buried near a rock on some wild coast. In the event, Jane was buried in plot 127 Kensal Green Cemetery on Wednesday 5 February with only Willie and his wife as mourners. Lily, writing to More Adey, explained that Jane 'had left us a private letter expressing very strongly the wish to be buried quite privately and for no one to come to her funeral'.[5] She went on to thank him for the beautiful wreath sent by Oscar's friends. Willie arranged for black-edged cards to be printed. They read: 'In Memoriam JANE FRANCESCA AGNES SPERANZA, Lady Wilde, Widow of Sir William Wilde, MD, Surgeon Oculist to the Queen in Ireland, Knight of the Order of the North Star in Sweden. Died at her residence, 146 Oakley Street, Chelsea, London, Feb 3rd 1896'.[6]

Many publications carried obituaries. The *World* of 12 February wrote: 'The note of her character was loftiness; she did not perceive small things; her soul was as high as her imagination was fervent, her enthusiasm fresh, and her heart tender and true.' The *Pall Mall Gazette* on 6 February praised her poetry. *The Times* of 7 February referred to her as 'a distinguished member' of Young Ireland and repeated the story of her standing up in court during the Charles Gavan Duffy trial to take the blame for the editorial 'Jacta Alea Est'. The *Athenaeum* of 8 February noted that 'under the mask of brilliant display and bohemian recklessness, lay a deep and loyal soul and a kindly and sympathetic nature'. It acknowledged with sympathy that she had to bear 'her heavy cross in silence and stoical patience under the cover of darkness and the cloak of oblivion'.

The Irish papers, too, gave over large amounts of space to the news of Lady Wilde's death. She had been a national figure in her day. The *Freeman's Journal* of 6 February called her 'A woman of the most versatile attainments, genuine intellectual power and commanding character.' Oscar's disgrace was only mentioned obliquely. The *Dublin Evening Mail*, also on 6 February, said that Jane 'had a great deal of the shadows of this life to encounter'.

The next problem was how to tell Oscar that his beloved mother had died. More Adey kindly volunteered when Willie told him that 'For many reasons he will not wish to see me.'[7] After consulting with Ernest Leverson, it was decided to ask Constance if she would come back to England and break the sad news to her husband. 'I am not strong', the ever-generous Constance replied, 'but I could bear the journey better if I thought that such a terrible thing could not be told to him roughly.'[8] Constance was by now suffering badly from the fall on the stairs in Tite Street but managed to make the journey from Italy.

Oscar was summoned to talk with his wife in a private room. He told her he already knew about his mother's death. He had seen a vision of her in his cell. She was dressed for out-of-doors and he asked her to take off her hat and cloak and sit down but she shook her head sadly and vanished. The day before, a warder had stepped on a spider and Oscar, always superstitious, told him that he would now hear bad news, worse than any he had yet heard.[9] Constance kissed him and comforted him and they spoke of the children. They also agreed practical issues. Oscar would receive an income of £200 a year from Constance's dowry when he was released and be reunited with his wife and family. Constance was deeply upset after the meeting and told her brother that Oscar was now an absolute wreck.

In July Oscar petitioned the Home Secretary for release. Writing in the third person, he referred to 'the despair and misery of this lonely and wretched life having been intensified beyond words by the death of his mother, Lady Wilde, to whom he was deeply attached'.[10] His petition was unsuccessful. Meanwhile, Lily Wilde sent Oscar's possessions to More Adey with a letter saying, 'I feel sure now his mother is dead he will not wish to hold any further communication with us.'[11] She also told him that they could no longer afford to stay on at Oakley Street and were moving to smaller rooms.

Not all of Oscar's possessions found their way to More Adey. The following year Oscar was upset to hear that his beautiful fur coat was missing. He had worn it in America and to opening nights and was attached to it for sentimental reasons. Willie had apparently pawned it. He was now pawning everything he could lay his hands on. Some rugs and two portmanteaux, among other items, had also been sold off. Lily must be given credit for managing to pass on as much as she did to More Adey, including some original manuscripts, for Willie could be very difficult when in need of a drink.

Oscar had more immediate problems. His big fear was of going mad. His friends grew alarmed and decided to try to get Oscar's sentence mitigated on health grounds. Haldane was also working on his case and the newly appointed chairman of the Prison Commission, Evelyn Ruggles-Brise, a man of more liberal views, agreed to meet with Frank Harris. Following this meeting Colonel Isaacson was told to allow Harris to meet with Wilde in private. Reports on Oscar's health were sought and eventually Ruggles-Brise was able to order more books for the prisoner. To Oscar's delight, he was also allowed at last a supply of writing materials.

Then, to improve the situation further, Colonel Isaacson was transferred to Lewes Prison and replaced by Major J. O. Nelson, a kinder individual. These developments greatly eased Oscar's situation as he faced into his second year behind bars. Nelson encouraged Oscar in his reading and writing. A more extensive list of books was ordered and Oscar, buoyed up a little by the improvements, began to study Italian and German. Relieved of the task of picking oakum, allowed more exercise and now provided with extra reading material, Oscar at last began to see some hope of a future life, even if in exile. He was also allowed to grow his hair for the last five months of his incarceration. This was important as it would allow the fallen celebrity to blend into society more easily upon his release.

These were actually extraordinary concessions given the harsh norms of the day. It has been suggested that Oscar was transferred to Reading Gaol, a comparatively obscure prison, because there was one member on that prison's Visiting Committee who might look out for his welfare.[12] This person was George W. Palmer, the eldest son of George Palmer, one of the founding partners of Huntley & Palmers, the famous biscuit makers whose factory was next door to the gaol. He had been MP for Reading from 1892 to 1895 and would be again from 1898 to 1904. By 1895 Huntley & Palmers was the largest biscuit manufacturing plant in the world, employing 5,000 people. George Palmer had a brother called Walter whose wife Jean liked to host literary parties at their home. Oscar and Constance were friendly with Walter and his wife and had been regular guests at Westfield, the Palmer's home. Documents in the Reading Museum refer to the fact that Oscar knew Jean Palmer so well that he liked to call her 'Moonbeam'. Oscar, together with friends George Meredith and the actress Louise Jopling, had visited the biscuit factory in 1892 and signed the visitors' book. It seems possible that Haldane, who had already secured concessions for Oscar and was aware of this connection with the Palmers, had Oscar transferred to Reading in the hope that he would receive some sort of protection from the influential member of the Visiting Committee.

Oscar now had unrestricted access to pen and ink, albeit with the stipulation that what he wrote had to be handed in to the warden every night and could not be returned the next day. This regulation was relaxed to a degree as the months passed and it became clear that Oscar was producing a work of value. In order to write something substantial and still keep within prison rules Oscar hit upon the plan of writing a long letter to Lord Alfred Douglas where he would reflect upon their friendship and their follies and discuss the path which led to ruin. Through the recording of the events and the exploration of motives and emotions, the fallen author might gain some form of redemption in the end.

38

Release

In January 1897 Oscar began writing the work that was to become known as *De Profundis*, an autobiographical account of the previous five years tracing his progress from pleasure to pain and remorse. It is here that Oscar wrote so poignantly of his mother's death:

> Three months go over and my mother dies. You know none better how deeply I loved and honoured her. Her death was so terrible to me that I, once a lord of language, have no words to express my anguish and my shame. Never, even in the most perfect days of my development as an artist, could I have had words fit to bear so august a burden, or to move with sufficient stateliness of music through the purple pageant of my incommunicable woe. She and my father had bequeathed me a name they had made noble and honoured not merely in Literature, Art, Archaeology and Science, but in the public history of my own country and its evolution as a nation. I have disgraced that name eternally. I have made it a low byword among low people. I have dragged it through the mire. I have given it to brutes that they might make it brutal, and to fools that they might turn it into a synonym for folly. What I suffered then, and still suffer, is not for pen to write or paper to record.

Oscar went on to write about 'the intolerable burden of misery and remorse that the memory of my mother placed upon me, and places on me still'. Perhaps hardest of all was his belief that his mother 'died broken-hearted because the son of whose genius and art she had been proud, and whom she had regarded always as a worthy continuer of a distinguished name, had been condemned to the treadmill for two years'.[1]

Lord Alfred Douglas would eventually write his own account of his time with Oscar and could always be relied upon to have the bitter word. Of Oscar and his mother he wrote: 'He was able to talk of his mother as Lady Wilde, and I have heard him refer to her in certain company as "her ladyship" with great effect. You would imagine from his manner that she was a grand dame of the first order with two or three large places to her name and retinues of servants. Of Papa Wilde we did not hear quite so frequently.'[2]

Oscar continued to work on his extended 'letter' from January into April and sought permission to send it out to Robbie Ross. Permission was denied but he was told he could bring it with him on release. The 50,000-word 'letter' now known as *De Profundis* is a remarkable, if flawed, document, written, as it was, without access to reference books and with minimum opportunity for revision. The history of its publication is complicated. Ross published an expurgated version in 1905 and a slightly longer version in 1908. He then donated the manuscript to the British Museum on the understanding that it would not be made public until 1960. Lord Alfred Douglas had, of course, opposed its publication but with his death in 1945 the last objection was removed and Oscar's son Vyvyan Holland published a version based on a faulty typescript bequeathed to him by Ross. The complete and correct version of *De Profundis* was not published until 1962 in *The Letters of Oscar Wilde*, edited and compiled by Rupert Hart-Davis, the book that according to Merlin Holland restored his grandfather's reputation.

De Profundis reflects unhappily on the negative effect Bosie had on Oscar's life. Nevertheless, during the process of writing, Oscar's great anger towards Bosie began to diminish. If Oscar's attitude towards Bosie began to change, Constance's attitude towards her husband also began to alter. She had been a loving and forgiving wife but an issue arose over Oscar's life interest in her dowry. The Official Receiver moved against this marriage settlement as being part of Oscar's estate and put it up for sale. In order to safeguard Oscar's interests Robbie Ross and More Adey bought it but Constance came to believe that they were in some way moving against her. Lawyers were involved and the issue became complicated. Constance reduced Oscar's annual allowance to £150 and inserted a clause stating that he would lose his allowance altogether if he visited his wife or his children without permission or if he should live notoriously on the Continent. Should he ever see the day of his release, Oscar could not now go to his wife without being invited and he could not go to see Bosie without losing the only source of income he would have.

A new warder appeared on C wing about seven weeks before Oscar was due for release. His name was Thomas Martin, a kindly Irishman who befriended his famous prisoner and treated him with respect. He broke the prison rules by giving Oscar ginger biscuits from the factory next door and provided his charge with the *Daily Chronicle* every morning. He even smuggled warm beef tea to Oscar's cell one morning after he found the prisoner still in bed and feeling unwell. All of this was completely against the rules. Thomas Martin was dismissed from his job as warder shortly after Oscar's release when it was discovered that he had given a biscuit to a hungry boy prisoner, one of three young children convicted of poaching. An inquiry was held into the incident and into the dismissal by the Prison Commission. Curiously, some of the papers were officially stamped 'Closed for 99 years'.

Anthony Stokes, author of *Pit of Shame: The Real Ballad of Reading Gaol*, himself a warder with twenty years' experience of working inside Her Majesty's prisons, much of it at Reading Gaol, raises some questions about the treatment of Oscar and about Thomas Martin. He suggests that somebody was watching out for Oscar. He believes his 'path into, through and out of Reading Gaol was made smoother than for other prisoners'. It was not customary for a junior warder to be placed on a long-term convict landing with someone like Oscar Wilde who was ready to be released. New warders, Stokes reveals, were given more difficult tasks in order to learn their trade while senior staff took the easier landings for themselves. Also, it was very unusual for a prisoner to be given any concessions – such as Oscar's books, writing materials, extra exercise and permission to grow his hair back to normal length – in those times. Stokes suggests that Warder Martin was a plant and a line from the aforementioned Prison Commission inquiry reads: 'As to Martin's dismissal this is a matter which obviously cannot be discussed in print.' Stokes certainly raises some interesting points about Oscar's treatment while incarcerated.

There is, of course, no suggestion that Oscar did not suffer greatly in prison even if there was somebody, such as George W. Palmer, trying to alleviate some of the more extreme conditions towards the end of his sentence. In fact, it was widely understood that a prison term of two years with hard labour for a man of Oscar's background and class was in effect a death sentence.

As the day of his release drew closer, Oscar's spirits began to rise and he searched about for a place where he could live, at least for the short term. Frank Harris wanted to bring him on a trip through the Pyrenees but Oscar felt that his friend's company might be too overpowering. He thought he might settle in Brussels or perhaps a town on the French coast and decided to use the name Sebastian Melmoth, the wanderer in Charles Maturin's story, in order to avoid any unwanted attention. As a further encouragement some of his good friends pledged sums of money to see him back on his feet.

On the evening of 18 May 1897 Oscar travelled by cab from Reading Gaol to Twyford station in the company of two prison officials. He was dressed in his own clothes and did not have to be handcuffed. When he saw a bush with fresh buds near the platform he exclaimed 'Oh beautiful world! Oh beautiful world.' The warder begged him to be quiet as he was sure to be recognised because 'you're the only man in England who would talk like that in a railway station'.[3] Oscar was then taken to Pentonville Prison in London where he was officially discharged at a quarter past six on the morning of 19 May. He was met by his loyal friend More Adey and also Stewart Headlam, the radical clergyman who had put up half the bail money for Oscar before his second trial. They drove to Headlam's house where he had a cup of coffee, the first in two years, and was soon joined by the Leversons. He talked excitedly and then sent a message to the Jesuits at Farm Street, asking if he could be allowed to enter there upon a six-month retreat but his appeal was refused on the grounds that a period of preparation would be required. Oscar was obviously emotionally very fragile for he wept at the failure of his unanticipated request. He regained his composure and spent the day talking with friends, then crossed to Dieppe in northern France on the night boat, never to return.

Robbie Ross and Reggie Turner were waiting for their friend on the pier at Dieppe even though it was four o'clock in the morning. Oscar handed Ross a package containing the letters that would become known as *De Profundis* and asked him to have copies made, one for himself and one for Alfred Douglas. The happy band of friends then retired to the Hotel Sandwich where a room had been prepared. Here they talked and laughed and drank until, exhausted, they collapsed to sleep.

Ross had managed to gather £800 for Oscar, which allowed him to move into a hotel in Dieppe. The first letter from Bosie soon arrived, asking if they could meet, but Oscar was not yet ready for a reunion, although the pair remained in touch by letter. Meanwhile, Oscar wrote a touching letter to Constance begging to see her and to see the children. He longed to be a husband and father once again. Constance was not fully convinced that Oscar had completely broken with Douglas and wrote a kind but hesitant reply. While Douglas bombarded Oscar with letters professing his love, Oscar clung to a hope of reuniting with his family. Constance, who was by now in serious pain and in need of an operation on her back, wrote to her husband every week but continued to postpone a meeting.

It was in Dieppe that Oscar first began to experience what was to become an all-too-regular occurrence. He was refused service in a restaurant and his friend Aubrey Beardsley, the young artist he had once championed, snubbed him by failing to turn up for a dinner engagement. He would receive such insults almost daily, both from acquaintances and from people who happened to recognise the notorious author, for the remainder of his life and they never lost their power to wound. Oscar decided to move to the small village of Berneval about 5 miles north of Dieppe. He lived there for a time under his assumed name of Sebastian Melmoth. Here Oscar entertained a succession of visitors, including André Gide and Leonard Smithers, the man who would eventually publish *The Ballad of Reading Gaol*. He also entertained young men, including the poet Ernest Dowson and painter Charles Conder. A young American-born writer, Vincent O'Sullivan, the son of Irish emigrants who had prospered, arrived for a visit. Many years later, Vincent O'Sullivan published an insightful memoir/biography, *Aspects of Wilde*.

There was much drinking and some carousing in Berneval and Oscar's £800 dwindled rapidly. On 22 June he threw a party for local children and villagers on the occasion of Queen Victoria's Diamond Jubilee. Perhaps it was his way of seeking comfort for the loss of his own family. Visits from friends continued into early autumn. Charles Wyndham came looking for a new play but Oscar was unable to commit. Robbie Ross arrived with Robert Sherard. Sherard, however, began to draw away from his old friend. Like most of Oscar's friends, he had always pressed him to reunite with his family but now it appeared that Oscar was edging closer to a reunion with Bosie instead. He had invited Bosie to visit in June but this was withdrawn when word got out and Oscar faced the danger of losing his allowance.

Oscar could have regained his wife and sons if he had laid constant siege to her affections. The ramparts behind which she tried to protect her battered heart and her bewildered sons were not strong and would have crumbled. Instead of decamping to within a stone's throw of his wife's base, Oscar was sending letters from far away in Berneval where he was drinking heavily and seeing a succession of young men. As summer turned to autumn and Constance still had not agreed to see him, Oscar began to blame his wife for not being able to forgive him and for causing him to turn once more towards Bosie.

Oscar and Alfred Douglas eventually met in Rouen at the end of August and they spent the night together. By now, the quiet rural village of Berneval had lost its charm and in September Oscar left for Paris where he borrowed some money from a friend. He then followed Bosie to Aix-les-Bains and there the pair made plans to live for a time together in Naples. With an advance of £100 for a work he probably never meant to attempt, Oscar and Bosie rented a villa just north of Naples. When Constance heard the news she was distraught and her solicitors cut off Oscar's allowance. Lady Queensberry was equally distressed and offered Oscar £200 if the pair would separate.

Oscar and Bosie lived together in Naples for almost three months but their great love affair, the one that had brought such ruin, was petering out in poverty. Oscar was no longer wealthy and he was no longer a famous dramatist. In fact, he was a social pariah with nothing now to offer Bosie, so the young Lord simply packed his bags and walked away in December. Oscar received the £200 from Lady Queensberry. He regarded it as part payment on the promise to cover the legal cost of his original suit. Then, on the urging of the staunch Robbie Ross, Constance restored her husband's allowance. Oscar and Bosie would later meet from time to time, usually in Paris, and Bosie occasionally gave Oscar money but their romance was at an end.

Oscar was now living the lonely life of an impoverished exile, left alone in Naples where he had to contend with being regularly and cruelly snubbed or insulted by people who happened to recognise him. Vincent O'Sullivan, who came to Naples and spent a few days with Oscar, later recorded how upset his friend could become as a result of such treatment. At one point, Oscar even contemplated ending his own life in a garden often used by people intent on suicide. He claimed he changed his mind when the souls of those who had taken their lives there came hovering about him and he knew they were condemned to remain in the gardens forever.

People in high places were still keeping an eye on the broken author. The British Consul in Naples, E. Neville-Rolfe, wrote to Lord Rosebery, who had a villa there, to tell him that the ex-prisoner was now living a secluded life under an assumed name in a rented villa outside the city 'fully two miles from you'. He looked 'thoroughly abashed, much like a whipped hound'. 'I really cannot think he will be any trouble to you,' the Consul continued, 'and after all the poor devil must live somewhere.' The Consul also told Rosebery that Oscar 'and Alfred Douglas have definitely parted'.[4] Oscar returned to Paris in February 1898 where he would at last receive some good news.

39

The Last of the Wildes

Even though the plays of Oscar Wilde are today staged regularly in capital cities all around the world, perhaps his most famous work remains *The Ballad of Reading Gaol*. As a poem it is not without its flaws. Yeats edited it severely before including it in his *Oxford Book of Modern Verse* but its haunting depictions of guilt and suffering remain etched on a reader's mind for life. If Oscar at times sounds like 'the kind of propagandist poet his mother had been fifty years before',[1] the verisimilitude contained in lines such as 'the wild regrets, and the bloody sweats, / None knew so well as I' retains the power of a knockout punch.

The poem itself is based on a real execution that took place in Reading Gaol on the morning of 7 July 1896. Oscar was just a month or so into his second year when the whisper spread that prisoner Charles Thomas Wooldridge, who had been a trooper in the Royal Horse Guards, was to be hanged at eight o'clock in the morning for the premeditated murder of his 23-year-old wife, Laura Ellen. Spurred on by jealousy, Wooldridge had borrowed a razor from a fellow soldier and went to the house near Windsor where his wife was staying with a friend. There had been a history of arguments and quarrels and he had beaten his wife a few weeks before in a fit of rage. In what he later admitted was a premeditated attack, he assaulted his wife at the door of her friend's house and followed her on to the road where he slit her throat three times. The crime was a horrible one but so too was the punishment. It reinforced Oscar's belief that 'each man kills the thing he loves'.

The idea of writing a ballad based on his prison experiences had been forming slowly in Oscar's mind but, not believing in autobiography, he required a more oblique approach. In the Wooldridge case he found a parallel. The soldier had given himself up immediately and upon receiving the death sentence requested that no appeal for clemency be made. He wanted to die for his crime.

It was in early July, six or seven weeks after his release, that Oscar began work on his poem. Robbie Ross suggested the title and encouraged Oscar as he worked through August on revisions. Further stanzas were composed and Oscar was still making less successful additions while living in the villa outside Naples. He wanted a long poem and was willing to compromise on quality to gain substance, believing it would need bulk if was to shake the sturdy walls of Reading Gaol itself. Leonard Smithers, the publisher, agreed that it was probably best if the name of Oscar Wilde did not appear on the book. When the first editions were published on 9 February 1898, the author's name appeared as C.3.3., Oscar's cell number in Reading representing the wing, the floor and the cell.

When Oscar eventually returned to Paris after his unsuccessful stay in Naples the news was that *The Ballad of Reading Gaol* was selling in substantial quantities. Even Smithers was taken by surprise and ordered further reprints. It was eventually decided to include Oscar's name on the cover and a deluxe edition was published. Oscar was pleased to be able to send inscribed copies to his friends. Although the poem's obvious weaknesses were recorded, reviews overall were good and some were excellent. Robbie Ross and others now hoped that Oscar would be able to take strength and courage from the success of his prison ballad and perhaps produce further work, but that was not to be. He could no longer hold his concentration for very long and knew only too well that the verses he had produced while in Naples were below standard. Smithers, delighted with the success of the long poem, went on to publish Oscar's last two plays, *An Ideal Husband* and *The Importance of Being Earnest*. They had not previously appeared in print because of the playwright's fall from grace.

Oscar was now spending much of the day in bed, rising in the afternoons to wander the cafés, drinking brandy and absinthe when he had money and talking to anybody willing to pass an hour in his company. He did make some temporary acquaintances as he moped about but they were only meaningless associations. One such new friend was a young homosexual soldier, Maurice Gilbert, whom Bosie would later take as a lover. Oscar enjoyed occasional evenings of good cheer but there were many lonely times and he continued to experience the hurt of being ignored or insulted by strangers or one-time friends who happened upon him on the street or in a café. Friends both old and new dropped away as they grew wary or weary of being asked for money. But Oscar did retain the friendship of a small core, which included Robbie Ross and Reggie Turner as well as Bosie who provided the occasional cheque. Frank Harris also kept in touch. But people had their own lives to live and friends could not always be on hand to offer support.

Further calamity arrived in April 1898 when Constance, who was becoming gradually paralysed from that fall on the stairs in Tite Street when Oscar was in Algiers, had to undergo a second operation on her spine. It did not go well and she died on 7 April. She was only forty years of age. Thirteen-year-old Cyril and twelve-year-old Vyvyan, children who had been through so much already, now had to face another huge upheaval in their young lives. They had been settling into life in their boarding schools but now had to return to England to be looked after by Constance's aunt, Mary Napier. Neither Cyril nor Vyvyan ever heard their father's name mentioned in that household as they grew up.

Bosie came to visit Oscar in his sorrow. However, Robbie Ross, who crossed from England, later commented that he did not find Oscar to be 'in great grief'. But any slim chance Oscar had of leaving the boulevards and returning to a traditional role of father and husband was now gone. 'My way back to hope and a new life ends in her grave,' Oscar told Frank Harris.[2] The following month Oscar had an operation on his throat and Bosie continued to visit for a while before deciding to risk a return to England and a meeting with his father. Queensberry and Bosie met and embraced but within a few short days the relationship had collapsed once again, never to be repaired.

With Bosie in England, Oscar took up an invitation from Frank Harris to visit the south of France for three months at his expense. Harris was hoping that he might be able to persuade Oscar to start writing again but then left his friend alone in La Napoule while he went to Monaco with the intention of buying a hotel and restaurant. It was in La Napoule that Oscar met a young, reclusive Englishman called Harold Mellor. He also became friendly with some local youths he described as being 'bare-limbed and strangely perfect'. Oscar was now determined to live to the full the life for which he had been so cruelly punished. Back from his business dealings, Harris was exasperated to find Oscar unwilling or unable to write. Nevertheless, he continued to support him for the agreed time.

Harold Mellor was the wealthy son of a Bolton cotton spinner who had a villa at Gland on Lake Geneva. Oscar accepted Mellor's invitation to come and stay with him in Gland but he never warmed to the dour, tight-fisted Englishman. Oscar drank his cheap wine and shared his roof but wrote disparagingly about him to his friends. Oscar was now becoming more and more like his brother, Willie, drinking heavily on borrowed money and becoming ever more willing to compromise his integrity for a bed, a meal or a bottle of wine. On the way to join Mellor in Gland, Oscar stopped off at Genoa to visit his wife's grave and was dismayed to see the bare inscription: 'Constance Mary, daughter of Horace Lloyd, QC'. It would be fifty years or more before 'wife of Oscar Wilde' was included on the stone.

While in Switzerland, news arrived that his brother, Willie, had died back in London on 13 April aged forty-six. The official cause of death was 'hepatic and cardiac disease' but in reality the years of heavy drinking had caught up with Willie and his liver gave out. 'I suppose it had been expected for some time,' Oscar wrote to Robert Ross. 'I am sorry for his wife, who I suppose, has little left to live on. Between him and me there had been, as you know, wide chasms for many years. Requiescat in Pace.'[3]

After Willie's death, the Moytura estate, Sir William's beloved lodge in the west of Ireland with its fields and its few tenants, should have passed without a hitch to Oscar, as Willie had no male heirs. But Oscar was a bankrupt and if the official receiver heard about the existence of the Irish property it would be seized. Oscar wrote to Robbie Ross from Mellor's villa wondering if a way could be found to have the rents from Moytura channelled through Lily Wilde. He would be willing to let her have £40 out of a total of £140 'as she has a child'. He wondered if it would be possible to sell Moytura or 'whether a private sale would be illegal. Of course, what one wants is a solicitor who will be able to show how one can escape the law . . . But I have not much hope of anything good.'[4] The receiver eventually learned about Moytura and it was sold to pay off some of Oscar's debts the year after his death.

Lily Wilde was in dire straits following her husband's death. She and Willie had had to give up the house on Oakley Street and move to rooms at 9 Cheltenham Terrace, a little side street close by, after Lady Wilde's death. One of Lily's sisters helped the destitute family pay the rent but Lily and her child were never to experience financial stability while Willie lived and for a period after his death. Lily's disastrous marriage had left her so poor that she could not afford to raise her own child. In a letter to Oscar dated 7 May 1899 she explains how 'One has always sad memories of what Willie might have been instead of dying practically unknown and leaving his child to be supported by my sister. She is well and happy in a country convent and I think will have a good share of the family brains.'[5]

Dorothy had been born into acute turmoil with an alcoholic father, a troubled mother, a failing grandmother and a family trauma-tised by disastrous events. A strange letter from Lily to More Adey, dated 13 March 1896, states that the baby was very sick so they, Lily and Willie, were leaving her at Cheltenham Terrace and going down to Kent.[6] Who was going to look after the child? Why were her parents taking off for Kent if the child was so sick? It all sounds very erratic. Later, Dorothy was 'put out to nurse and was only returned to the household when she was three years old'.[7] Then, after her father's death, the toddler was placed 'in a country convent', probably a religious orphanage or foster home either in England or possibly Ireland. Dolly, as she was known, in later years never spoke about her unstable childhood and rarely mentioned her father. The troubled woman preferred instead to be linked to her notorious uncle with whom she bore an uncanny resemblance in manner and inclination as well as appearance. And Dolly did not hesitate to play upon that physical resemblance in order to entertain her wealthy companions. One is reminded of the antics of her father in New York, which so annoyed Oscar.

Lily Wilde remarried within eighteen months of Willie's death. Her new husband, Alexander Teixeira de Mattos, was a journalist and translator of Dutch-Jewish descent whose family had settled in England when he was nine years old. He had been Willie Wilde's best man when he married Lily but did not share Willie's indolent habits. He worked hard, was disciplined and humorous, and was well respected as the official translator of many writers including Gaston Leroux. His translation of Leroux's *The Phantom of the Opera* is still in print today. Lily deserved some comfort in life if only for her kindness towards Lady Wilde and her attempts to save some of Oscar's possessions from falling into her drunken husband's hands. Her second marriage was a happy one although their only child, a boy, died within hours of birth. Alexander made a settled home for Lily and her daughter and Lily loved him. When the First World War broke out Alexander was appointed head of the intelligence section of the Department of War Trade Intelligence. His health, however, was never very strong. He suffered from serious heart problems and died while still a relatively young man on 5 December 1921. A grieving Lily, who was six years older than her husband, outlived him by only one year, dying at the age of sixty-two in 1922. Her gravestone today can be seen in the Catholic section of Kensal Green Cemetery.

Even though Lily's second husband provided much-needed stability, Dorothy Wilde never experienced any level of real security as a child and as an adult would never have a true 'home life'. Instead, like Oscar in his last years, she spent her life wandering about, staying in the homes of wealthy companions when she could get an invitation or staying in good hotels in London or Paris when she had funds. The £2,000 she inherited when her mother died, probably from her stepfather's estate, did not last her very long. Known to her friends in the wealthy lesbian literary world she inhabited as Dolly Wilde, she could be charming and brilliantly witty and was celebrated for her lightning-quick retorts. She could also experience times of deep depression and on more than one occasion became so desperate that she attempted to take her own life. Famous or influential people liked to have her around and were willing to support her both emotionally and financially. Victor Cunard, the witty cousin of the poet and heiress Nancy Cunard of the shipping-line family, was a particularly close friend as were Lady Carnarvon and others who mixed in the high society of Paris and London in the 1920s and 1930s.

In 1914, while still in her teens, Dolly ran away to France, sending her mother a curt wire – 'sailing!' She drove ambulances during the First World War and also began a series of lesbian relationships, the Standard Oil heiress Marion 'Joe' Carstairs being her first lover. Between the wars she often stayed at the home of multimillionaire Natalie Clifford Barney in Paris. For almost fifty years this address at 20 rue Jacob was the centre of a literary lesbian circle and salon that included Gertrude Stein, Elisabeth Eyre de Lanux and Dolly's arch-rival for the attentions of Natalie Barney, Djuna Barnes. Dolly drank heavily like her father and Oscar. She also had the extra burden of being addicted to heroin and her many attempts at detoxification were unsuccessful.

Dolly Wilde was found dead in her London apartment at 20 Chesham Place, Belgravia, by the chambermaid on the morning of 10 April 1941. She was only forty-five years of age. The coroner's report states that the cause of death was unascertainable but a drug overdose was suspected. Vyvyan Holland, Oscar's son and Dolly's first cousin, believed that her death was more than likely suicide but there is no medical evidence to support the theory of a drugs overdose and she was also being treated for breast cancer at the time. Vyvyan did not have a close relationship with Dolly and did not attend her funeral. They had been estranged for some time. Perhaps her flaunting of what Vyvyan would have understood to have been well-known family weaknesses made him feel uncomfortable. He certainly believed that her life had been somewhat sordid and did not appreciate the fact that her room was found to be stuffed full with prescription drugs and that an old syringe was also found in the flat. Dolly, officially the last of the Wildes, was buried with her mother in Kensel Green Cemetery.

40

Outcasts Always Mourn

After tiring of Mellor and Switzerland, Oscar moved south to Liguria, the coastal strip around Genoa beloved of Byron and Shelley. He quickly ran up debts and the ever-faithful Robbie Ross had to come to his rescue. He settled Oscar's bills and took his impoverished friend back to Paris where he once more resumed the life of a ruined exile, ghosting through the streets, scrounging drinks and trying to borrow money from those he encountered along the way. Occasionally, Oscar bumped into figures from his past life as he wandered about. He once exchanged a silent glance with Whistler at the door of a restaurant and Edward Carson told of colliding with a large man on the street and being surprised to find it was Oscar. Ellen Terry took him for a meal when they met but, for the most part, he was ignored or insulted when recognised.

Oscar stayed for a time at the Hotel Marsollier where the proprietor refused to let him have his belongings until the bill was paid. Jean Dupoirier, who ran a hotel on the Left Bank called Hotel d'Alsace, lent Oscar some money to clear his bills and allowed him to move into his own hotel in August 1899. Oscar had little money apart from the small marriage allowance and occasional donations but Dupoirier was flexible and generous so Oscar managed to survive through the winter and was well looked after by the kindly hotelier. In April he once again accepted an invitation from Harold Mellor to accompany him to Italy. They visited Palermo, Naples and Rome, where Oscar stood in a crowd at St Peter's on several occasions to receive a Papal blessing. Another of Oscar's unexpected encounters with people from his past occurred in Rome when John Grey, now a seminarian, came walking past with a group of colleagues. They stared at each other but did not speak.

Back in Paris, Oscar once more took up residency in the Hotel d'Alsace and again was well looked after by Dupoirier, enjoying late breakfasts and even later nights at the Café de Paris or at the Calisaya with his new acquaintances. Then news arrived that the Marquess of Queensberry was dead and that Percy and Alfred Douglas had come into their inheritance. There was a suggestion that Bosie should now provide Oscar with an annual allowance to top up the £150 he received from his wife's bequest. Bosie refused to agree to any such thing, preferring instead to pass on an occasional handout.

George Alexander arrived with news that he had bought the rights to Oscar's last two plays and, now that the plays were once again being staged, was willing to make some payments to the author even though he was not obliged to do so. He also said he would bequeath the rights of the two plays to Oscar's sons, a very generous gesture that pleased Oscar greatly. Frank Harris approached Oscar with the idea that they write a play together and share the royalties. The result, *Mr and Mrs Daventry*, had to be written entirely by Frank in the end. When it was finally staged in London, Frank Harris was exasperated to find that much of the royalties had to go to pay back advances Oscar had accepted from others to whom he had promised a play.

In the autumn of 1900 Oscar's health began to be a cause of concern. He had not been taking care of himself as he wandered around Paris drinking absinthe and brandy and keeping late hours. He was, for the most part, gloomy and dispirited and was finding life as an impoverished exile to be almost as difficult as his life behind bars. Then Oscar began to experience a severe pain in his right ear. Even before his arrest he had been complaining of deafness and a discharge but damage could also have occurred when he took a heavy fall in the prison chapel shortly after commencing his sentence. By the end of September 1900 Oscar was feeling too ill to get out of bed. His doctor, Maurice a'Court Tucker, at first had difficulty pinpointing the problem. He then decided that an operation on the ear was urgently required. The hotel bedroom was prepared and Dr Paul Cleiss performed the surgery there on 10 October. He was paid with borrowed money. Six days later Robbie Ross arrived and found Oscar had improved. Other friends visited, including Reggie Turner. Then, surprisingly, Lily, Willie's widow, arrived with her new husband on 16 October. They were honeymooning in Paris and Lily wanted to see her former brother-in-law who had always been kind to her. Oscar told her he was 'dying beyond my means'.

Oscar left his sick bed and made his way laboriously to a nearby café on 29 October where he drank absinthe against everybody's wishes. He told Claire de Pratz that 'My wallpaper and I are fighting a duel to the death. One or the other of us has to go.' Ross told his friend that he would surely kill himself with his imprudent behaviour, reminding him that the doctor had issued a warning against absinthe. Oscar simply replied: 'And what do I have to live for?' The following day the pain in his ear had increased and a drive to the Bois de Boulogne in sunshine was recommended but Oscar began to feel dizzy and they returned to the hotel in the afternoon. He had developed a serious abscess in his inner ear. Richard Ellmann, Oscar's biographer, believed this ear infection to be a tertiary symptom of advanced syphilis picked up originally as a student at Oxford, but there is no evidence for this theory and is not now accepted as fact. As the pain in Oscar's ear increased, the loyal hotelier Dupoirier gave him regular injections of morphine but this eventually proved to be ineffective. Oscar believed he was dying and became very concerned about his debts of about £400 and also about *De Profundis*, which he hoped, if eventually published, might go some way towards redeeming his tarnished reputation. Robbie Ross was charged with this task.

As the November days passed the patient lay in bed with the ever-faithful Robbie Ross and then Reggie Turner in attendance. Oscar was now occasionally slipping into periods of delirium and his speech began to ramble. He spoke incoherently of his children and of the steamboat *The Munster* that sailed between Holyhead and

Ireland. The doctor's report of 25 November told of 'significant cerebral disturbances stemming from an old suppuration of the right ear'. It goes on to say that 'the symptoms became much graver. The diagnosis of encephalitic meningitis must be made without doubt.' When Robbie Ross returned from a short visit to his mother in the south of France he realised that Oscar was dying. Reggie Turner had been growing ever more alarmed as he nursed his friend with the help of an exhausted attendant while Robbie was away. Reggie realised that practicalities such as contacting relatives and making funeral arrangements would soon need to be taken in hand and was glad to see Robbie return. The pain was now so severe that Oscar, who could no longer speak, kept his hand in his mouth to avoid crying out.

Robbie Ross was a Catholic and knew that Oscar had held a lifelong interest in converting. After some hesitation he decided to try to find a priest for his dying friend. As well as providing spiritual succour the presence of a priest might have the practical advantage of ensuring that a proper burial with full obsequies would take place. At the Passionate Fathers he located a priest willing to come to his dying friend. Fr Cuthbert Dunne asked Oscar if he wished to be received into the Roman Catholic Church. Oscar could not speak and perhaps was not even fully conscious at this stage but he was able to hold up his hand. Upon receiving this response Fr Dunne blessed and baptised Oscar and anointed him with holy oils in the sacrament for the dying.

At half past five in the morning of 30 November 1900 a strong death rattle began and at ten minutes to two in the afternoon Oscar Wilde died in his bedroom at the Hotel d'Alsace. Dupoirier laid out the body of his friend and Fr Dunne put a rosary in his hands. They spread palm fronds on the body and Maurice Gilbert took a photograph. Life had become a misery for the fallen author and death was a release.

Two years of imprisonment had left Oscar in a weakened condition and likely to succumb to an infection. His broken spirit and nomadic life since gaining liberty did not help. Perhaps medical historian J. B. Lyons puts it best in his study *What Did I Die Of?*, where he concludes that 'syphilis did not topple Oscar Wilde, a victim in all probability of the more brutally lethal pyogenic cocci. By one of the recurring ironies of medical history, the Dublin aurist's son died of a complication within the field of his father's endeavours ... There is no convincing evidence that Oscar Wilde had tertiary syphilis. A chronic infection of the right ear antedated his imprisonment. An intra-cranial complication – pyogenic meningitis – led to his death following an acute illness.'[1]

Complications immediately arose following his death because Oscar was registered under the name of Melmoth. The distraught Robbie Ross had to see the police commissioner several times and then he had to go to the funeral director for the British Embassy. Gesling, the undertaker, told Robbie that the body might have to be taken to the morgue since its identity would need to be established. Some years later in an article in the *New York Times* Robbie explained how this was avoided: 'After the physician had examined the body and cross-examined each and every one at the hotel, and after a series of drinks and inappropriate jokes and a fair-sized tip he signed the death certificate.'[2] Robbie then describes the arrival at the hotel of 'different poets and authors who sent in their cards: Raymond de la Tailhade, Terdieu, Charles Sibleigh, Jehan Rictus, Robert d'Humières, George Sinclair, and a number of Englishmen who gave fictitious names. Also two veiled ladies. They all had to register their names before seeing the body.' One is reminded of the mysterious veiled lady who, it was said, came to sit by Sir William's bedside as he died.

Robbie goes on to describe the funeral: 'On Monday, Dec 3 at nine o'clock in the morning, the funeral procession started from the hotel. We walked all behind the bier to the church of St Germain-des-Prés: Alfred Douglas, Reggie Turner, I (Robert Ross), Dupoirier (the hotel keeper), Henri (the attendant), Jules (the servant), Hennion, and Maurice Gilbert, with two others whom I did not know.' The vicar said a 'quiet mass at the altar' and 'Reverend Cuthbert Dunne completed the funeral ceremony. The porter said that fifty-six people were present at the funeral, among them five women in deep mourning: Mdme Stuart Merrill, Countess de Bremont, her maid, an old servant girl of Oscar Wilde's wife, and another woman whom

I did not know.' The article goes on to say that 'twenty-four wreaths were sent, several of them anonymously'.

Oscar was then taken from the church, where only the side door was opened for the mourners, to go to his place of rest. Four carriages made up the funeral procession, with Bosie, who had arrived two days after Oscar's death, in the leading carriage behind the hearse with Robert Ross, Reginald Turner and the hotelier Dupoirier. Oscar was buried in the seventh row of the seventeenth section of Bagneux Cemetery on 3 December. The simple stone bore a Latin inscription from the Book of Job: 'To my words they durst add nothing, and my speech dropped upon them.' There was some fracas or unpleasant incident at the graveside, probably involving Robbie Ross and Alfred Douglas, but the details were never made public. However, for years after Oscar's death, Douglas vindictively pursued Ross and made repeated attempts to have him arrested for homosexuality.

In 1909 Oscar's remains were removed to Père Lachaise Cemetery and his grave marked by Jacob Epstein's famous monument, commissioned by Ross and paid for by Sir Coleridge Kennard's mother Mrs Carew. It bears an inscription from *The Ballad of Reading Gaol*:

> And alien tears will fill for him
> Pity's long-broken urn,
> For his mourners will be outcast men,
> And outcasts always mourn.

In the tragic story of Oscar Wilde's fall, Robbie Ross stands out for his unswerving devotion and for his loyalty to his friend in life and in death. As Oscar Wilde's executor he eventually managed to secure Wilde's entire literary legacy. He tracked down manuscripts and restored copyrights lost to the family at the time of the bankruptcy. It took Robbie six years to satisfy creditors, a feat he was able to accomplish largely because France and Germany continued translating and selling Oscar's books and performing his plays. England, by contrast, did its best to ignore the great writer for many years. All of this painstaking work was undertaken for the benefit of Oscar's two sons, Cyril and Vyvyan, the latter of whom had never even heard of

Robbie until he was introduced to him in 1907. They became firm friends.

When Sir Jacob Epstein was designing Oscar's tomb, Robbie Ross asked if he would include in the construction a small compartment for his own ashes. Robbie died suddenly in 1918 as he was preparing to travel to Australia to open an exhibition at the National Gallery. He was only forty-nine years old but had been put under a lot of stress by Douglas and a right-wing MP called Noel Pemberton Billing who had accused members of Robbie's circle of being homosexual traitors during the First World War. Eventually, in 1950 – the fiftieth anniversary of Oscar's death – Robbie's ashes were placed in the Epstein tomb at Père Lachaise Cemetery as he had wished.

Lord Alfred Douglas led a long and controversial life. He married Olive Custance, a poet, in 1902 and they had a son, Raymond, who later had to be hospitalised after a mental breakdown. The marriage did not last. Douglas converted to Roman Catholicism in 1911 and became highly litigious, spending a lot of his time trying to distance himself from Oscar. His 1914 biography, *Oscar Wilde and Myself*, was basically an attempt to repudiate Oscar's memory and to distance himself from homosexuality, which he now went out of his way to condemn. In 1923 Douglas served six months in Wormwood Scrubs Prison after Winston Churchill took a successful criminal libel action against him. This experience made Douglas a little more aware of what Oscar had gone through although prison conditions had improved in the intervening thirty years. In 1928 Douglas published another book, *Autobiography*, where he tried to clear up what he considered to be misunderstandings about his role as an *homme fatal* in Oscar's life. But no matter how hard he tried to present himself as a serious poet and a person much maligned, the shadow of his great affair and his part in bringing down Oscar Wilde continued to hang over the aristocrat even into old age. He died in 1945 at the age of seventy-four.

As for Alfred Taylor, Douglas is reported to have told how once in the 1920s when he was staying in a hotel in Chicago he rang the bell for the waiter and to his surprise the person who arrived was none other than Alfred Taylor. His reaction to the chance encounter is unrecorded.[3]

Cyril Holland, Oscar's eldest son, who was born on 5 June 1885, was sent by his mother to an English-speaking school in Germany after his father's ruin. Later, after his mother's untimely death, Cyril attended Radley College, a public school in Oxfordshire, England. He became a cadet at the Royal Military College, Woolwich, and served as a lieutenant in England and India before being promoted to the rank of captain on 13 October 1914. He was posted back to Europe when the First World War broke out and took part in the battle for Neuve-Chapelle. Cyril was killed by a sniper's bullet during the battle for the village of Festubert on the Western Front on 9 May 1915. He was buried at St Vaast Post Military Cemetery, Richebourg-l'Avoué.

Vyvyan Holland, Oscar's second son, was not happy at the school in Germany and so was sent to a Catholic school in Monaco. When his mother, Constance, died the young boy's life was once again thrown into turmoil. A priest from Monaco took him back to England to be cared for by his mother's aunt. It was decided to keep the brothers apart, perhaps in the vain hope that they would escape recognition and harassment and would not get to hear about their troubled father. Vyvyan was sent to the prestigious Stonyhurst College, a Jesuit school in Lancashire, England, while Cyril remained at Radley School. The brothers saw little of each other from then on; however, they did correspond regularly. Vyvyan was led to believe that his father's life had been insignificant and that he was now dead. Oscar's name was never mentioned and the brothers were to forget that they were ever called Wilde. Vyvyan was only eleven years of age when he came back to England but already he felt there was some terrible disgrace hanging over him and over his family.

Cyril knew a little more about his father's disgrace but did not share his knowledge with his younger brother. Cyril dedicated his life to retrieving by what he saw as manly activities a name so dishonoured. He became an outstanding athlete and found his niche in the army even though by nature he appreciated the artistic and the cultural. He was a solitary, reflective figure, somewhat distanced from his more boisterous fellow officers. At the outbreak of the First World War he desperately wanted to see action and was even willing to switch regiment and sacrifice nine years of seniority in order to be at the front. Cyril believed that by fighting bravely and, if necessary, dying for king and country he would redeem his family's besmirched honour. The sniper's bullet granted Cyril the honour he so craved.

The young Vyvyan was very shocked when in 1900 the Rector of Stonyhurst informed him that his father had died because, as far as he knew, his father had been dead for years. Vyvyan finally learned the full truth two years later when he read the newly published book by Robert Sherard, *Oscar Wilde, the Story of an Unhappy Friendship*. Vyvyan was then sixteen years old. Guilt, shame, bewilderment and even fear would have been the justifiable emotions of a young boy who had lived through such upheaval and indeed Vyvyan experienced all of these. He tried to come to terms with his life and applied for entry to Oxford but was refused and instead went to Cambridge to study law. However, he could not settle and left before completing his degree. In 1907 he eventually met Robbie Ross for the first time and was introduced to many of the people who knew and respected his late father. At last he began to understand the truth and his constant fear of discovery and of ridicule, which had clung to him since boyhood, began to slowly fade.

Robbie Ross took it upon himself to watch over the younger son of his great friend and when Vyvyan turned twenty-one he hosted a magnificent dinner party to mark his coming of age. Cyril was there, as were many of Oscar's old literary friends who were all delighted to meet the great writer's two sons. The boys began at last to feel accepted by the world. Jean Cocteau stated that he met Vyvyan Holland in Venice in September 1908 at a time when he had resumed the name of Wilde as a two-week experiment but that 'So many Italian journalists wanted interviews with him when they heard the name "Wilde" that he gave up the painful trial.'[4]

Vyvyan was in Paris with Robbie Ross on 20 July 1909 to witness his father's remains being transferred from Bagneux to Père Lachaise Cemetery and after Robbie went to bed the younger man took himself off to Montmartre where he joined in the local revelries which lasted well into the night. Ross sent him packing back to London the following day but the two were by now firm friends. After a short spell in Spain travelling about, Vyvyan returned to England and completed his degree. He was called to the bar in 1912 although law would not be his life. The following year he met Violet Mary Craigie, the daughter of Edmund Warren Craigie, an officer with the 2nd Dragoon Guards, and they married in January 1914 at St Mary's Catholic Church, Cadogan Street, Chelsea, not far from the Cadogan Hotel, the scene of Oscar's arrest. It is just one more coincidence that the officiating priest was a Fr Maturin who was descended from Charles Maturin, Lady Wilde's eccentric uncle and author of *Melmoth the Wanderer*. Best man was Robbie Ross and among the guests at the reception was Lady Wilde's old friend the Comtesse de Brémont.

Vyvyan served as an officer with the Royal Field Artillery during the First World War and spent much of the war at or near the front. He was only a few miles away on the day that Cyril was killed but he did not know about his brother's tragic death until he received a letter from his wife who was back in England. 'The last link with Tite Street and the spacious days had snapped,' he later wrote.[5] Vyvyan was given his brother's bridle, field glasses and his revolver, which later saved his life when he used it to shoot a German officer who had sent a bullet through his cap from close range.

Vyvyan was on leave in Paris just before the end of the war when he read in a newspaper that Robbie Ross had died. 'He was my greatest friend,' Vyvyan later wrote in his memoir, 'and whenever I got in trouble, which I did with great frequency, he always came to the rescue. I was devoted to him and I wonder how he could have put up with me; his death was a great blow to me, and I felt that another of the strings that bound me to life had snapped.' Vyvyan had now lost his brother and his best friend but the fates were still not finished dealing out the hammer blows to this tortured family. A few weeks before the Armistice in 1918 Vyvyan received a telegram at his company's billet at Tournai just inside the Belgium border: 'Your wife dangerously injured by fire. Police, Pimlico.' Violet had recently moved from Southsea up to London and had taken a flat in

St George's Road, Pimlico. The couple had no children and perhaps she missed the city. In a terrible accident that recalls the fearful events in Monaghan all those years ago when Sir William's two illegitimate daughters were burned to death, Violet caught her dress in a gas fire on returning to her flat after an evening at the theatre. She ran to the bathroom to try to extinguish the flames but she sustained very serious burns to her body and died at Westminster Hospital before her husband could reach her from the front. Vyvyan read of her death in the *Evening News* as he hurried from Folkstone to London. 'I sat in the train and thought of the people who had died in such a short space of time: my brother, Robbie Ross and now Violet, and I felt that I was once more alone in the world, as I had been years before on my return to England from Monaco. I do not think I mourned particularly, I was too numb, and it all seemed to be fatalistic and pre-ordained.'[6] The idea of the fates being cruel reminds one of his extraordinary grandmother's beliefs years before.

Vyvyan received an OBE upon demobilisation. He then became an author and translator and mixed in high society throughout the 1920s and into the 1930s. His cousin, Dolly Wilde, had been social secretary to Lady Carnarvon in the 1920s and Vyvyan became friendly with some of the country's leading aristocracy, including the Birkenheads. Like his father and grandfather he had the same ability to get to know people in high places. Later, when the Second World War came, he worked as a translator for the BBC. In August 1942 Vyvyan met Dorothy Thelma Helen Besant (a beautician from Melbourne, Australia). They married a year later in September 1943 at St Margaret's Church, Westminster, with the Earl of Birkenhead as best man. They had one son, Christopher Merlin Vyvyan Holland, born in London in December 1945 and known today as Merlin Holland. According to Vyvyan, 'never was a more welcome child brought into this world'.[7]

In 1947 Vyvyan's wife, Dorothy, was invited by Cyclax Cosmetics to deliver a series of lectures in Australia and New Zealand to be illustrated by original costumes of the late nineteenth century. They sailed south and the tour, which lasted just over a year, took the couple and their child to many interesting places. Back in England

Dorothy became managing director of the Slenderella group of beauty salons and for a time was cosmetician and beauty adviser to Queen Elizabeth II. Vyvyan, encouraged by his vivacious wife, at last felt sufficiently comfortable to begin piecing together facts about his father and incidents from his own early life and what emerged was the autobiography *Son of Oscar Wilde* published in 1954. This was followed by a second autobiography, *Time Remembered, after Père Lachaise*. The boy who was told never to mention his father's name was at last telling the world who he was and who his great father had been. 'Starting with the presumption that no one is entitled to happiness as a right', Vyvyan wrote, 'and that the lot of man is to strive painfully through sorrow and frustration to the merciful release of death, I count my blessings. I have my health, a good home, a good wife and a good son. What more can I ask of life?'

Vyvyan lived happily with his wife and son in London and survived to see his father's name rise once more to take its rightful place among the world's greatest writers. He died on 10 October 1967 at the age of eighty. His wife, Dorothy, who was much younger than her husband, died in London in 1995. Merlin Holland, Vyvyan's son, today lives mostly in Burgundy. He is an author and an expert on his grandfather's life and works. Merlin has one son, Lucian. Born in London in 1979, he lives today in Oxford and is a computer programmer. On 30 November 1998 both Merlin and Lucian were present in Adelaide Street on the edge of London's Theatreland when actor Stephen Fry unveiled a memorial in honour of the great playwright in the city he enchanted over a hundred years before. The statue by the artist Maggie Hambling depicts Oscar's bronze head emerging, cigarette in hand, from a green polished-granite sarcophagus to engage anyone who cares to sit for a moment in some witty conversation. On the base is inscribed one of Oscar's most famous quotations taken from *Lady Windermere's Fan*: 'We are all in the gutter, but some of us are looking at the stars.'

And what had the stars in store for others in the cast of this story of Oscar Wilde and his famous family? Within five years of the triumphant opening night of *The Importance of Being Earnest* most of the main players in the drama then unfolding offstage were dead –

Oscar, Willie, Jane, Constance and Queensberry. None of Sir William's family joined him in the Wilde tomb at Dublin's Mount Jerome Cemetery. Mrs Frank Leslie, Willie's first wife, who by now had styled herself Baroness de Bazus, tried to find her ex-husband's grave while on a visit to England but nobody could tell her where it was. Lady Wilde was buried in Kensal Green Cemetery, plot 127, but as Willie failed to buy a headstone or make a payment for a permanent marker, her remains were removed to an unknown grave after seven years. Nothing today marks the spot where Speranza's bones rest.

> And all men kill the thing they love,
> By all let this be heard,
> Some do it with a bitter look,
> Some with a flattering word,
> The coward does it with a kiss,
> The brave man with a sword!

Appendix 1

Sir William Wilde's Publications

1839   *Narrative of a Voyage to Madeira, Teneriffe, and along the shores of the Mediterranean, including a visit to Algiers, Egypt, Palestyne, Tyre, Rhodes and the Holy Land* (William Curry, Dublin)

1841   Census – Report of Medical Advisor to the Irish Census and Tables of the Causes of Death from the Earliest Times to Present Day.

1843   *Austria, its Literary, Scientific, and Medical Institutions* (William Curry, Dublin)

1849   *The Closing Years of Dean Swift's Life* (Hodges and Smith, Dublin)

1850   *The Beauties of the Boyne and Blackwater* (James McGlashan, Dublin)

1851   *An Essay on the Epidemic Ophthalmia which has prevailed in . . . Tipperary and Athlone* (James McGlashan, Dublin)

1851, 1861, 1871 Census – Report of Medical Commissioner to the Irish Census

1852   *Irish Popular Superstitions* (James McGlashan, Dublin)

1853   *Practical Observations on Aural Surgery and the Nature and Treatment of Diseases of the Ear* (Churchill, London)

1854   *On the Physical, Moral and Social Conditions of the Deaf and Dumb* (Churchill, London)

1857   *A Descriptive Catalogue of the Antiquities in the Museum of the Royal Irish Academy, Vol. I* (Royal Irish Academy, Dublin)

1861   *A Descriptive Catalogue . . . Vol. 2* (Royal Irish Academy, Dublin)

1862   *A Descriptive Catalogue . . . Vol. 3* (Royal Irish Academy, Dublin)

1863   *An Essay on the Malformations and Congenital Diseases of the Organs of Sight* (Churchill, London)

1867   *Lough Corrib, its Shores and Islands* (McGlashan and Gill, Dublin)

Appendix 2

Lady Jane Wilde's Publications

1849   Translation of J. William Meinhold, *Sidonia the Sorceress* (The Parlour Library, London)

1850   Translation of Alphonse de Lamartine, *Pictures of the First French Revolution* (Simms and McIntyre, London)

1851   Translation of Alphonse de Lamartine, *The Wanderer and his Home* (Simms and McIntyre, London)

1852   Translation of Alexandre Dumas, *The Glacier Land* (Simms and McIntyre, London)

1853   Translation of Emmanuel Swedenborg, *The Future Life* (James McGlashan, Dublin)

1863   Translation of M. Schwab, *The First Temptation or 'Eritis Sicut Deus'* (T. Cautley Newby, London)

1864   *Poems* (James Duffy, Dublin)

1867   *Poems: Second Series: Translations* (James Duffy, Dublin)

1880   *Memoir of Gabriel Beranger* (Richard Bentley and Son, London)

1884   *Driftwood from Scandinavia* (Richard Bentley and Son, London)

1888   *Ancient Legends, Mystic Charms and Superstitions of Ireland* (Ward and Downey, London)

1890   *Ancient Cures, Charms and Usages of Ireland* (Ward and Downey, London)

1891   *Notes on Men, Women and Books* (Ward and Downey, London)

1893   *Social Studies* (Ward and Downey, London)

Appendix 3

Oscar Wilde's Publications

(Major works, including first staged plays and first published plays, in bold)

1876   'From Spring Days to Winter', poem published January in the *Dublin University Magazine*

'The Dole of the King's Daughter', poem published June, in the *Dublin University Magazine*

'Graffiti d'Italia (Rome Unvisited)', poem published September in *Month and Catholic Review*

'Graffiti d'Italia I. San Miniato', published in *Dublin University Magazine*

'By the Arno Part II of Graffiti d'Italia', published in *Dublin University Magazine*

1877   'Lotus Leaves', poem published February in *Irish Monthly*

'Salve Saturnia Tellus', poem published June in *Irish Monthly*

'Sonnet on Approaching Italy', poem published June in *Irish Monthly*

'Urbs Sacra Aeterna', poem published June in the *Illustrated Monitor*

'Sonnet Written During Holy Week', poem published July in the *Illustrated Monitor*

'The Tomb of Keats', article containing poem 'Heu Miserande Puer', published July in *Irish Monthly*

'Wasted Days', poem in *Kottabos*

'A Night Vision,' poem in *Kottabos*

1878   'Ravenna', poem wins Newdigate Prize. Published March, Thomas Shrimpton & Sons, Oxford.

'Magdalen Walks', poem published April in *Irish Monthly*

'Ave Maria Gratia Plena', published July in *Irish Monthly*

1879   'Athanasia', poem published April in *Time*

'To Sarah Bernhardt', poem published June in *The Word*

'Easter Day', poem published June in *Waifs and Strays*

'The New Helen', published July in *Time*

'Queen Henrietta Maria', published July in *The World*

'La Belle Marguerite. Ballade du Moyen Age' published in *Kottabos*

1880   First cartoon of Oscar Wilde by George du Maurier appears in *Punch*

Vera or The Nihilist, Oscar's first play limited bound edition, Rankin and Co.

'Portia', poem published January in *The Word*

'Impression de Voyage', published March in *Waifs and Strays*

'Ave Imperatrix', poem published August in *The Word*

'Libertatis Sacra Fames', published in November in *The Word*

1881   **Poems**, Oscar's first collection of poetry published by David Bogue

'Serenade', poem published January in *Pan*

'Impression du Matin', published March in *The World*

'Impressions: 1 les Silhouettes, 2 La Fuite de la Lune', poems published April in *Pan*

1883   **The Duchess of Padua** completed in March (not produced until November 1891, as it was rejected by Mary Anderson, the actress for whom it was originally intended).

Vera was produced in New York in August but was taken off after only one week

1885   'The Harlot's House', poem published April in *The Dramatic Review*

'The Truth of Masks', essay published May in *The Nineteenth Century*

1887   'The Canterville Ghost', story published 23 February and 2 March in *The Court and Society Review*

'Lady Alroy or The Sphinx Without a Secret', short story published May in *The World*

'The Model Millionaire', short story published June in *The World*

'Fantaisies Decoratives:1 Le Paneau. 2 Les Ballons', poem published December in *Women's Journal*

'Lord Arthur Savile's Crime', published in December in *The Court and Society Review*

1888　　***The Happy Prince and Other Tales,*** short story collection published May by David Nutt.

'Canzonet', poem published April in *Art and Letters*

'The Young King', short story published December in *The Lady's Pictorial*

1889　　'The Decay of Lying', essay published January in *The Nineteenth Century*

'Pen, Pencil and Poison', essay published January in *The Fortnightly Review*

'Symphony in Yellow', poem published February in the *Centennial Magazine*

'The Birthday of the Infanta', short story published March in *Paris Illustre*

'The Portrait of W. H.', story published July in *Blackwood's Edinburgh Magazine*

'In the Forest', published December in *The Lady's Pictorial*

1890　　***The Picture of Dorian Gray,*** published June as lead story in *Lippincott's Magazine*

'The Critic as Artist', essay in dialogue form published July and September in *The Nineteenth Century*

1891　　'The Soul of Man Under Socialism', essay published February in *The Fortnightly Review*

'A Preface to Dorian Grey', article published in March in *The Fortnightly Review*

Intentions, four previously published essays collected. Published May James R. Osgood, McIlvaine

Lord Arthur Savile's Crime and Other Stories published by James R. Osgood, Mc Ilvaine

The Picture of Dorian Grey, Oscar's only novel published April by Ward, Lock & Co.

A House of Pomegranates, short stories published James R. Osgood, Mc Ilvaine

The Duchess of Padua staged New York anonymously at first under title *Guido Ferranti*

1892   *Lady Windermere's Fan,* first staged 20 February at St James's Theatre, London

Salome, June production scheduled in Palace Theatre, London, cancelled when licence refused

1893   'The House of Judgement', prose poem published February in the Oxford undergraduate magazine *The Spirit Lamp*

Salomé, published (in French) February by Librairie de l'Art Independent

A Woman of No Importance first staged 19 April, the Haymarket Theatre, London

'The Disciple' prose poem published in June in *The Spirit Lamp*

Lady Windermere's Fan published November by Elkin Mathews and John Lane, The Bodley Head Publishers.

'To My Wife – With a Copy of my Poems', a poem in *Book-song, An Anthology of Poems of Books and Bookmen from Modern Authors* published by Elliot Stock, London

1894   *Salome*, English translation with illustrations by Aubrey Beardsley published February by John Lane and Elkin Mathews, The Bodley Head

'**The Sphinx**', poem published June by Mathews and Lane, The Bodley Head Publishers.

'Poems in Prose', the collective title of six prose poems published July in *The Fortnightly Review*

A Woman of No Importance, published in October by Mathews and Lane, The Bodley Head

'Phrases and Philosophies for the Use of the Young', article published in December in the Oxford student magazine *Chameleon*

1895   *The Ideal Husband*, first produced 3 January at the Theatre Royal, Haymarket, London

The Importance of Being Earnest, first produced 14 February at St James's Theatre, London

The Soul of Man (under Socialism), essay previously published in 1891. Published May in book form in a limited run of 50 copies by Arthur L Humphries

1896   *Salomé*, produced in February at the Theatre de L'Oeuvre, Paris by Sarah Bernhardt

1898   *The Ballad of Reading Gaol*, poem published February by Leonard Smithers, London

1899   *The Importance of Being Earnest*, published February by Leonard Smithers, London

An Ideal Husband published July by Leonard Smithers, London

1905   *De Profundis*, incomplete version of the last prose work of Oscar Wilde written in the form of a letter to Lord Alfred Dougles while Oscar was in Reading Goal, edited by Robert Ross and published by Methuen, London

1908   *De Profundis*, a second incomplete version edited by Robert Ross and published by Methuen & Co., London

Oscar Wilde, Collected Works, published by Methuen & Co., London

1949   *De Profundis*, the first complete but inaccurate version published, produced from a copy given to Vyvyan Holland by Robert Ross and published by Methuen, London

1962   ***The Letters of Oscar Wilde***, includes among Oscar's letters the full
        text of *De Profundis* based on the original manuscript, edited by
        Rupert Hart–Davis published by Hart–Davis, London

2000   ***The Complete Letters of Oscar Wilde***, edited by Merlin Holland
        and Sir Rupert Hart–Davis, published by Fourth Estate, London
        and New York

2003   ***Oscar Wilde, A Life in Letters***, edited by Merlin Holland published
        by Fourth Estate, London and New York

References

Prologue

1   *Oscar Wilde, his Life and Confessions*, Frank Harris (Garden City, New York, 1932)

2   *The Real Trial of Oscar Wilde*, Merlin Holland (Fourth Estate, London, 2004)

3   *De Profundis and Other Writings*, Oscar Wilde (Penguin Books, London, 1954)

4   *Ibid.*

5   *Ibid.*

6   *Ibid.*

7   Young Ireland was a political and cultural movement in mid-nineteenth-century Ireland. It emerged from a constitutional movement led by Daniel O'Connell to repeal Ireland's Act of Union with Great Britain. It grew ever more militant an eventually led to an abortive rebellion in 1848.

8   *Life of Sir William Rowan Hamilton*, vol. 3, Robert Perceval Graves (Longmans, Green, London, 1889)

Chapter 1

1   *Oscar Wilde and Myself*, Alfred Lord Douglas (John Long, London, 1914)

2   'Oscar Wilde and the Wildes of Merrion Square', Davis Coakley, in *The Wilde Legacy*, Eiléan Ní Chuilleanáin (ed.) (Four Courts Press, Dublin, 2003)

3   *The Parents of Oscar Wilde*, Terence de Vere White (Hodder and Stoughton, London, 1967)

Chapter 2

1   'Sir William Wilde, 1815–1876: Demographer and Irish Medical Historian', Peter Froggatt, in *The Wilde Legacy*, Eiléan Ní Chuilleanáin. Peter Froggatt acknowledges his indebtedness to Mr Fergus O'Connor FRCS, ophthalmic surgeon, Bury, and Dr Norman Reid, Keeper of the Manuscripts and Monuments, University of St Andrews, for unpublished facts about Sir William Wilde's father's medical qualifications.

2   *Oscar Wilde, a Life in Letters*, Merlin Holland (ed.) (Fourth Estate, London, 2003)

3   While in Portugal with Mr Meiklam, Wilde's party were entertained by Major General Sir Ralph Ouseley. Young William made much of his rather tenuous connections with their host.

4   *Victorian Doctor*, T. G. Wilson (Methuen, London, 1994)

5 The Edge, guitarist with the rock band U2, was the owner of Moytura House for a number of years. It changed hands in 2003.

6 *More Letters of Oscar Wilde*, Rupert Hart-Davis (John Murray, London, 1985)

Chapter 3

1 *Irish Popular Superstitions*, William Wilde (James McGlashan, Dublin, 1852)

2 *Ibid.*

3 Letter to A. H. Sayce, Bodleian Library, Oxford, in *Oscar Wilde*, Richard Ellmann (Hamish Hamilton, London, 1987)

4 *Lough Corrib, its Shores and Islands*, William Wilde (McGlashan and Gill, Dublin, 1867)

5 The King's Evil was scrofula, a form of tuberculosis affecting the lymph nodes and presenting in a variety of skin diseases. Historically known as 'the King's Evil' because sufferers believed they could be cured if touched by the monarch, a belief and practice that continued in England into the eighteenth century.

6 *Lough Corrib, Its Shores and Islands,* William Wilde

7 It was crafted by Maoiliosa O'Echan whose name is also found engraved on the side.

8 Professor McCullagh persuaded the new parish priest to sell the cross to the Royal Irish Academy in 1839 for 100 guineas and have it safely placed among their artefacts. Even though the money received from the sale was used to put a new roof on the church at Cong, the local people were outraged at the loss of their beautiful and valuable relic. The ill-feeling lingered and years later there was an almost farcical attempt made by the succeeding parish priest, the outspoken and rebellious Fr Pat Lavelle, to snatch the cross back from the Royal Irish Academy and return it to its rightful place in Cong but the bizarre theft failed.

9 In his book *Lough Corrib, its Shores and Islands*, published in 1867, Sir William credits Sir Benjamin with saving the ruins of Cong Abbey from total collapse even if some of this restoration work was carried out without due care. Sir William shows a rare understanding of the delicate nature of conservation by not including a drawing of the Abbey's northern doorway in his book because, as he says, it is 'of the "composite order" having been made up some years ago of stones taken from another arch in this northern wall'.

10 Sir William tells his readers in *Lough Corrib, its Shores and Islands* that 'this charming little ruin, which stands in the middle of a very ancient burial ground, and is surrounded by antique hollies and thorns, is highly

venerated by the people, among whom there is a tradition, that from it was brought the clay with which the Abbey of Cong was consecrated'.

1 *Narrative of a Voyage to Madeira, Teneriffe, and along the shores of the Mediterranean, including a visit to Algiers, Egypt, Palestyne, Tyre, Rhodes and the Holy Land* , William Wilde, (Curry, Dublin, 1840)

2 *Ibid.*

1   A letter dated 8 February 1882 from W. F. Wakeman, who had been a student of Petrie's and a friend of William Wilde's, to the antiquarian James Graves throws some light on the relationship between the young Wilde and the more senior Petrie. In this letter Wakeman is enquiring if he should now proceed with sketching and describing the finds at Lagore Crannog: 'I believe I am the only man now living to do the latter which should have been done long ago, and would certainly have been done but for the mutual jealousies of Petrie and Wilde'. W. F. Wakeman was for a time an art teacher at Portora School and taught Oscar and Willie Wilde. Published in *The Journal of the Royal Society of Antiquaries of Ireland*, Vol. 120 in 1990 pp. 112–119. Article by Siobhan de hOir.

2 *Austria, its Literary, Scientific and Medical Institution*, William Wilde (Curry, Dublin, 1843)

3 William Wilde had observed the instrument being used by its original inventor, Ignaz Gruber, in Vienna. Home in Ireland, Wilde continued to refine Gruber's specula and helped gain international acceptance for the instrument. Gruber himself did not publish his invention.

4 'Robert J. Graves', William Wilde, in *Dublin University Magazine* (1842)

5 *The Parents of Oscar Wilde,* Terence de Vere White

Chapter 8

1 *Irish Popular Superstitions*, William Wilde

2 Title of a ballad composed by Thomas Davis in 1845

1 'Irish Poets of 1848', lecture given by Oscar Wilde at Platt Hall, San Francisco, 5 April 1882

2 'Tribute to Thomas Davis', speech delivered by W. B. Yeats, 20 November 1915

3 *Hearth and Home*, 30 June 1892

4 *Freeman's Journal*, 4 February 1896

5 *Nation*, 8 July 1848

6 The Fenian Brotherhood was an Irish Republican organisation founded in the United States in 1858 with the aim of overthrowing British rule in Ireland by force of arms. It was a precursor of the Irish Republican Brotherhood, itself a forerunner of the Irish Republican Army or IRA.

7 Letter to an unknown correspondent, University of Reading

8 *Ibid.*

9 *Ibid.*

10 *Ibid.*

11 *Ibid.*

Chapter 10

1 Letter to an unknown correspondent, University of Reading

2 *Ibid.*

Chapter 11

1 'Speranza's Secret', Terence de Vere White, *Times Literary Supplement*, in *Mother of Oscar Wilde*, Joy Melville (John Murray, London, 1994)

2 Letter to an unknown correspondent, University of Reading

3 *Letters of J. B. Yeats*, J. M. Hone (ed.) (Faber, London, 1944)

4 'The Bondage of Women', in *Social Studies*, Jane Wilde (Ward and Downy, London, 1893)

5 *Ibid.*

6 *Ibid.*

7 'Genius and Marriage', in *Social Studies*, Jane Wilde

8 *Memoir of Gabriel Beranger*, William Wilde, Introduction by Jane Wilde (Richard Bentley and Son, London, 1880)

9 Letter to an unknown correspondent, University of Reading

10 *Practical Observations on Aural Surgery and the Nature and Treatment of Diseases of the Ear*, William Wilde (Churchill, London, 1853)

11 Letter to an unknown correspondent, University of Reading

12 *Life of Sir John T. Gilbert*, R. M. Gilbert (Longmans, Green, London, 1905)

REFERENCES

Chapter 12

1 The Fenians also took their name from this mythological band of warriors.

2 Letter to an unknown correspondent, University of Reading

3 *Life of Sir William Rowan Hamilton*, vol. 3, Robert Perceval Graves

4 Letter to an unknown correspondent, University of Reading

5 Today the still-impressive house at 1 Merrion Square is part of the American College. Regular tours are available.

6 *Oscar Wilde*, Richard Ellmann

7 *Ibid.*

8 Letter to an unknown correspondent, University of Reading

9 *A Chronicle of Friendship*, Luther Munday (T. Werner Laurie, London, 1912)

10 *Memoir of Gabriel Beranger*, William Wilde

11 Founded in 1785 with the aim of promoting study in the sciences, humanities and social studies in Ireland, the Royal Irish Academy was, and still remains today open for membership to those who have attained distinction in science or other branches of scholarship as evidenced by their published work. Candidates must be proposed and recommended by five or more members. Wilde had been elected to the Academy as early as June 1839.

Chapter 13

1 'Författaren Oscar Wilde's Föräldrahem i Irlands Hufvudstad', Lotten von Kraemer, *Ord och Bild* (1902), in *Oscar Wilde*, Richard Ellmann

2 *Ibid.*

3 Letter to an unknown correspondent, University of Reading

4 Sir John Gilbert's Correspondence, National Library of Ireland, Dublin

5 Letter from Reginald Turner to A. J. A. Symons, William Andrews Clark Library, University of California, in *Mother of Oscar Wilde*, Joy Melville

6 'People I Have Met', L. C. P. Fox, in *Donahoe's Magazine* (1905)

7 *The Letters of Oscar Wilde*, Rupert Hart-Davis (ed.) (Hart-Davis, London, 1962)

Chapter 14

1 Letter to Lotten von Kraemer, Royal Library of Sweden

2 From the records of the Medico-Philosophical Society, in *The Parents of Oscar Wilde*, Terence de Vere White

3 Letter to Lotten von Kraemer, Royal Library of Sweden

4 *The Parents of Oscar Wilde*, Terence de Vere White

5 Letter to Lotten von Kraemer, Royal Library of Sweden

6 From a manuscript memoir by Dr Conor Maguire given to de Vere White by Conor A. Maguire, SC, in *The Parents of Oscar Wilde*, Terence de Vere White

Chapter 15

1 Letter from L. C. Purser to A. J. A. Symons, William Andrews Clarke Library, University of California

2 *Oscar Wilde*, Frank Harris (New York, 1918)

3 *Oscar Wilde, a Life in Letters*, Merlin Holland

4 *Ibid.*

5 *Irish People*, 2 May 1864

6 *Poems*, Speranza (James Duffy, Dublin, 1864)

Chapter 16

1 *Saunders' Newsletter*, 29 January 1864

2 *The Irish Times*, 29 January 1864

3 Letter to Rosalie Olivecrona, National Library of Ireland, Dublin

Chapter 17

1 *Freeman's Journal* and *Saunders' Newsletter*, accounts of the trial, December 1864

2 *Mother of Oscar Wilde*, Joy Melville

3 *Freeman's Journal*, 16 December 1864

4 *Victorian Doctor*, T. G. Wilson

Chapter 18

1 *Freeman's Journal*, 14 December 1864

Chapter 19

1 *Victorian Doctor*, T. G. Wilson

2 *The Parents of Oscar Wilde*, Terence de Vere White

REFERENCES

Chapter 20

1 Letter to Lotten von Kraemer, Royal Library of Sweden

2 *New York Herald*, 18 August 1881

3 *The Life of Oscar Wilde*, Robert Sherard (T. W. Laurie, London, 1906)

Chapter 21

1 *The Corrib Country*, Richard Hayward (Dundalgan Press, Dundalk, 1943)

2 *Ireland Before the Vikings*, Gearoid Mac Niocaill (Gill & Macmillan, Dublin, 1972)

3 *Lough Corrib, its Shores and Islands*, William Wilde (McGlashan and Gill, Dublin, 1867)

4 *Ibid.*

Chapter 22

1 *Portora Royal School*, W. Steele, (Hely, Dublin, 1891)

2 *Oscar Wilde, the Importance of Being Irish*, Davis Coakley (Town House, Dublin, 1994)

3 *Ibid.*

4 *Oscar Wilde*, Richard Ellmann

5 The University of California and the town that grew up around it are named in Bishop Berkeley's honour as is the library in Trinity College, Dublin

6 *Life of Sir John T. Gilbert*, R. M. Gilbert

7 *Melancholy Madness, a Coroner's Casebook*, Michelle McGoff-McCann (Mercier Press, Dublin, 2003)

8 *Letters of J. B. Yeats to W. B. Yeats*, J. M. Hone (ed.) (Faber, London, 1944)

9 *The Letters of John Stuart Blackie to His Wife*, John Stewart Blackie (William Blackwood, London, 1910)

Chapter 23

1 'Unpublished Lecture Notes of Oscar Wilde,' Michael J. O'Neill, in *Irish University Review* (1955)

2 *Oscar Wilde as I Knew Him in Victorian Days and Other Papers*, G. H. Blair (Longmans, Green, London 1939)

3 *Autobiographies*, W. B. Yeats (Macmillan, London, 1955)

4 *Oscar Wilde, a Life in Letters*, Merlin Holland

Chapter 24

1 The Larcom Papers, National Library of Ireland, Dublin

2 *Victorian Doctor*, T. G. Wilson

3 Letter to Lotten von Kraemer, Royal Library of Sweden

4 *The Life of Oscar Wilde*, Robert Sherard

5 Letter to Oscar Wilde, William Andrews Clark Library, University of California

6 The Larcom Papers, National Library of Ireland, Dublin

7 Five years later Undersecretary Burke met a violent death as he walked towards the Vice-Regal Lodge with the new Chief Secretary for Ireland Lord Frederick Cavendish in what became known as the Phoenix Park murders.

8 The Larcom Papers, National Library of Ireland, Dublin

9 The Larcom Papers, National Library of Ireland, Dublin

Chapter 25

1 *The Letters of Oscar Wilde*, Rupert Hart-Davis

2 *Ibid.*

3 Letter to Oscar Wilde, William Andrews Clarke Library, University of California

4 *The Letters of Oscar Wilde*, Rupert Hart-Davis

5 Letter from Reverend H. S. Bowden to Oscar Wilde, William Andrews Clark Library, University Of California

Chapter 26

1 Letter from Willie Wilde to Margaret Campbell, William Andrews Clark Library, University of California

2 Letter to Rosalie Olivecrona, National Library of Ireland, Dublin

3 *Impressions That Remained*, Ethel Smyth (Longmans, Green, London, 1919)

4 Letter to Oscar Wilde, William Andrews Clark Library, Univeristy of California

5 *Ibid.*

6 Letter to Rosalie Olivecrona, National Library of Ireland, Dublin

Chapter 27

1 'Oscar Wilde and His Mother,' *T. P's Weekly*, 25 April 1913

2 *The Art of Herbert Schmalz*, Trevor Blakemore (George Allen, London, 1911)

3 *Entr'acte*, 1 September 1883

4 *Oscar Wilde and His Mother*, Anne, Comtesse de Brémont (Everett, London, 1911)

5 'Brother to Oscar,' James Edward Holroyd, in *Blackwood's Magazine* (1979)

6 *The Works of Arthur M. Binstead*, Arthur Binstead (T. W. Laurie, London, 1927)

7 *Max and Will*, Mary M. Lago and Karl Beckson (eds.) (John Murray, London, 1975)

8 Letter to Oscar Wilde, William Andrews Clark Library, University of California

Chapter 28

1 *Oscar Wilde, a Life in Letters*, Merlin Holland

2 Letter to Oscar Wilde, William Andrews Clarke Library, University of California

3 Letter to Oscar Wilde, William Andrews Clark Library, University of California

Chapter 29

1 *The Duchess of Padua* was completed in March but rejected by actress Mary Anderson for whom it was intended. It was eventually produced in New York in November 1891. Twenty copies were produced and privately circulated for this production. Two copies survived, one with the author's corrections. The original manuscript was taken from Oscar's house in Tite Street in April 1895. The play was first published in Germany in 1904 by Egon, Fleishel and Co., Berlin. The translation into German by Dr Max Meyerfeld was based on the author's copy from the 1891 New York production.

2 '"I See it is My Name That Terrifies": Wilde in the Twentieth Century,' Alan Sinfield, in *The Wilde Legacy*, Eiléan Ní Chuilleanáin (ed.)

3 Letter from Constance Wilde to Otho Lloyd, Holland Family Private Papers

Chapter 30

1 Letter to Oscar Wilde, William Andrews Clark Library, University of California

2 Letter to Oscar Wilde, Lady Eccles Oscar Wilde Collection, British Library

3 *Oscar Wilde, a Life in Letters*, Merlin Holland

4 Letter to Rosalie Olivecrona, National Library of Ireland, Dublin

5 *Queen*, 7 June 1884

6 Letter to Oscar Wilde, William Andrews Clark Library, University of California

Chapter 31

1 Letter from Reginald Turner to A. J. A. Symons, William Andrews Clark Library, University of California

2 *Both Sides of the Curtain*, Elizabeth Robins (Heinemann, London, 1940)

3 Letter to Constance Wilde, William Andrews Clark Library, University of California

4 *Athenaeum*, 29 March 1890

Chapter 32

1 *The Lost Historian, a Memoir of Sir Sidney Low*, Desmond Chapman- Huston (Murray, London, 1936)

2 Letter to Oscar Wilde, William Andrews Clark Library, University of California

3 *The Life of Oscar Wilde*, Hesketh Pearson (Methuen, London, 1946)

4 Letter to Oscar Wilde, William Andrews Clark Library, University of California

5 André Gide won the Nobel Prize for Literature in 1947

6 *The Pilgrim Daughters*, Hesketh Pearson (Heinemann, London, 1961)

7 *Ibid.*

8 *Purple Passage, the Life of Mrs Frank Leslie*, Madelene B. Stern (University of Oklahoma Press, Oklahoma, 1953)

9 *Ibid.*

10 *Ibid.*

11 *The Pilgrim Daughters*, Hesketh Pearson

Chapter 33

1 Letter to Oscar Wilde, William Andrews Clark Library, University of California

2 *Ibid.*

3 *The Parents of Oscar Wilde*, Terence de Vere White

4 *New York Times*, 18 September 1893

5 Letter from A. Mynous to Constance Wilde, William Andrews Clark Library, University of California

6 Letter to Oscar Wilde, William Andrews Clark Library, University of California

7 *Ibid.*

8 Letter from Mrs Frank Leslie to Lady Jane Wilde, William Andrews Clark Library, University of California

9   *The Adventures of a Novelist*, Gertrude Atherton (Jonathan Cape, London, 1932)

10 *Ibid.*

Chapter 34

1   Letter to Oscar Wilde, William Andrews Clark Library, University of California

2   D. J. O'Donoghue, in *The Irish Book Lover* (1921)

3   *Oscar Wilde*, Richard Ellmann

4   *The Secret Life of Oscar Wilde*, Neil McKenna (Century, London, 2003)

5   Letter in possession of Richard Ellmann, in *Oscar Wilde*, Richard Ellmann

6   Letter from Constance Wilde to Robbie Ross, William Andrews Clark Library, University of California

7   Letter to Oscar Wilde, William Andrews Clark Library, University of California

8   *Son of Oscar Wilde*, Vyvyan Holland (Hart-Davis, London, 1954)

Chapter 35

1   *Oscar Wilde, a Life in Letters*, Merlin Holland

2   *The Letters of Oscar Wilde*, Rupert Hart-Davis

Chapter 36

1   *New York Times*, 5 May 1895; *Letters and Leaders of my Day*, T. M. Healy (Thornton Butterworth, London, 1928)

2   *The Life of Oscar Wilde*, Robert Sherard

3   *Oscar Wilde, the Story of an Unhappy Friendship*, Robert Sherard (Hermes Press, London, 1902)

4   *Oscar Wilde*, Frank Harris

5   *Ibid.*

6   *Autobiographies*, W. B. Yeats

7   *The Life of Oscar Wilde*, Robert Sherard

8   *Ibid.*

9   *Autobiographies*, W. B. Yeats

10 *Oscar Wilde and his Mother*, Anna, Comtesse de Brémont

11 *The Real Oscar Wilde*, Robert Sherard (T. W. Laurie, London, 1917)

12 *Oscar Wilde, the Story of an Unhappy Friendship*, Robert Sherard

13 *Oscar Wilde and his Mother*, Anna, Comtesse de Brémont

Chapter 37

1 Letter to an unknown correspondent, University of Reading

2 Letter from Lily Wilde to Governor of Pentonville Prison, William Andrews Clark Library, University of California

3 *The Letters of Oscar Wilde*, Rupert Hart-Davis

4 Letter from Lily Wilde to More Adey, Bodleian Library, Oxford, in *Truly Wilde, the Unsettling Story of Dolly Wilde, Oscar's Unusual Niece*, Joan Schenkar (Virago Press, London, 2000)

5 Letter from Lily Wilde to More Adey, William Andrews Clark Library, University of California

6 *The Life of Oscar Wilde*, Robert Sherard

7 *Ibid.*

8 Letter from Constance Wilde to Lily Wilde, William Andrews Clark Library, University of California

9 'The Story of Oscar Wilde's Life and Experiences in Reading Jail', *Bruno's Weekly*, 22 January 1916

10 *The Letters of Oscar Wilde*, Rupert Hart-Davis

11 Letter from Lily Wilde to More Adey, William Andrews Clark Library, University of California

12 *Pit of Shame, the Real Ballad of Reading Gaol*, Anthony Stokes (Waterside Press, Winchester, 2007)

Chapter 38

1 *De Profundis*, Oscar Wilde

2 *Oscar Wilde et quelques autres*, Alfred Lord Douglas (Paris, 1932)

3 *New York Times*, 19 May 1987

4 'A Note on Oscar Wilde, Alfred Douglas, and Lord Rosebery, 1897,' Joseph O. Baylen and Robert L. McBath, in *English Language Notes* (1985), in *Oscar Wilde*, Richard Ellmann

Chapter 39

1 *The Redress of Poetry*, Seamus Heaney (Farrar, Straus and Giroux, New York, 1995)

2 *Contemporary Portraits*, Frank Harris (London, 1915)

3 Letter from Oscar Wilde to Robert Ross, William Andrews Clarke Library, University of California

4 *Oscar Wilde, a Life in Letters*, Merlin Holland

5 Letter from Lily Wilde to Oscar Wilde, William Andrews Clark Library, University of California

6 Letter from Lily Wilde to More Adey, William Andrews Clark Library, University of California

7 *Truly Wilde, the Unsettling Story of Dolly Wilde, Oscar's Unusual Niece*, Joan Schenkar

Chapter 40

1 *What Did I Die Of?*, J. B. Lyons (Lilliput Press, Dublin, 1991)

2 *New York Times*, 13 March 1910

3 *Oscar Wilde*, Richard Ellmann

4 *Cocteau, a Biography*, Francis Steegmuller (Atlantic-Little, Brown, Boston, 1970)

5 *Times Remembered, after Père Lachaise*, Vyvyan Holland (Victor Gollancz, London, 1966)

6 *Ibid.*

7 *Ibid.*

Bibliography

The Wildes of Merrion Square, Patrick Byrne (Staples Press, London, 1953)

Oscar Wilde, the Importance of Being Irish, Davis Coakley (Town House, Dublin, 1994)

Talk on the Wilde Side, Ed Cohen (Routledge, London, 1993)

The Parents of Oscar Wilde, Terence de Vere White (Hodder and Stoughton, London, 1967)

The Anglo-Irish, Terence de Vere White (Victor Gollancz, London, 1972)

Oscar in the Wilds, Anthony Dudley (Ashfield Publishing Services, Dublin, 2003)

Oscar Wilde, Richard Ellmann (Hamish Hamilton, London, 1987)

The Corrib Country, Richard Hayward (Dundalgan Press, Dundalk, 1943)

Oscar Wilde, a Life in Letters, Merlin Holland (ed.) (Fourth Estate, London, 2003)

The Real Trial of Oscar Wilde, Merlin Holland (Harper, London, 2004)

Son of Oscar Wilde, Vyvyan Holland (Hart-Davis, London, 1954)

Times Remembered, after Père Lachaise, Vyvyan Holland (Victor Gollancz, London, 1966)

The Trials of Oscar Wilde, H. Montgomery Hyde (William Hodge and Co, London, 1948)

Mad with Much Heart, Eric Lambert (Muller, London, 1967)

What Did I Die Of?, J. B. Lyons (The Lilliput Press, Dublin, 1991)

Wilde the Irishman, Jerusha McCormack (ed.) (Yale University Press, New Haven, CT, 1998)

Ireland Before the Vikings, Gearoid Mac Niocaill (Gill & Macmillan, Dublin, 1972)

Mother of Oscar Wilde, Joy Melville (John Murray, London, 1994)

The Wilde Legacy, Eiléan Ní Chuilleanáin (ed.) (Four Courts Press, Dublin, 2003)

Truly Wilde, the Unsettling Story of Dolly Wilde, Oscar's Unusual Niece, Joan Schenkar (Virago Press, London, 2000)

Reflections on Lough Corrib, Maurice Semple (Maurice Semple, Galway, 1973)

By the Corribside, Maurice Semple (Maurice Semple, Galway, 1981)

Where the River Corrib Flows, Maurice Semple (Maurice Semple, Galway, 1988)

The History of Galway, Sean Spellissy (The Celtic Bookshop, Limerick, 1999)

Famous Irish Writers, Martin Wallace (Appletree Press, Belfast, 1999)

The Complete Works of Oscar Wilde, Oscar Wilde (Magpie Books, London, 1993)

Victorian Doctor, T. G. Wilson (Methuen, London, 1942)

Index

The following abbreviations are used throughout the index:
JW: Lady Jane Wilde; OW: Oscar Wilde; WW: Sir William Wilde